Silence at Boalt Hall

Silence at Boalt Hall

The Dismantling of Affirmative Action

Andrea Guerrero

UNIVERSITY OF CALIFORNIA PRESS

Berkeley / Los Angeles / London

University of California Press
Berkeley and Los Angeles, California

University of California Press, Ltd.
London, England

Library of Congress Cataloging-in-Publication Data

Guerrero, Andrea
    Silence at Boalt Hall : the dismantling of affirmative action / Andrea
Guerrero.
        p.   cm.
Includes index.
    ISBN 0-520-22893-6 (Cloth : alk. paper)—ISBN 0-520-23309-3 (Paper : alk.
paper)
    1. University of California, Berkeley. School of Law—
Admission. 2. Affirmative action programs—Law and legislation—
California. 3. Discrimination in education—Law and legislation—
California. I. Title.
    KF292.C353 A54 2002
    340'.071'179467—dc21   2002002313

Manufactured in the United States of America

11   10   09   08   07   06   05   04   03   02

10   9   8   7   6   5   4   3   2   1

The paper used in this publication is both acid-free and totally chlorine-free
(TCF). It meets the minimum requirements of ANSI/NISO Z39.48-1992
(R 1997) (*Permanence of Paper*). ⊚

I believe that what self-centered men have torn down, men other-centered can build up.

Martin Luther King Jr.

Contents

Tables

Preface

I was among the last beneficiaries of affirmative action at Boalt Hall—
the prestigious law school at the University of California at Berkeley.
Though I was a strong student and scored well on the law school entrance exam, my grades and test scores alone were not enough to win me
a seat at the highly selective law school. However, I was accomplished in
many other ways, and I had more to offer than just good grades and test
scores. In addition, I was Mexican American and viewed the world from
a different perspective. I came from a bicultural and bilingual background
and in part because of this fact I was admitted to Boalt Hall.

For thirty years, Boalt had used affirmative action to admit others like
me—historically underrepresented minorities—who were capable of succeeding in law school but were not able to survive the extremely competitive admissions process. As a result of race-conscious policies, the law
school became one of the most diverse in the country, educating a generation of minority—as well as nonminority—lawyers, judges, politicians,
professors, and civic leaders. However, in 1995, the Board of Regents
voted to end affirmative action at the University of California, and, one
year later, the electorate voted to do the same across the state of California. Consequently, my class was the last to be admitted under affirmative
action at the law school.

In my three years at Boalt, I watched the law school as it was forced
to dismantle its affirmative action program—a program from which I had
benefited—and I watched the numbers of minority students plummet. I
joined student activists in the struggle to maintain diversity. From policy
proposals to public protests and political campaigns, we poured our en-

ergy into keeping the doors of the law school open. Although these efforts helped to prompt important changes in the admissions policy, they were not enough to keep those doors from whispering shut for many minority students.

Though California was the first state to end affirmative action in higher education, other states have since followed suit. By ballot initiative, court order, and regent vote, at least four other states—Texas, Washington, Florida, and Georgia—have eliminated race-conscious admissions policies at their public universities. At the most competitive of these campuses, "race-blind" policies have yielded far fewer underrepresented minorities than previous race-conscious policies. In the worst instances, the numbers of underrepresented minorities have fallen by more than half, prompting a closer examination of traditional admissions criteria.

The results of "race-blind" policies have been far from race-neutral and have raised the question that first led to the implementation of affirmative action: How can a highly competitive university admit a talented and diverse student body? The answer to this question may lie somewhere in the past. By design and by default, traditional admissions criteria have failed to adequately identify promising minority candidates. The two principal criteria—grade point averages and standardized test scores—have been shown to be neither sufficiently valid nor truly objective measures of merit. Standardized test scores in particular appear to correlate more with race than with academic or professional success and seem to have a disparate and discriminatory impact on minority students. Nevertheless, schools such as Boalt continue to use them.

Before it was eliminated, affirmative action countered the prejudicial effects of traditional criteria by allowing school administrators to look beyond sheer numbers to admit talented minority students. Race-conscious policies were constructed to be a temporary measure that would end when racial bias was eradicated and racial diversity occurred naturally in the admissions process. But affirmative action programs were cut short in California, and university administrators have since been unwilling or unable to address the bias in traditional admissions criteria, resulting in the decimation of the minority population at Boalt and other competitive campuses of the University of California.

At a time when admissions criteria are coming under closer scrutiny, the issue of affirmative action appears headed for the U.S. Supreme Court. Several reverse discrimination cases are currently making their way through the judicial system and challenging university race-conscious admissions policies. Two of these cases—both brought against the University of Michigan—are expected to become the national vehicles for deciding whether and how universities can use affirmative action. The Supreme Court has not considered race-conscious admissions policies since the *Bakke* case in 1978, when the court upheld the use of such policies on very narrow grounds. Recently, however, several lower federal district courts and courts of appeals have differed on the interpretation of *Bakke,* using it both to affirm and negate the continuing permissibility of race-conscious policies. With an interest in resolving these differences, the Supreme Court is likely to review the matter in the near future.

With so much at stake in the evaluation of affirmative action, an examination of how it has worked and who it has affected is essential. This book is my attempt to tell the story of one institution—Boalt Hall—as it has struggled to make itself more representative of and more relevant to a changing populace. I have done my best to provide the context necessary to understand this story, even though in some instances my access to information was limited. I have also tried to include a range of perspectives on the issue of affirmative action, but in no way are these perspectives comprehensive. This book is not a general history of affirmative action, nor is it a rigorous study of admissions criteria. Instead, nestled between the arguments for and against race-conscious policies, it is the story, told over thirty years, of those who benefited from affirmative action and those who suffered from its removal. It includes the voices of various students, faculty, and administrators who ground a theoretical debate in reality—the reality of an institution that was among the first to implement affirmative action policies and among the first to be forced to remove them. The voices from Boalt Hall inform the debate.

As the nation confronts one of the most pivotal and controversial issues of our time—racial diversity in higher education—the story of Boalt Hall provides insights into the future as well as the past. The antecedents and outcomes of this story have implications for educational institutions across the country. It is my hope that the reader will use this story to rethink the dismantling of affirmative action and help set the country on a path that will open wide the doors of higher education for students of all racial backgrounds and not just the privileged few. In an increasingly diverse nation, we cannot afford to do otherwise.

Acknowledgments

I owe many thanks to my friends and family—especially my parents—who supported me with love and encouragement throughout this endeavor. A special thanks to my husband, Beston, who not only endured the countless hours of writing and rewriting and made room for this project in our around-the-world honeymoon, but also provided editorial comments and love songs when I needed them most. I am grateful to Khaldoun Shobaki for parting with his laptop computer so that I could travel and write at the same time. I am also grateful to the people that housed and fed me in various locales—Javier and Carol in San Diego, Mike and Vanita in San Francisco, Krista and Peter in Berkeley, Martha in Nashville, Sid in Toronto, Peter in New York, Junaldo Duarte in Salvador, and the Talbot family in Montpellier.

This book would not have been possible without the willingness of students, alumni, and faculty to share their memories, insights, and experiences. To all the people I interviewed, I owe a heartfelt thanks. May your collective stories serve as a guide to others. I am especially grateful to Herma Hill Kay, Richard Delgado, Dirk Tillotson, Daniel Tellalian, Lydia Chavez, Henry Ramsey Jr., and the many others who read the manuscript and provided me with helpful comments, suggestions, and changes. I extend *mil gracias* to Robert Cole and William Kidder, who went beyond the call of duty, reading multiple drafts and giving me extensive feedback. A special thanks to Bill Earner for inspiring the tables and to John Edgerton for giving me a crash course on how to find a publisher—the plan worked. Last but not least, I want to thank the University of California Press for giving me this opportunity and letting my voice be heard.

CHAPTER I

Balancing the Scales

On April 4, 1968, amid news of war abroad and revolt at home, came the devastating report that Dr. Martin Luther King Jr. was dead. The thirty-nine-year-old civil rights leader had been killed by a sniper outside his hotel room in Memphis, Tennessee. Sadness mingled with frustration and demoralization as the nation mourned the loss of yet another figure—after President John F. Kennedy, Malcolm X, and Medgar Evers—in America's crusade for racial justice and equality. The victories for which King and others had fought so hard—school desegregation, antidiscrimination legislation, and minority hiring programs—had been slow to produce the opportunities promised to blacks and other minorities in this country.[1]

Several years earlier, on the hundredth anniversary of the signing of the Emancipation Proclamation, King had delivered his powerful "I Have a Dream" speech on the steps of the Lincoln Memorial. He spoke longingly of a world in which his children might be judged by the "content of their character" rather than the color of their skin. But he reminded the nation that America had fallen short on its promise "that all men, yes, black men as well as white men, would be guaranteed the unalienable rights of life, liberty, and the pursuit of happiness." Wearing a button that said "Jobs and Freedom," King stated,

It is obvious today that America has defaulted on this promissory note in so far as her citizens of color are concerned. Instead of honoring this sacred obligation, America has given the Negro people a bad check; a check which has come back marked "insufficient funds." We refuse to believe that there are insufficient funds in the great vaults of opportunity of this nation. And so we've come to cash this check, a check that will give us upon demand the riches of freedom and the security of justice.[2]

One year later, the United States Congress passed the Civil Rights Act of 1964, prohibiting discrimination based on race, sex, ethnicity, and national origin.[3] This legislation achieved important equalities under the law but failed to achieve equality as a result, leaving the underlying ideals of the civil rights movement unfulfilled. Dr. King spent the last years of his life advocating affirmative action programs that would realize the promise of equality. He compared affirmative action programs to the GI Bill of Rights and stated that the policy of special treatment that America had adopted for millions of veterans after World War II had "cost far more than a policy of preferential treatment to rehabilitate the traditionally disadvantaged Negro would cost us today."[4]

At his death, Dr. King's message of unfulfilled promises sat heavy on the public conscience. From the U.S. president on down, officials across the country vowed to extend the promised opportunities so long denied to blacks and other minorities. Administrators at the University of California were no exception. Like universities across the nation, the University of California remained predominantly white and male, despite the charter of the university to admit a "representation of students...[so] that all portions of the state shall enjoy equal privilege therein."[5] The assassination of Dr. King served as a catalyst for action and led UC President Charles Hitch to declare, "Dr. Martin Luther King was one of the great Americans. His courage and his character inspired the world. One of his great services to our Nation was to remind us by word and deed, that the Nation's constitutional rights had not yet been extended to all our citizens. We must now honor his memory by assuring that the opportunity and justice he sought for that 'other America' be realized."[6] Echoing President Hitch, Berkeley Chancellor Roger Heyns called on the faculty to lead the fight against discrimination in education and employment. The chancellor stated, "It is my personal belief that we must develop a sense of urgency. We have to grab hold of these problems where we are—it is not a question of what someone else should do. Let us re-examine our consciences, then our priorities, and then act."[7] And at the law school on campus, known as Boalt Hall, Dean Edward Halbach and the law school faculty "renewed and expanded [their] commitment to increase the representation of minority groups in the law school."[8] The law school had opened its doors in 1911 and had enrolled through the years more than six thousand students, but[9] only twenty-two had been African American, twenty had been Latino,[10] and far fewer had been Asian American and Native American.[11] A group of administrators, faculty, and students at Boalt sought to change that.

The previous five years had been an awakening—a process of realization that racial inequalities in this country ran deep and wide. Beginning in the summer of 1963, small groups of law students from Boalt—mostly white, as were almost all Boalt students then—traveled to places like Georgia, Mississippi, and North Carolina to work with black lawyers who were challenging racial prejudice and discriminatory practices. Recounting their experiences in the student newspaper, the *Writ,* they described the inequities of having to drive forty-five miles round-trip just to be served a hamburger if you were black, and they detailed the constant apprehension that black civil rights lawyers felt of being shot or beaten. They told of the prejudice of the courts that allowed segregated courtrooms, permitted witnesses to be addressed as "niggers," and sustained "the most absurd objections."[12]

One student also related his experience of being an "other" as a white student working in a black community. Describing the conditions in which a law clerk lives in the South, he wrote, "Life is confined to the Negro community, physically, morally, and culturally. [The student] becomes what I like to call an 'obvious person.' . . . This is not to imply constant hostility, rather the same kind of attention that a Negro would receive in one of the 'better' social spots in San Francisco. When the experience is new it is uncomfortable to say the least. I don't know that anybody ever gets used to it, but the initial apprehension seems to be the worst part."[13]

Boalt students who traveled to the South helped to create an awareness in the law school of racial problems and a climate of opinion on what should be done to alleviate them.[14] But one did not have to look as far away as the South to understand discrimination. The city of Berkeley had recently undergone a racial transformation that had turned a virtually all-white suburb into a racially mixed city with numerous tensions and frustrations. By 1960, as a result of black migration from the South after World War II, the city was one-fifth black. As one historian recounted, "Berkeley's blacks lived in a corner of the city remote from the University. One seldom saw a black on campus, black shoppers were not welcome in downtown Berkeley, and both school segregation and discrimination in employment and housing were common."[15] Eugene Swann, a black student who graduated from Boalt in 1962, knew this all too well. While in law school, he and his wife had been discriminated against in the rental of an apartment on Hillegass Street in Berkeley and brought suit under the newly enacted Unruh Civil Rights Act—a California statute prohibiting discrimination in housing.[16] Though he was successful in his case, racial discrimination in Berkeley and the surrounding Bay Area remained prevalent.

Drawing heavily from the southern movement organized by black college students who called themselves the Student Non-violent Coordinating Committee (SNCC), Berkeley student activists formed the Berkeley Congress of Racial Equality (CORE) to protest job discrimination.[17] Throughout much of 1964, CORE and its allies sponsored demonstrations at Lucky's stores in Berkeley, at the Sheraton-Palace Hotel, along auto row in San Francisco, and at the *Oakland Tribune*. In September 1964, possibly because of pressure from the business community, the University of California banned students, including CORE, from passing out literature, soliciting funds, or organizing support from card tables set up at the edge of campus. This ban led civil rights workers and other student activists to attack the new rules and move their activities onto the campus. Following the administration's reprisals, students demanded and won the right to conduct all sorts of political activity throughout the campus. The student uprising was known as the Free Speech Movement and, coupled with the civil rights movement, antiwar movement, and equal rights movement, prompted students at Berkeley and across the nation to question the assumptions underlying the social order in America.[18]

Though formal equality had been granted in the Fourteenth Amendment—which promised equal protection—and again in the Civil Rights Act of 1964—which prohibited discrimination—the doors of opportunity remained largely closed to minorities. Racial inequality clearly had much deeper roots and was not simply the product of racial prejudice and intentional discrimination. Rather, inequality appeared to be an almost unavoidable outcome of patterns of socialization that were "bred in the bone." Discrimination, "far from manifesting itself only (or even principally) through individual actions or conscious policies, was a structural feature of U.S. society, the product of centuries of systematic exclusion, exploitation, and disregard of racially defined minorities."[19]

In 1965, the recognition of this led President Lyndon B. Johnson, in a speech delivered at Howard University, to describe the Civil Rights Act of 1964 as merely a beginning. "That beginning," he said, "is freedom.... [It] is the right to share fully and equally in American society—to vote, to hold a job, to enter a public place, to go to school. It is the right to be treated in every part of our national life as a person equal in dignity and promise to all others." But he went on to say that "freedom is not enough":

It is not enough to just open the gates of opportunity. All citizens must have the ability to walk through those gates. This is the next and more profound stage of the battle for civil rights. We seek not just freedom but opportunity—not just legal equity but human ability—not just equality as a right and a theory, but equality as a fact and as a result.....

Equal opportunity is essential, but not enough. Men and women of all races are born with the same range of abilities. But ability is not just the product of birth. Ability is stretched or stunted by the family you live with, and the neighborhood you live in, by the school you go to and the poverty or the richness of your surroundings. It is the product of a hundred unseen forces playing upon the infant, the child, and the man.[20]

At Boalt, this recognition—that inequalities resulted from structural features and not just individual actions—led a group of students to examine how the admissions process at the law school worked or did not work to exclude minorities.[21] Boalt had never prohibited minority students from entering the law school, but minorities had been effectively excluded by other means. The students formed the Committee on Aid to Minority Groups and, with the help of the dean of admissions and a few law professors, identified several problems in enrolling more minority students at the law school. First, they discovered "a serious lack of information about educational opportunities" in minority communities, which contributed to a lack of interest in the legal profession. Second, they found that interested minority students were often deterred from pursuing a legal career, because employment customs and prejudice in the legal profession would make it difficult for them to obtain jobs.

In addition to these problems, the committee identified two other hurdles for potential minority applicants: entrance requirements for the law school and the financing of three years of legal education. Noting that many law schools relied heavily on past grades as well as scores from the Law School Admission Test (LSAT), the committee observed that these two factors were especially disadvantageous to minority students. With respect to grades, the committee found that an "economically deprived student coming from a minority group is usually concerned with 'getting by' financially rather than with competing for honors." With respect to the LSAT, they asserted, "it is well known that Negroes tend to score lower because of their socioeconomic backgrounds. Many don't even have the $15 to take the test." In addition, "they are unaccustomed to taking multiple choice tests." In view of these considerations, the committee devoted itself "primarily to getting qualified applicants interested in law, and providing financial assistance to those in need."[22]

The awakening that was taking place at the law school did not escape the attention of Edward Halbach, who had been appointed dean of Boalt Hall in April 1966.[23] At age thirty-four, he was the youngest dean in the history of the law school, and he was coming to his own deeper understanding of racial problems. Dean Halbach had grown up in a small city in Iowa with little awareness of the continued seriousness of racial issues. Not until 1953, when a good friend declined an invitation to his wedding in a Chicago suburb because he thought he would feel uncomfortable as possibly the only black guest, did Halbach realize "how life was for blacks." There were few minority students at Boalt, and professors and students alike had limited exposure to issues of race and ethnicity. "Like universities elsewhere," Halbach recalled, "without the benefit of more minority students we were all running behind."

Halbach recognized the need to take affirmative steps to increase minority representation at the law school and encouraged student and faculty efforts to do so. Efforts to increase minority enrollment were motivated by "a desire to be responsive to the lack of adequate representation of minority persons in the profession, and . . . by a belief that the presence of members of minority groups would add to the educational quality of the school." Nationally, minorities constituted just over 1 percent of the bar and 1 percent of the law school population. In 1964, the total minority enrollment in accredited American law schools was 700—out of a total of more than 54,000—and 267 of these (more than a third) were enrolled in historically black schools. At Boalt, the situation was much the same; the presence of a single minority student was exceptional.[24]

The perceived problem at Boalt was the lack of minority applicants, and so a small group of administrators, faculty, and students conducted outreach to minority students at college campuses. This early effort resulted in a small increase in the number of minority applicants in 1966, but it was not enough. In the spring of 1967, Dean Halbach entered into a conversation with Homer Mason (class of 1969)—one of four black students in the first-year class—about what more could be done to increase minority applications, particularly through the black organizations in which Mason was active or had good contacts.[25] Mason had some ideas and was eager to help. He was the third in his family to pursue a legal career. His grandfather had been the first. After being emancipated from slavery, his grandfather had pursued higher education, and in 1893 he became the third black lawyer in Texas. His father followed in his grandfather's footsteps and became one of the small number of black attorneys in the country.

Mason brought Dean Halbach into the black community to speak about Boalt and the value of a legal education. Together they went to black fraternities, sororities, churches, and other student and community groups to get the word out that Boalt was a good place to go to law school. Mason recalled, "We wanted to let them know that we were looking for outstanding students, and that they were welcome."[26] The outreach paid off, and the number of black applicants increased, even if only incrementally. Reflecting on the effectiveness of this limited but targeted outreach, Dean Halbach remarked, "The time I spent with Homer was extremely valuable and eventually had a multiplier effect."[27]

Dean Halbach found the few minority students enrolled at Boalt to be very effective at contacting potential minority applicants and recruiting those applicants to come to the law school. Albert Moreno (class of 1970) was a notable example.[28] Moreno was a student from Calexico, California, who entered Boalt as the only Latino in his class in 1967. He worked with two other Latinos in the school at the time to contact undergraduate students through organizations such as MEChA (Movimiento Estudiantil Chicano/a de Aztlan) and encourage them to apply to law school. Moreno and his colleagues were advocates for promising Latino applicants in the admissions process and persuaded them to come to Boalt if they were admitted. These efforts helped to increase the number of Latinos in the student body and, in turn, helped to sustain outreach and recruitment efforts at the law school.[29]

Halbach relied on the judgment of minority students such as Albert Moreno and Homer Mason regarding how best to approach applicants: "Who else would get to them; who else would be as credibly enthusiastic to have them come to Boalt?"[30] While the few enrolled minority students reached out to minority applicants, the dean and several faculty members solicited scholarship money to enable admitted students to come to Boalt. Together, these efforts were important steps in increasing minority enrollment. They constituted what would later be described as "soft" affirmative action—outreach, recruiting, and financial aid. As had been pointed out by the Committee on Aid to Minority Groups in 1965, however, "soft" affirmative action was not enough. The admissions process itself presented obstacles to minority applicants, suggesting a need for "hard" affirmative action—that is, race-conscious admissions.

Minority students did not generally have grades and LSAT scores as high as those of their white peers. That is not to say that they were unprepared for law school—they had strong college grade point averages and respectable LSAT scores. But they were not competitive in the admissions process—they did not often have honors grades, and their LSAT scores did not reach the upper national percentiles. In the late 1960s, Boalt had become a highly competitive place. The baby-boom generation was coming of age, and the protest movements of the time had fueled student interest in the law. In addition, women had begun to apply to law school in unprecedented numbers.[31] These factors led to a threefold increase in applications to Boalt between the years 1960 and 1967.[32]

With a dramatic increase in demand, the qualifications for acceptance rose. In 1960, any applicant who had a B average as an undergraduate could obtain admission to Boalt without regard to his or her LSAT score. In 1967, the median LSAT score of those admitted to Boalt was 638 (out of a possible scaled score of 800), and the median undergraduate grade point average for the entering class was 3.5 (out of 4.0).[33] When they applied to Boalt Hall in 1967—the year that the numbers of minority applications first began to grow—many minorities found that their qualifications, which would have been sufficient in 1960, were no longer enough to win them a spot at the highly selective law school.

Recognizing that escalated standards would exclude even promising minority applicants, the faculty and the Admissions Office flexibly modified the standards for minority applicants. At the time, admissions decisions were made through the Admissions Office with faculty consultation and sometimes student consultation. If a minority applicant had a lower grade average and test score, relatively speaking, but was "suitably qualified to pursue a legal education," and had something to offer the law school in terms of a different life experience, then the Admissions Office would give special consideration to that applicant.[34] In this way, the Admissions Office acted in a race-conscious manner, giving rise to "hard" affirmative action.

The informal affirmative action program that emerged by early 1968 was slowly making headway, but remained limited in scope. The program depended on a few minority law school students to conduct outreach and recruiting, and on several administrators to identify and admit a small number of promising law school candidates. In April 1968, however, the assassination of Martin Luther King Jr. gave further impetus to the affirmative action program, leading the faculty to formalize and greatly expand the program, which they referred to as the "Special Admissions" program.

As news of the assassination spread across the country, the nation seemed ready to erupt. The country was sinking deeper into the Vietnam War and drafting a disproportionate number of soldiers from urban minority communities where tension was high and morale was low. In the previous four years, racial riots had broken out in a number of major cities across America. A National Advisory Commission appointed by President Johnson to determine why the riots had taken place and what could be done to prevent further riots issued a report in March 1968, which stated that the riots were the result of a "reservoir of unredressed grievances and frustration in the ghetto."[35] The commission's report stated bluntly, "What white Americans have never fully understood—but what the Negro can never forget—is that white society is deeply implicated in the ghetto. White institutions created it, white institutions maintain it, and white society condones it."[36] To respond to the despair and discrimination facing blacks and other minority communities in the country, the commission recommended broad reforms that included a minimum national income, the establishment of a welfare system based on need, and the creation of three million low-cost housing units and two million jobs in the next three years. The commission stated, "[O]nly a commitment to national action on an unprecedented scale can shape a future compatible with the historic ideals of American society."[37]

By April 1968, the president had received the report but had not yet acted on it. However, confronting the possibility of a new wave of riots in reaction to King's death, President Johnson called for "constructive action instead of destructive action in this hour of national need" and urged the passage of legislation adopting many of the recommendations made by the National Advisory Commission.[38] In mourning her slain husband, Coretta Scott King pleaded with the nation to make real his dream of racial equality.[39] A leader of the National Council of Churches stated, "Grief at a time like this is not enough."[40] He asked Americans to deliver "the greatest outpouring of cards, letters, and telegrams to Washington the nation has ever known," to bring about change in America. And at Boalt, a student writing for the *Writ* called for action: "We need no more reports." Reflecting the frustration of many, she wrote, "[Despite the] avalanche of words...on the subject of America's race problem,...amazingly little has been done."[41]

It was certainly true that very little had been done in the legal profession. In 1968, the legal profession remained almost entirely white and male. African Americans constituted not much more than 1 percent of the bar, and the numbers of other minority lawyers were so small that they were not even tallied.[42] And although Boalt had begun to take affirmative steps to increase minority enrollment, the total number of minorities ever enrolled at Boalt was little more than the age of the law school.[43]

Professor Herma Hill Kay was one of many faculty members at Boalt who found this disquieting. Kay had grown up in the South and understood how pervasive racial inequality was in America. She was also one of the first female law professors in the country—hired in 1960 as the second woman ever to teach at Boalt—and was acutely aware of the extent of white male privilege in the legal profession.[44] "It was clear," she stated, "that we needed to change the face of the profession and that we needed to make a special effort toward that end."[45]

In the spring of 1968, following King's assassination, Boalt renewed and expanded its commitment to increase the number of minorities at the law school. The dean of admissions recounted this history in a memo to the faculty one year later. He wrote, "It was quickly apparent that there were relatively few applications from minority groups in the previous years—a number so small as to frustrate our goal. Our first step . . . was to stimulate applications. . . . [W]e accelerated our efforts to inform undergraduates from minority groups of the opportunities available in the law."[46] Minority student organizations at Boalt designed and operated outreach and recruitment programs in consultation with the Dean's Office, which provided financial support in conjunction with the Boalt Hall Student Association.

In addition to expanded outreach and recruitment efforts, at the prompting of Boalt professors Larry Stone and Adrian Kragen, the faculty established the Martin Luther King Fund, to which law firms throughout California contributed, making available scholarships and financial aid to students choosing to attend Boalt.[47] As the dean of admissions later observed, financial aid played a pivotal role in enabling minority students to attend Boalt:

[It was] apparent . . . [that] [w]ithout the financial assistance, most [minority] students would probably not have been able to attend law school at all, or, if they did attend, would have been required to work an excessive number of hours each week in order to earn the amounts required to survive. The need [for] and importance [of] financial assistance cannot be overstated. Effectively none of the students have outside sources of financial assistance. Most have been self-supporting throughout their undergraduate years.[48]

Increased financial aid coupled with aggressive student outreach and recruiting constituted the "soft" elements of an affirmative action program that was conceived in the years prior but came into full operation following Martin Luther King's death. The "hard" elements of the affirmative action program involved the admissions process itself. Outreach and recruitment were only effective if qualified minorities were admitted to Boalt. Because the law school had become increasingly competitive and many minority applicants had relatively lower grades and test scores,

Boalt was compelled to give special consideration to these students if it was to increase the representation of minorities in the law school. In fall 1968, the Special Admissions program was formally put into place.

Under the Special Admissions program, the rapidly increasing work of examining individual applications was given to an Admissions Committee, staffed initially by faculty members who were later assisted by students appointed by the Boalt Hall Student Association. All applicants were evaluated primarily on the basis of their predicted grade average (PGA), which was based on a formula that weighted an applicant's undergraduate grade point average (UGPA) and his or her LSAT score. At the time, the formula weighted LSAT scores 70 percent and UGPAs 30 percent.[49] The PGA had been designed by the Educational Testing Service to predict the first-semester grades of a law student. Boalt used the PGA to select students who were likely to successfully complete their first semester and, by logical extension, their three years of law school. In a large applicant pool, with more students capable of completing law school than there were seats, Boalt also used the PGA to distinguish between capable applicants. The use of the PGA in this way had a disparate impact on minority students.

Some believed that the PGA was useful in predicting the obvious — that an applicant with a 700 LSAT and a 3.8 UGPA was likely to excel academically, and an applicant with a 500 LSAT and a 3.0 UGPA might have trouble competing. But it was not as useful in differentiating the middle — the hard ones — and was unreliable in predicting the applicants at the lower extremes.[50] More important, the PGA seemed to under-predict the performance of many minority students, partly because the UGPA did not adequately reflect the potential of minority applicants to do well in law school — many minority students had to work as undergraduates to an extent that might have affected their grades. This was also due to the limited ability of the LSAT to predict performance in the first place. On a validity scale of .00 (no relationship between test scores and first-semester grades) and 1.00 (complete congruence of the two), the LSAT produced a validity down in the .33–.35 range.[51]

This low validity meant that the LSAT was limited in its ability to explain the variance in first-year grades. Statisticians often square the validity correlation coefficient to measure the percentage of variance in performance that a predictor explains.[52] With a validity of .33 to .35, the LSAT could be said to explain only 11 to 12 percent of the variance in first-year grades, leaving about 88 percent unexplained. To put this in perspective, one could more accurately predict a person's height on the basis of weight than a person's first-year grades on the basis of an LSAT score.[53] Heavy reliance on the LSAT, with its limited predictive validity, subjected minority applicants to a substantial "selection bias," even when the predictive validity of the LSAT was about the same for all racial groups.[54]

The LSAT—far from adequately predicting success in law school—produced results that bore an uncanny resemblance to the social hierarchy in America. This was no accident. The LSAT had been derived from IQ (intelligence) tests designed by eugenicists in the early part of the century, who believed that the test measured a biologically grounded, genetically inherited quality that was tied to ethnicity.[55] Henry H. Goddard, who brought the IQ test to America, hoped to use it to "recognize limits, segregate, and curtail breeding to prevent further deterioration of an endangered American stock, threatened from without and by prolific reproduction of its feeble-minded from within."[56] The first large-scale use of the test occurred during World Wars I and II, when the military used IQ tests to sort soldiers by their "inherent abilities." Not surprisingly, the tests faithfully reproduced the social order. "Officers scored higher than enlisted men, the native-born scored higher than the foreign-born, less recent immigrants scored higher than more recent immigrants, and whites scored higher than Negroes."[57] The results of the tests led directly to new laws curbing immigration and were used by segregationists to argue that "the education of whites and colored in separate schools may have justification other than that created by racial prejudice."[58]

Following World War II, the military tests were adapted to university admissions and transformed by the newly formed Educational Testing Service (ETS) into standardized entrance exams. In 1947, the ETS developed the LSAT at the request of several prestigious law schools, including Harvard, Yale, and Columbia, who were beginning to experience a greater demand for admissions.[59] Far from being color-blind, the test was developed at a time when the legal profession affirmatively sought to exclude people based on their race and ethnicity.[60] The LSAT was pretested on a population almost entirely composed of upper-class white men.[61] This proved to be a distinct liability for women and particularly for minorities. Minorities sat low in America's social hierarchy, and their LSAT scores reflected their position. While the LSAT had a correlation with first-year law school grades in the .33–.35 range, the test had a correlation with racial group membership (as between blacks and whites) in the .52–.68 range. To compare, first-year grades had a correlation with race in the .31–.47 range. Such bias in a test whose predictive ability was based on its prejudicial impact on racial minorities meant that the LSAT was better at predicting the race of an applicant than it was at predicting first-year grades. [62]

Despite scoring low on a test supposedly designed to predict "inherent ability," minority students who were given the opportunity to study law showed that they could outperform the predictions of the LSAT. John Huerta (class of 1968), a Mexican American transfer student to Boalt Hall, was a case in point.[63] Huerta had grown up in the Watts area of Los Angeles and graduated with honors from Los Angeles State College, where he had been elected student body president and "outstanding man of the year." In 1965, upon graduating, Huerta applied to Boalt, but was denied admission because his LSAT score was low—in the fourteenth percentile. So he went to law school at Hastings, across the bay in San Francisco, and made the top 1 percent of his class. After his first year, Huerta transferred to Boalt, where he excelled and soon became an associate editor of the *California Law Review*—the prestigious law journal at Boalt.

As a third-year student, John Huerta gave an interview to the student newspaper, during which he discussed the limited predictive value of the LSAT and questioned its continued use for some minority students. He stated, "There [is] substantial and persuasive evidence that the tests are culturally biased. Therefore, most minority applicants will make a poor showing on [them]." He recommended waiving LSAT scores unless they would help the minority applicant, pointing out that the few minorities who do well on the test demonstrate that they are adept within both cultural frameworks—the mainstream white cultural framework and their own—and should be admitted. However, Huerta suggested, "the decision to admit the minority student who scores low on the LSAT should be based on other factors, say grades and recommendations."[64]

Recognizing the disparity of opportunities between minority and non-minority applicants, and acknowledging the limitations of the LSAT in identifying promising candidates, the Admissions Committee considered the particular circumstances of minority applicants. As one admissions officer noted, a minority applicant's grades "may reflect a clash with his education[al] institution or an effort finally to catch up after an inferior educational background." In addition, the officer stated, "standardized tests such as the LSAT [may not be]...accurate predictors of ability of those whose background is not mainstream American."[65]

Minority applicants were given special consideration, which meant disregarding lower grades and test scores, and admitting minorities based on other information in their files that indicated an ability to succeed in law school. If the Admissions Committee felt confident that a minority applicant could handle the work, then that applicant was admitted. The expanded affirmative action program was immediately effective. In its first year, 1968–69, Boalt enrolled more African American students than it had graduated in all its prior years. The same could be said for Latino students.[66] The faculty and administration were encouraged by the results and sought to increase the number of minority students to approximate "a fair representation of ethnic groups in the state and nation."[67]

In reviewing the affirmative action program after its first year of operation, the Admissions Office reported that, as had been expected, "the students admitted so far perform in law school better than the standard predictors indicated."[68] The dean of admissions noted in a memo to the faculty that "most of the students who started in September 1968, are still with us."[69] Only two had withdrawn, for reasons unrelated to academics, and only two appeared to be in serious academic difficulty, but the dean observed that these two "would likely be able to cure their deficiencies by the end of the year." The dean counted the program as a success, not only in terms of the increased numbers of minority students, but also in terms of the contributions of these students to the law school and to the legal profession. He stated,

[T]he attitude of the students toward law school, toward legal education, and toward the profession of law is one of serious enthusiasm and determination. Of equal importance . . . are the contributions of those students to the school itself. Their presence has contributed incalculably to the enrichment of the educational experience of the other 90% of the student body. Nor is the enrichment limited to the students. The faculty, both in the subject matters of their instruction and individually, have been challenged and stimulated by the ideas and experiences of these students. The long-run benefits in terms of curricular reform and improvement and in terms of social awareness can only be measured at some future date.

Ultimately, the greatest contributions remain to be made by these students as leaders in all the ways Boalt graduates serve. We expect that, in the tradition of our profession, these men and women will be an important source of political and business leadership, some for their communities, some for other "communities" in society, and some for society as a whole.[70]

In the following years, Boalt admitted an increasing number of minority students, including not only African Americans and Latinos, but also Asian Americans and Native Americans. For example, Asian Americans, who had numbered only one or two per class in the 1960s, increased to eight in the class that entered in 1969. Neil Gotanda (class of 1972) was one of the Asian American students admitted that year. Gotanda was a

TABLE 1. Minority Students Entering Boalt Hall, 1967–1971

	1967	1968	1969	1970	1971
Percentage of Class	2	7	14	24	34

SOURCE: "Statement of Faculty Policy Governing Admission to Boalt Hall and Report of the Admissions Policy Task Force," August 31, 1993, p. 11 (for years 1968–1971); Boalt Hall Registrar's Office (for year 1967).

Japanese American from Stockton, California, whose family had been interned during World War II. He had grown up with a mother who was outspoken about the unfairness of the internment, and her willingness to speak out, coupled with the climate of the 1960s, fueled an interest in activism. In his first year at Boalt, 1969–70, Gotanda helped organize Asian Americans into a student group that, among other things, focused on the need to increase Asian American representation at the law school. The new student group identified promising Asian American candidates and served as an advocate for them in the admissions process. Due in part to these efforts, Asian admissions more than doubled in the subsequent two years.[71] By 1971, the percentage of minorities enrolled at Boalt had reached an unprecedented 34 percent (see table 1). Leading the nation in the inclusion of students previously unrepresented in law schools, Boalt enrolled more minority students that year than did any other American law school, with the exception of historically black law schools.[72]

The increased number of minority students at Boalt had an appreciable effect on the law school. For the first time in its history, the norms and assumptions underlying the historically white male institution came under fire. Reflecting the tension in the newly diverse law school, a minority student wrote in the student newspaper, "Admitting non-whites to the system means more than taking black, brown and yellow bodies and putting them into slots tailored for whites—it means changing the very nature of that system. And this I assure you we are determined to do."[73]

Minority students at Boalt, as well as at universities across the country, called attention to the need for change in the traditional curriculum. In a series of strikes known as the Third World Movement that began at San Francisco State University in the fall of 1968 and arrived in Berkeley in late January 1969, minority students demanded more relevance in their curriculum.[74] A black law student at Boalt explained that traditional education "has had the effect of reinforcing the values of the [white] majority, while negating the contributions and cultural roles of [minorities]."[75] He further explained that in traditional education the minority student feels that his own experiences and background are "insignificant, if not irrelevant," and he feels alienated as a result.

Referring specifically to legal education, another black student stated, "Since there is only one system of law in this society it should embrace the frailties and conflicts of all people. A law school curriculum should be relevant to the needs of [minorities], and those needs should be the subject of academic discussion and study." He asserted that white students had a stake as well in learning from other cultural perspectives and in learning alongside students of different cultural backgrounds. "We can learn to live together and respect each other *only* as equals," the student stated.[76]

This sentiment had been expressed by John Huerta in his 1968 interview with the school newspaper about the affirmative action program.[77] Huerta justified affirmative action not only in terms of closing the opportunity gap in America, but also in terms of closing the "understanding" gap. He remarked,

A few weeks ago Bobby Seale, a leader of the Black Panthers, spoke at this law school. During the questioning that followed his speech, a student asked him to explain what he meant by "police brutality." No student in law school should have to ask that question. Yet most students here don't have any idea what "police brutality" is all about.... If we had the number of minority students here proportionate to those that exist in the out-of-law-school world, then white students might understand why minorities dislike the police, vomit at the thought of installment contracts, scoff at much civil rights legislation and a whole host of other matters.

He added, "White law students should want to be in a 'real life' situation; they won't learn about the lives and attitudes of minorities out of casebooks. To learn this they will either have to live and practice in minority communities or have a dialogue with minority classmates and professors."[78]

To the extent that professors responded to the concerns of minority students, courses at Boalt became more relevant, making room for discussion about how the law affected different communities. In addition, Boalt began to offer new courses such as "Corrections and Sentencing," "Slavery as an American Legal Institution," "Consumer Protection Seminar," "Children and the Law," "Patterns in Collective Bargaining," and "Civil Disobedience, Self Help, and Coercion."[79]

Outside of the classroom, minority students found relevance in community legal work. Latino law students were particularly active on this front, forming their own community legal clinic in Oakland. Like the black population in the area, the Latino population had also grown over the last decade, concentrating itself in the Fruitvale District of East Oakland. The Latinos living in Fruitvale, and across the state of California, suffered from an acute lack of legal services based in the Spanish-speaking community. Though Latinos numbered some two million in California, Boalt students estimated that there were no more than sixty Latino professionals (lawyers, doctors, and dentists) in the entire state. To alleviate at least part of the lack of legal services in Fruitvale, Boalt students formed La Raza Centro Legal. Through this legal clinic and with the support of community lawyers, Latino and non-Latino students familiarized themselves with the legal problems of the community and supplemented a formal education with real-life experience.[80]

The greater number of minority students at Boalt brought a new awareness of racial issues to the law school. Dean Edward Halbach, who had led the development of a formal affirmative action program at Boalt, recalled that prior to affirmative action, "We had only the benefit of a few minorities in our law school classes. The more minorities there were around and the more comfortable they became, the more we understood the extent and complex nature of racial problems in our society."[81]

Increased exposure to minority students had an effect on Robert Cole, a young professor who had been hired to teach at Boalt in 1961. Cole was Jewish and had come into the legal profession at a time when explicit barriers against Jewish people were just being removed. He was familiar with religious discrimination and sensitive to racial discrimination. Growing up in Chicago, he had Japanese friends who suffered through internment during World War II, and this affected him profoundly. But in a racially segregated city, he knew very few African Americans. He reflected, "Black people were far less visible to most whites then, and poor blacks were virtually invisible to them."[82] It was not until affirmative action brought significant numbers of minorities into the law school that Cole was able, at a more profound level, to understand the problems of blacks and other minorities and to realize the breadth and depth of racial disparity in this country.

The transition made by the law school from being virtually all white and male to being diverse, both in terms of race and gender—for at that time women were also enrolling in significant numbers, though without the assistance of affirmative action—was a difficult one. Common ground was needed to overcome the racial divide, and that ground did not come easily. Minority and nonminority students and faculty alike

were unfamiliar with one another and had to bridge the gap in understanding. Minority students had to adapt to a culture still unfamiliar to
many of them: that of the middle- to upper-class white. For example, in
his third-year class in corporate law, John Huerta remembered the professor asking who among the students owned stock, and "everyone
raised their hands" except him. "I felt there was a whole culture gap...
and that there was a lack of understanding of working-class people, immigrant families, and minority communities." Moreover, "the subject
matter that I studied was intellectually remote and not grounded in my
own experiences."[83]

White students and professors had to become a "great deal more sensitive" to minority students.[84] Individuals who before had made racist
and sexist jokes or were too casual in their language now thought more
about what they said. There was a heightened awareness, recalled Professor Cole, "that things that you took for granted could be insulting."
John McNulty, a young professor who had been hired the year the Civil
Rights Act was passed, agreed, and did what he could to make the students in his class feel comfortable at the law school.[85] McNulty had
grown up in Buffalo, New York, which had received successive waves of
immigrants, mostly from Europe, and was conscious of welcoming out-
siders. Arriving at Boalt in the same year that the law school hired its first
African American professor, John Wilkins, McNulty and his wife found
they had a lot in common with Wilkins and his wife, and the two couples
became friends.

Several years later, as minority students, particularly black students,
began to enroll in significant numbers, McNulty was "conscious of treat-
ing every student with respect, from correctly pronouncing student
names to responding to student concerns." One concern involved grading. At the house of a visiting African American law professor and her
husband, a number of black students expressed concern that they were
being discriminated against in the grading process. They also discussed
their feelings and concerns about being a minority in a primarily white institution. The professor's husband (himself African American) em-
pathized with the students, and told them that the toughest dilemma they
would face in life would be knowing whether certain things happened to
them because they were black or for some other reason. Professor Mc-
Nulty was present and drew from the conversation an insight into the
position of a minority person. This insight, he reflected, "revealed to me
and verbalized the reality and difficulty of that position in a way better
than I had ever heard it put before." He subsequently made a point of ex-

plaining the grading process to his students in class and clarifying to them that grading was blind.[86]

Despite the conscious effort by some to make Boalt a more welcoming environment for new students, minority students still had trouble adjusting to the predominantly white male law school. Students complained of continuing "insensitivity" and, in some cases, "latent hostility" toward minorities and women.[87] For Richard Delgado (class of 1974), a Latino law student who entered Boalt in 1971, the real divide seemed to be between young minority students and older white professors. He recalled feeling "tolerated, but not welcome" by many of the professors. Delgado was the son of Mexican immigrants and had been inspired to come to law school by the civil rights movement and the antiwar movement. He embraced the diversity of the law school, and was pleased to find students from different racial, economic, religious, and ideological backgrounds with whom he could relate. He had difficulty, however, relating to the majority of law professors at Boalt. "They seemed unapproachable and uninterested in minority students."[88]

Though Delgado earned high marks during his three years, he recalled that "not one professor encouraged me to try out for law review, to apply for a clerkship, or go into teaching." In his second year he won a coveted spot on the staff of the *California Law Review*. Delgado remembered that one day, when he was checking citations on an article for the journal, a professor came into the *Law Review* office and was startled to see a brown face. The professor's eyes looked at Delgado in surprise, seeming to ask, "What are you doing here?" Delgado felt uncomfortable. He felt like he didn't belong—he knew that he had entered a world that was historically reserved for the white elite. Delgado turned outside the law school for support and found a mentor in a young Latino law professor at another university who encouraged him to go into teaching, which he did, becoming one of the most prolific contemporary legal scholars in the country.[89]

Though most faculty and students agreed that the law school needed to reflect more accurately the community in which it existed, the means by which it would become more diverse were questioned from the outset, if not publicly then privately. Professor Jesse Choper, for one, held serious reservations about the affirmative action program at the law school.[90] Choper was a constitutional law scholar who had joined Boalt in 1965 after clerking for Supreme Court Chief Justice Earl Warren. Choper believed that Boalt had a moral interest in being race-inclusive, but he was not sure that that interest overpowered the constitutional interest in neutrality.

Choper interpreted the constitutional interest in neutrality found in the Fourteenth Amendment—ensuring every individual the "equal protection of the laws"—as not allowing for the award of benefits or burdens based on race. He questioned whether affirmative action was constitutional, troubled as to whether the special consideration accorded to minority applicants was a benefit and the lack of special consideration accorded to white applicants was a burden. However, the concept of affirmative action in education was relatively new in the country. Boalt had been one of the first institutions to implement a race-conscious admissions policy aimed at increasing minority enrollment, and the courts had not yet considered the validity of such a policy. Choper maintained his reservations, but he did not actively oppose the new policy at Boalt.

Immediately following the formal adoption of the affirmative action program in the spring of 1968, some began to question whether race-conscious admissions policies discriminated against whites. Foreshadowing cries of reverse discrimination, an interviewer for the *Writ* had asked John Huerta whether the efforts to recruit and help minority students reflected "racism in reverse." Huerta answered,

Minorities have been disadvantaged in every way as a group when compared with the white majority. The average black or brown person is caught very early in a vicious circle of discrimination, joblessness, poor housing, and inferior schooling. . . . [E]qual opportunity will not be realized by suddenly removing one or two of the barriers. An inequality has already been perpetrated. To remove that inequality requires special attention to be given in all respects . . . [to compensate for] harmful attention or inattention. [A] minority student must be recruited, tutored, and financed if he is just to have a "fighting chance" to compete academically with his middle-class and rich Anglo classmates who have not suffered an inferior education and environment all their lives.[91]

Claims of reverse discrimination were based on the difference in LSAT scores and undergraduate grade point averages between minority and nonminority students. Even though these differences did not consistently translate into success or failure at the law school, given the limited ability of grades and tests to predict performance, some white students and faculty resented the special consideration given to minority students. Competition for law school seats was getting fierce, and opponents of affirmative action objected to the fact that minority students were gaining admission with relatively lower scores.

In December 1971, after the law school had enrolled the highest percentage of minorities in its history—34 percent—the faculty quietly voted to curb the Special Admissions program. Responding to concerns that minority students were overrepresented at the law school, the faculty imposed a limit of 25 percent on minorities admitted under the Special Admissions program.[92] Boalt had previously admitted as many minority students as the Admissions Committee found qualified to attend the law school. With a dramatic rise in minority applications—from 60 in 1968 to 564 in 1971— the faculty found it necessary to put some limits on the Special Admissions program, just as it had found it necessary beginning in 1961 to put some limits on the regular admissions program.[93]

Partly because they were not included in the decision-making process, minority students protested the faculty decision, viewing the new policy as a rollback of the school's commitment to increasing minority representation at the law school. The Black Law Students Association called for a boycott of classes, which 80 percent of the student body honored. At a press conference, a spokesperson for the Asian American Students Association stated, "The administrators promised us earlier that there would be no cutbacks in the special admissions program, and they have gone back on their promise." The student noted that the Special Admissions program had been pivotal in increasing Asian representation in the legal profession, particularly for Filipino students, who were the fastest-growing minority group in America but only numbered eight in American law schools, two of whom were at Boalt. Congressman Ron Dellums, an African American representing the Oakland area, lent student protesters his full support "in their attempt to impress upon the school administration the importance of continuing to recognize their obligation to serve the needs of all the people of the state rather than a select elite portion thereof."[94]

Students also garnered the support of several faculty members, such as Professor Robert Cole, who advocated the continued admission of significant numbers of minority students. He said that the larger number of minority students had raised the quality of his classes. He explained to other faculty members that minority students appeared to question his premises more closely than did their white counterparts. In previous years, when there had been fewer minority students, they appeared to be less willing or able to do so.[95] Professor Cole also argued for a more significant student role in the decision-making process. Admissions was one of many areas where the faculty was limiting student participation, and Cole felt strongly that as stakeholders in the development of the law school, student voices should be incorporated into the decision-making structure.[96]

A spokesperson for the Black Law Students Association demanded that the faculty call an emergency open meeting, declaring, "This is not a racial issue.... The real issue is arbitrary decision making." Students challenged the lack of a stated rationale behind the 25 percent and the lack of a student participatory role. "We know of no decision-making body in a state institution comparable for the secretiveness and unrecorded nature of the process by which it reaches decisions."[97] The faculty agreed to form a student-faculty committee to study special admissions. Professor Herma Hill Kay suggested that students on the committee have voting power, but her suggestion had so little support among the other professors that it was never brought to a vote.[98]

In 1973, the faculty adopted the "Faculty Policy Governing Admission to Boalt Hall." The policy established the general rule for the selection of applicants: "[A]pplicants shall be accepted for admission who on the basis of their academic achievement, LSAT scores and other data appear to have the highest potential for law study and for achievement in and contribution to the legal profession, legal scholarship or law-related activities."[99] The policy also provided for the special consideration of minority applicants, but limited the admission of such applicants to no more than 25 percent of the entering class. Special admission was to be given to members of racial or cultural groups "which have not had a fair opportunity to develop their potential for academic achievement and which are in need of adequate representation in the legal profession." The policy stated that the number of those specially admitted should vary with shifts in the quality and availability of applicants and also with the number of applications from the groups given special consideration who gained admission under the general rule.[100]

Under the 1973 policy, regular admissions and special admissions were conducted separately. Minority applicants with a PGA above a certain level were first considered in the regular admissions process. If not admitted through that process, they were considered in the special admissions process. However, minority students—with the notable exception of Japanese American and Chinese American students—were rarely admitted through the regular admissions process. Because Japanese American and, to a lesser extent, Chinese American students were successful in gaining admission through the regular process, the faculty decided in 1975 to eliminate and reduce, respectively, special consideration for these Asian subgroups.[101]

Competition for admission to Boalt stiffened significantly in the early 1970s, and many minority students found that their numerical qualifications kept them from being considered in the regular admissions process. While the entering class of roughly 270 students had been selected in 1960

from an applicant pool of approximately 700, and in 1964 from an applicant pool of approximately 1,500, the entering classes from 1972 on were
selected from applicant pools of almost 5,000.[102] By 1972, the average
LSAT score of those admitted under the regular admissions program was
706—a score which represented the top 3 percent of all those taking the
LSAT—and the grade point average remained high: 3.5.[103]

The PGAs of African American, Native American, and Latino applicants, and of Asian American applicants other than Japanese and Chinese
Americans, continued to be substantially lower than those of other applicants. It was clear to the Admissions Committee at Boalt that without
a Special Admissions program that evaluated these groups separately,
there would be little minority presence at the law school. To maintain
more than a token minority presence, Boalt would have to give special
consideration to groups that would otherwise be excluded.[104]

What was true at Boalt was true at other highly selective law schools
and professional schools in the country—because of a disparity in grades
and especially test scores between minority and nonminority students,
affirmative action was necessary to achieve a racially diverse student population. Nevertheless, the special consideration accorded minority students angered those who had opposed affirmative action from the outset. Critics of race-conscious measures rejected the use of race to remedy
the condition of minority groups in America, viewing any form of race
consciousness as discriminatory. They failed to distinguish between race-
inclusive affirmative action programs and race-exclusive segregation practices. They urged a return to a conception of racism that was based on
specific acts of discrimination resulting in injury to an individual, rather
than on structural forms of discrimination resulting in injury to a group.
This view tended to rationalize racial injustice as a supposedly natural
outcome of group attributes in competition.[105] In the context of highly
competitive university admissions, this view supported the argument that
the playing field was fair and that therefore minority students did not de-
serve to be admitted in preference to white students because they had
lower grades and test scores.

In 1971, a white applicant to law school used this argument to sue the
University of Washington Law School, lodging the first legal challenge to
affirmative action. In *DeFunis v. Odegaard,* a white applicant denied admission to the law school charged the University of Washington with reverse discrimination when minority students with PGAs lower than his
were admitted.[106] The state court ruled in favor of Marco DeFunis—the
white applicant—and directed the law school to admit him. The Univer-

sity of Washington appealed, and in 1974 the case reached the U.S. Supreme Court. By that time, DeFunis was about to graduate, and the Court, with eight of the nine justices in agreement, held that the case was moot.

Justice Douglas, however, dissented and asserted that the case was not moot, and that, given the significance of the issues raised, it was important to reach the merits of the case.[107] His dissent focused partly on the use of the LSAT in an admissions process that in every way resembled the admissions process employed at Boalt. Minority students were given special consideration; as a result, thirty-six of these students were admitted to the law school despite having lower PGAs than DeFunis's. Notably, forty-eight *nonminority* applicants with PGAs lower than DeFunis's were also admitted—twenty-three of them were returning veterans, and the remainder were admitted "because of other factors in their applications that made them attractive candidates despite their relatively low PGAs."[108] But what DeFunis objected to was not just the admission of students with lower PGAs, but the special consideration accorded minorities simply because of their race.

Douglas argued, however, that the presence of the LSAT in the admissions decision was sufficient to warrant the special consideration of minority candidates. The law school had not raised the argument of deficiencies in the test in its defense of affirmative action. Nevertheless, Douglas questioned the continued use of traditional criteria, especially the LSAT, in law school admissions. Quoting from a law journal article, he stated,

[L]aw school admissions criteria have operated within a hermetically sealed system; it is now beginning to leak. The traditional combination of LSAT and [U]GPA...may have provided acceptable predictors of likely performance in law school in the past...[but] [t]here is no clear evidence that the LSAT and [U]GPA provide particularly good evaluators of the intrinsic or enriched ability of an individual to perform as a law student or lawyer in a functioning society undergoing change.[109]

He asserted that the law school's admissions policy could not be reconciled with the goal of increasing minority representation, "unless cultural standards of a diverse rather than a homogenous society are taken into account." In his view, because the LSAT "reflects questions touching on cultural backgrounds," a law school may properly give minority applicants special consideration. Suggesting that the test was culturally biased as a result of its being norm-referenced to a majority white population, Justice Douglas added, "[M]inorities have cultural backgrounds that are vastly different from the dominant Caucasian...[and] a test sensitively tuned for most applicants would be wide of the mark for many minorities." He reasoned that special consideration of these applicants was warranted, "lest race be a subtle force in eliminating minority members because of cultural differences."[110] In his dissent, Douglas concluded that the case should be remanded for a new trial to consider, among other things, "whether the established LSAT should be eliminated so far as racial minorities are concerned." He contended that "[t]he reason for the separate treatment of minorities as a class is to make more certain that racial factors do not militate *against an applicant or on his behalf.*"[111]

Immediately after the Supreme Court ruled in *DeFunis,* another white applicant—this time at the University of California Medical School at Davis—filed charges of reverse discrimination, bringing affirmative action programs under scrutiny once again.[112] Allan Bakke—the white applicant in *Regents of the University of California v. Bakke*—had been denied admission to medical school while minority students with lower grades and test scores had been admitted under an affirmative action program. The state court ruled in favor of Bakke, and in 1978 the case was appealed all the way to the U.S. Supreme Court. Affirmative action was on the block, and three of the best legal minds at Boalt—Professors Paul Mishkin, David Feller, and Jan Vetter—helped write three briefs on behalf of the University of California, the Association of American Law Schools (AALS), and the public law schools in California, defending affirmative action.[113] In the brief to the Supreme Court defending its program, the University of California articulated the necessity of a race-conscious admissions program to increase diversity not only at the medical school, but also at other highly competitive professional schools across the country:

Today, only a race-conscious plan for minority admissions will permit qualified applicants from disadvantaged minorities to attend medical schools, law schools and other institutions of higher learning in sufficient numbers to enhance the quality of the education of all students; to broaden the professions and increase their services to the entire community; to destroy pernicious stereotypes; and to demonstrate to the young that educational opportunities and rewarding careers are truly open regardless of ethnic origin.

Applicants for admission to professional schools greatly outnumber the available places. Until their cultural isolation is relieved by full participation in all phases of society, historically alienated minorities would be screened out by all racially blind methods of selection. There is, literally, no substitute for the use of race as a factor in admissions if professional schools are to admit more than an isolated few applicants from minority groups long subjected to hostile and pervasive discrimination.[114]

With respect to law schools in particular, the AALS filed an *amicus* brief, stressing the importance of affirmative action programs in increasing minority enrollment. Over the previous decade, minority enrollment had increased from seven hundred (approximately 1 percent) in 1964 to more than ninety-five hundred (approximately 8 percent) in 1976.[115] Special admissions programs, the AALS asserted, had been pivotal in increasing not only the number of law students, but also the number of minority lawyers—a number that still remained "inordinately small at under 2 percent of the entire bar."[116]

According to the AALS, law schools were created and supported by the state to meet its needs for lawyers and legal services. Lawyers played a critical role in the public as well as private governance of our society, and the inclusion of minorities in the bar was required to achieve their participation in the governance of our society, public as well as private.[117] The AALS emphasized the public importance of the profession in decisions made daily by zoning boards of appeal, transportation departments, regulatory agencies, and all other bodies affecting the lives of people in a racially diverse society: "At times, perhaps often, these decisions will have a different impact upon minority communities than upon the white community. A minority presence in the decision-making process increases the likelihood that those differences will be recognized and taken into account."[118] The AALS added that in light of the need to understand and work across racial differences in a diverse society, significant minority enrollment at the law schools was important to increase understanding of minority groups and effective communication across racial lines.[119]

When the decision in *Bakke* came down, a majority of the Supreme Court justices upheld race-conscious admissions programs. The University of California had offered several theories justifying affirmative action, and the five justices finding affirmative action to be constitutional adopted two of these theories, although no one theory had a majority in the Court. Four of the five justices—Justices Brennan, White, Marshall, and Blackmun—focused on the theory that effective compensation for unequal opportunities caused by previous societal discrimination required that adjustments be made through race-conscious admissions programs. In an individual opinion, Justice Marshall, the first African American appointed to the Supreme Court, reviewed the history of state-sponsored discrimination in this country in relation to the present condition of minorities and of African Americans in particular. Marshall noted that, compared to whites, black Americans suffered from twice the rate of infant mortality, lived five years less, faced more than twice the rate of unemployment, and, when they were fortunate enough to earn a college degree, earned little more than a white high school graduate.[120] Justice Marshall wrote, "At every point from birth to death the impact of the past is reflected in the still disfavored position of the Negro. In light of the sorry history of discrimination and its devastating impact on the lives of Negroes, bringing the Negro into the mainstream of American life should be a state interest of the highest order. To fail to do so is to ensure that America will forever remain a divided society."[121]

Justice Powell—the other justice holding affirmative action constitutional—dismissed this theory, viewing "societal discrimination" as "an amorphous concept of injury that may be ageless in its reach into the past."[122] Powell stated that any finding of discrimination would have to be based on a specific injury and could not be drawn from a general history of discrimination. At one point, however, he suggested that the cultural bias in admissions criteria might constitute a specific injury sufficient to justify making adjustments based on race. In a footnote, he observed,

Racial classifications in admissions conceivably could serve [another] purpose, one which petitioner does not articulate: fair appraisal of each individual's academic promise in the light of some cultural bias in grading or testing procedures. To the extent that race and ethnic background were considered only to the extent of curing established inaccuracies in predicting academic performance, it might be argued that there is no "preference" at all. Nothing in this record, however, suggests either that any of the quantitative factors considered by the [University of California] were culturally biased or that petitioner's special admissions program was formulated to correct for any such biases.[123]

Minority students had implored the University of California to detail the racial bias of traditional admissions criteria, namely, grades and standardized test scores, but the university refrained from raising bias as an issue or introducing any evidence to that effect into the record,[124] despite detailed evidence of bias in a substantial body of research, part of which was supplied to the court by *amici*.[125] Not without reason, the university seemed to believe that building a record of culturally biased admissions criteria would invite litigation by minorities who were denied admission.[126] But in not raising racial discrimination embedded in traditional admissions criteria as a justification for its affirmative action program—as suggested by Justice Douglas in *DeFunis* and again by Justice Powell in *Bakke*—the university did a great disservice to minority students. In his critique of the university in its handling of the case, Derrick Bell, an African American professor at New York University Law School, wrote, "Given the choice of acknowledging that their admissions practices disadvantaged racial minorities in that they did not accurately predict minority applicants' performance in medical school, or casting doubt on the intellectual abilities of minority students by implying that the tests were valid but that minorities simply had trouble with them because of some vague, undefined disadvantage, the [university] chose the latter. In doing so, they committed [a] kind of group defamation."[127]

The university explained in great detail the large gaps in grades and test scores between white and minority applicants, concluding that without a special program, most minorities could not compete successfully with white applicants. However, the university provided no reason for the gap, and Justice Powell, who might otherwise have cast the deciding vote to uphold affirmative action as a remedy for discrimination, was left to ascribe the gap to a vague injury caused by indeterminate societal discrimination rather than a specific injury caused by identifiable racial bias. Furthermore, the Court was left to accept without question the use of grades and test scores as a neutral and proper measure of qualification through which minorities were determined to be "less qualified" and in need of preference, and whites were determined to be "more qualified" and subject to reverse discrimination. As a consequence, criticized Bell, "In what was potentially the most important civil rights case since *Brown v. Board of Education,* racial disadvantage, like a birth defect, was treated as an unfortunate accident of nature for which charity was appropriate, not as a massive, historic, and intentional racial crime for which virtually all institutions are responsible and for which a compensatory remedy is essential."[128]

Feeling that minority students had been forsaken by the university in its defense of affirmative action, the Black Law Students Association (BLSA) at Boalt filed an *amicus* brief challenging the assumption that standardized tests were objective measures of merit and that minorities were "less qualified" to attend medical and professional schools.[129] In its brief, BLSA reviewed the published research indicating that in the instance of medical schools, the Medical College Admission Test (MCAT) was not a valid indicator of performance for a medical student, an intern or resident, or a practicing physician.[130] The research also showed that the test had a discriminatory impact on minorities, partly because it was normed on a virtually all-white test-taking population.[131] Consequently, the BLSA asserted, the MCAT was neither a proper nor a neutral measure of "qualification." Under an earlier Supreme Court case, *Griggs v. Duke Power Co.,* a test with racially disparate results had to "bear a demonstrable relationship to successful performance" in the field for which applicants were screened.[132] Because the MCAT bore no such relationship, the BLSA argued that the test should justify neither rejecting minority candidates nor disparaging the qualifications of those who were accepted.[133]

When factors other than MCAT scores were considered, the BLSA argued, minority students were just as "qualified" to attend medical school as white students.[134] This was borne out by the successful completion of medical school by minority students, but it was also evident in the comparable undergraduate grades and personal qualities elicited in medical school interviews. Therefore, the BLSA concluded, the continued reliance on the MCAT as the primary screening device for medical school was a form of racial discrimination that warranted remedial action in the form of affirmative action.[135] The BLSA noted that under *Sweatt v. Painter,* the Court had required that racial minorities be admitted to professional schools without prejudice to their race, and under *Brown v. Board of Education,* it had guaranteed racial groups the opportunity to learn and compete in integrated schools.[136] However, the use of standardized tests thwarted the goal of integration in higher education, and the full realization of that goal still required that a "race-neutral" admissions process be race-conscious. The BLSA asserted that, given the bias found in the MCAT and other standardized tests such as the LSAT, race consciousness did not constitute a preference for racial groups but a means of avoiding racial discrimination which would otherwise occur.[137]

Though the BLSA and other *amici* raised the issue of ongoing racial discrimination, this was not enough for the Court to consider it in this case.[138] The university had not placed any evidence of test bias or other forms of discrimination into the record at the trial level, nor had it raised discrimination as an issue. Justice Powell did not further discuss the issue, embracing instead the theory offered by the university in its defense of affirmative action, that the educational interest in diversity was sufficient to justify race-conscious admissions. Using this theory of diversity, Justice Powell issued an individual opinion, which became the accepted opinion in the case.

Powell stated that a diverse student body was crucial to a university education because it produced an "atmosphere of speculation, experiment, and creation—so essential to the quality of higher education."[139] Citing *legal* education as an example of the type of program that would benefit from a diverse student body, Powell quoted the 1950 case of *Sweatt v. Painter,* which had invalidated a Texas statute excluding African American students from the University of Texas Law School: "The law school, the proving ground for legal learning and practice, cannot be effective in isolation from the individuals and institutions with which the law interacts. Few students and no one who has practiced law would choose to study in an academic vacuum, removed from the interplay of ideas and the exchange of views with which the law is concerned."[140]

In affirming race-conscious admissions programs, however, Powell imposed some limitations. He held that an affirmative action program was constitutionally permissible if it considered the race of an applicant as only one among many factors and did not employ strict quotas. In addition, Powell held that in the admissions process, minority and nonminority applicants could not be separated into different pools. Though race could be taken into account in evaluating what each applicant brought to the law school, all applicants—minority and nonminority—had to be compared against one another in a single applicant pool.

The diversity rationale of *Bakke* allowed highly competitive law schools such as Boalt to admit minority students by considering race as a "plus" factor in their files. However, the sizable difference in the PGAs of minority and nonminority applicants remained unaddressed. A growing body of evidence suggested that the use of the LSAT in admissions decisions had a disparate impact on minority applicants. David White, who had been working at Boalt during the *Bakke* case, conducting research on credentialism, was well versed on this evidence and the politics surrounding it. He had offered his assistance on the testing issue to the law professors preparing the UC defense but had been repeatedly rebuffed.[141] He had helped the BLSA at Boalt prepare its brief and had submitted it to the Supreme Court on behalf of the students, hoping to bring attention to the issue of test bias. But for the most part—with the exception of Powell's acknowledgment that test bias might justify a race-conscious remedy—this effort had been unsuccessful. Following *Bakke*, in an attempt to bring public awareness to the issue, White wrote a law journal article in which he used national data submitted to the Supreme Court in the *Bakke* case to demonstrate the disparate impact of the LSAT on the admissions opportunities of minority students (see table 2).[142]

The data showed that getting high grades or high test scores was a comparable feat for whites. For example, 40 percent of white applicants had college grades of 3.25 or higher, and 37 percent had LSAT scores above 600. In contrast, high test scores were much rarer for top black college students. While 13 percent had 3.25 or better grade averages, only 3 percent scored above 600 on the LSAT. When high test scores were considered in conjunction with high grades—as done in determining the

TABLE 2. Percentage of Black and White Applicants at or above Selected Levels of LSAT Scores and Undergraduate Grade Point Averages

	LSAT at or above 600	UGPA at or above 3.25	Combined LSAT and UGPA
Black	3%	13%	1%
White	37%	40%	20%
	LSAT at or above 500	UGPA at or above 2.75	Combined LSAT and UGPA
Black	19%	45%	11%
White	77%	75%	61%

SOURCE: David M. White, "Culturally Biased Testing and Predictive Invalidity: Putting Them on the Record," 14 *Harvard Civil Rights-Civil Liberties Law Review* 89–132, 119 (1979).

PGA of an applicant—half of the top whites were eliminated, while the top blacks were virtually decimated.[143] Consequently, the LSAT acted as a bar to admission for many black students. The analysis indicated that many black and other minority students deemed "inadmissible" under a combined LSAT and UGPA index would be considered "admissible" on the basis of UGPA alone.[144]

Given the consistently large gap in test scores between minority and nonminority students, David White suggested that the LSAT might be culturally biased. He identified several sources of possible bias, which varied "from the intentional to the indiscernibly subtle and accidental."[145] Intentional discrimination was the first source of bias. Given the racist origins of aptitude testing, it may not have been mere coincidence that the LSAT acted to disproportionately exclude minority students. White suggested that a second source of bias might be found in test questions that required knowledge of information more familiar to one cultural group than to another, such as questions pertaining to polo matches or regattas. The speed with which tests had to be completed constituted a third possible source of bias. The time requirement, White explained, might adversely affect certain groups whose apprehensions prompted them to be meticulous in taking the test. A fourth source of bias might arise from unfamiliarity with standardized tests themselves. Minority students were less likely to have the resources or the opportunity to familiarize themselves with the test by taking a test preparation course or sitting for the LSAT multiple times.

A fifth source of possible bias lay in unrecognized assumptions implied in test questions—where one cultural group might make the necessary assumptions to answer a question correctly while another cultural group might make the opposite assumption. For example, in an LSAT question asking the test taker to find a query similar in logic to the query, "Do you think that our university ought to go on discriminating against disadvantaged students by continuing its current admissions policies?" students from different cultural groups were likely to answer differently. A white student who assumed discrimination by its name was wrong and should be stopped, was likely to choose the "correct" answer, selecting the query, "Should your neighbor stop beating his wife?" A minority student, however, who assumed that the current discriminatory policies to which the question referred was actually affirmative action, a force which was necessary to admit disadvantaged minority students, was likely to select the "wrong" query: "Should force be used to prevent a person from committing suicide?"[146]

Finally, White contended that cultural bias could be expected as a result of the process by which tests were developed. Potentially discriminatory questions were withdrawn only when they yielded inconsistent results from a majority of students. Because the test-taking population remained majority white, the LSAT disadvantaged minority students who regularly answered a particular question differently. Because minority students did not make up a majority of test takers, the test continued to be norm-referenced to a white population.

In the aftermath of *Bakke*, at least some of the faculty at Boalt acknowledged the limitations of performance indicators, of which the LSAT was one. In a report assessing the admissions program at Boalt in light of *Bakke*, a faculty committee stated, "Predictions of probable performance are only predictions in gross and are subject to a wide margin of error in individual cases."[147] But in recognizing this, the committee did not question the continued use of the LSAT, partly because few other predictors were available to enable the law school to differentiate between talented students. This was also due to Boalt's increased reputation as the premier public law school in the country. Its competitive standing rested in part on the high ranking of its student body under the very performance indicators—namely the LSAT—that were detrimental to minority students.

In 1978, the average UGPA of students admitted to Boalt was 3.69, and the average LSAT was 728. However, the differences between minority and nonminority students remained substantial, particularly with respect to LSAT scores. Relative to admitted white students, who in 1978 had an average UGPA of 3.72 and LSAT score of 734, admitted African American students had an average UGPA of 3.23 and LSAT score of 616.

Admitted Latino students had an average UGPA of 3.28 and LSAT score of 583. Admitted Native American students had an average UGPA of 3.20 and LSAT score of 594. And admitted Asian American students, *including* Japanese and Chinese students, had an average UGPA of 3.55 and LSAT score of 701.[148]

Due to heightened competitiveness, the lower undergraduate grade averages and test scores of minority students, though exceeding the average grades and test scores of white students a decade earlier, required "special" consideration if these students were to be represented in the student body.[149] To this end, in 1978 the Boalt faculty adopted a new admissions policy providing for the continued special consideration of applicants from "those racial and cultural minority groups which [have] not had a fair opportunity to develop their potential for academic achievement and which lack adequate representation within the legal profession."[150] However, pursuant to *Bakke,* the regular and special admissions programs were combined so that all applicants would be compared against one another. In addition, the maximum 25 percent limit on students admitted through special consideration—which resembled a quota—was replaced with a target range of 23–27 percent. Subtargets that approximated percentages in the national population were set at 8–10 percent African American, 8–10 percent Latino, 5–7 percent Asian American, and roughly 1 percent Native American.

The faculty otherwise affirmed its 1973 admissions policy. The committee appointed to assess the former admissions program stated in its report that the 1973 criteria "were and remain valid."[151] The admissions policy adopted in 1978 would remain the policy at Boalt until the 1990s. At that time, opponents of affirmative action would turn their attention toward Boalt and charge in a more sophisticated argument that affirmative action policies discriminated not only against whites, but also against Asians. Moreover, they would argue, affirmative action compromised "academic excellence."

CHAPTER 2

Pursuing Excellence

In 1978, following the revision of the affirmative action policy at Boalt, attention at the law school shifted from student diversity to faculty diversity. With that shift came new arguments opposing affirmative action that centered on "academic excellence" and used the language of "merit." Opponents of affirmative action refashioned themselves as "neoconservatives" who were concerned with the *means* for best achieving equality. They asserted that color-blind measures, which measured merit, were the best means to achieve equality and ensure academic excellence at our premier universities. They contended that such measures were also consistent with the goals of the civil rights movement.[1]

As conceptualized by neoconservatives, merit was evaluated by traditional criteria that had consistently awarded seats to white students and tenure to white faculty. The more merit that students and faculty had, the more excellent was the university. Merit, in their view, was the ultimate arbiter of opportunity and the measure of a university. This conceptualization, however, ignored embedded preferences for whites and accorded admissions and hiring criteria an undeserved objectivity. But once detached from the realities of past and present discrimination, the notion of merit was a powerful one that posed a formidable challenge to affirmative action.

At Boalt, the idea that academic excellence was compromised by affirmative action was first asserted in the context of a debate over diversity in faculty hiring. In 1978, racial minorities made up less than 5 percent of the tenured faculty (2 out of 42) and women constituted just over 5 percent (3 out of 42).[2] The lack of diversity in the faculty stood in stark contrast to the diversity of the student body, which in that year was 26 percent minority and 33 percent female.[3] A group of students formed a new organization called the Coalition for a Diverse Faculty (CDF) to advocate the hiring and tenuring of more minority and female faculty. They urged the law school to act affirmatively—as it had done with student admissions—to increase the numbers of minorities and women on the faculty. Women had not needed affirmative action to gain entrance into the law school as students, but it now seemed necessary in order to increase the number of women on the faculty.

In the hiring process, the law school faculty evaluated each candidate on the basis of academic scholarship and employment résumé. At this time, the faculty looked particularly favorably upon candidates who had earned high grades, held a position on law review, clerked for a judge, and worked at a prestigious job. As at other top law schools, the faculty at Boalt tended to hire the candidates most resembling themselves. Thus, newly hired faculty were most likely to have graduated from the same elite private schools, been mentored by the same notable law professors, participated on the same exclusive law journals, clerked in the same high court, and maintained the same traditional interests in the law as existing Boalt faculty. The new hires were also likely to have traveled in the same social circles and to be, like their senior colleagues, white and male. The "old boys network" was alive and well at Boalt and there was little room for new faces in the legal academy.

The CDF urged the faculty to consider diversity *along with* academic and employment criteria in order to increase minority representation. But their concerns went unheard, and in March 1978, the CDF sponsored an all-day strike and teach-in to draw attention to the lack of diversity in the faculty. In the course of the day, more than two hundred students attended a rally in which they called on the faculty to take "immediate and concrete action" to guarantee the hiring of more minorities and women. Dean Sanford Kadish—who had been appointed dean of the law school in 1975 after Dean Edward Halbach stepped down—responded in a statement that echoed the emerging rhetoric of neoconservatives. Unwilling to change the faculty hiring criteria, he stated, "In time, the standards will yield minorities as well as women. Our prime function is to advance legal scholarship and contribute to that scholarship, and to maintain traditions of *absolute excellence* in at least a few institutions in the country."[4]

In adopting the notion that top academic institutions should concentrate on excellence *rather than* diversity, Dean Kadish abdicated responsibility for increasing minority representation at the law school, at least within the faculty. Professor Herma Hill Kay, one of the three female professors at the time, joined several other professors in supporting an active effort to increase the numbers of women and minorities on the law school's faculty—but the lack of leadership on this issue was disheartening. Students sought to influence hiring decisions by gaining a participatory role on the faculty appointments committee. But Dean Kadish let students know that they were unwelcome. He stated, "Students lack background and experience in law. While they bring a point of view, they are not seasoned professionals and cannot pass professional judgements." Ignoring the structural preferences for white men in the hiring process, the dean asserted that the "objective" search for excellence would in time yield a more diverse faculty. However, he did not appear to value faculty diversity independently and did not actively pursue it. A student at the law school who had not been involved in the hiring protests blindly observed, "The faculty is making its best efforts to hire women and minority faculty members."[5] The Boalt administration adopted this mantra, and, for the next ten years, "best efforts" yielded no increase in the number of tenured minority or women faculty.

Students involved in the CDF were discouraged by the unresponsiveness of the Boalt administration and subsequently disbanded. The political climate was changing, becoming more conservative, and affirmative action was beginning to be viewed as an inappropriate or unnecessary tool, or one that had to be used under great constraints. In a series of cases that included *Bakke,* the majority of the Supreme Court indicated that affirmative action could not be used to address general societal discrimination. Confronted with widespread institutional practices of discrimination, Justice White, in *Washington v. Davis,* explained the unwillingness of the Court to address societal discrimination through its judicial rulings. With reference to the validity of statutes in particular, Justice White stated that if the Court were to rule that a statute designed to serve neutral ends was invalid merely because "in practice it benefits or burdens one race more than another," such a ruling would be "far reaching." Furthermore, such a ruling "would raise serious questions about, and perhaps invalidate, a whole range of tax, welfare, public service, regulatory, and licensing statutes that may be more burdensome to the poor and to the average black than to the more affluent white."[6]

Ironically, this same understanding of widespread discrimination led Justice Marshall to conclude that far-reaching affirmative action programs *were* necessary to eradicate entrenched racial prejudice.[7] But his was the minority view. The Supreme Court left room for affirmative action to redress specific instances of discrimination. However, the mood of the country was changing, and outside of the courtroom and in the political arena, public willingness and ability to see discrimination were diminishing. Republicans were assuming control of the White House, and neoconservatives were assuming control of the affirmative action debate.

In 1981, Ronald Reagan became president of the United States. His record on racial issues was not an enlightened one. He had opposed every major civil rights measure considered by Congress, including the Civil Rights Act of 1964, calling it "a bad piece of legislation," and the Voting Rights Act of 1965, regarding the legislation as "unnecessary." President Reagan took his cue from the new right and from neoconservatives, arguing that the important forms of racial discrimination had been eliminated. In his view, most civil rights remedies and mechanisms for achieving racial equality were no longer needed, and their perpetuation constituted discrimination against whites.[8]

President Reagan rewrote history to suggest that discrimination against racial minorities had been drastically curbed, and he radically transformed the public institutions that were previously mandated to protect racial minority interests. Under his leadership, the attorney general dropped desegregation appeals in some states and slowed integration efforts in others; the secretary of labor substantially weakened affirmative action requirements attached to federal contracts; and the Justice Department urged the voluntary modification of affirmative action plans to remove numerical goals and quotas, hinting that failure to comply might result in court action. Most unnerving, however, was the position of the U.S. Civil Rights Commission, whose chair characterized supporters of civil rights as the new racists who "treat blacks differently than whites" in their advocacy of race-conscious programs. With Reagan in power, the federal government appeared to switch sides on racial policy.[9]

Not only was Reagan unwilling to see discrimination, but he also attempted to limit the ability of others to see it. In his second term, he tried to eliminate record-keeping in a number of federal programs that kept track of the race and ethnicity of Americans receiving benefits from the government. He also opposed the inclusion of "hate crime" categories, which, among other things, tracked crimes motivated by racial hatred in national crime statistics. This attempt to blind the public to instances of discrimination led one administrator of a federal program to comment that the lack of information "will put us in the position where, if abuse exists, we will not be able to find it."[10]

Though Reagan attempted to deny and dismiss the existence of continuing discrimination in this country, the relative inequalities faced by racial minorities remained visible. The state of black America, in particular, was worsening when measured by indicators such as unemployment rates, numbers of families falling below the poverty line, and the widening gap between white and black infant mortality rates. Yet despite these problems, the American populace seemed callous about the situation of blacks and other racial minorities. A new mood of "social meanness" pervaded the United States, and many Americans resented having to provide for the "underprivileged." Indeed many felt that, far from being the victims of deprivation, racial minorities were unfairly receiving "preferential treatment" with respect to jobs and educational opportunities.[11]

Neoconservatives asserted that programs benefiting minorities were by definition discriminatory vis-à-vis whites. Affirmative action programs that were instituted to remedy a long history of discrimination against racial minorities were described as instances of "reverse discrimination." In describing affirmative action programs as such, neoconservatives appropriated the demand for equality articulated by the civil rights movement of the 1960s and stood it on its head.[12] They rearticulated the meaning of equality in such a way as to preserve the status quo, and central to this rearticulation was the idea of merit, which legitimated the allocation of benefits. To neoconservatives, only merit justified the granting of privilege.[13]

However, merit was not an objective concept and could be defined and redefined to achieve the desired distribution of benefits. Such was the case for Asian undergraduates at Berkeley, who suffered from a manipulation of standards in the mid-1980s that demonstrated the malleability of merit. In 1984, Berkeley professor Ling-chi Wang was scanning undergraduate admissions data when he discovered that Asian enrollment had dropped a sudden 21 percent in a single year (from 1983 to 1984). Suspicious that the drop was the result of a deliberate policy to reduce Asian enrollment, Professor Wang and other Asian faculty, students, and administrators formed a task force to investigate the issue. The task force ultimately charged the university with instituting a series of unannounced policy changes that intentionally discriminated against Asians.[14]

Asian Americans constituted the fastest-growing minority group in higher education, and, as a group, competed directly with white students for coveted spots at the most competitive universities. As a result of a series of changes in the immigration laws, beginning with those in the Immigration Act of 1965, the United States lifted a long-standing, nearly total ban on Asian emigrants. The combination of the new laws that allowed in Koreans, Filipinos, and Taiwanese, whose opportunities back home were severely limited, and the flood of refugees from the Vietnam War fueled a dramatic increase in the Asian American population, which grew from 1.5 million in 1970 to 3 million in 1980. In 1990, it would reach 7 million.[15] Consequently, Asian Americans pursued higher education in substantially higher numbers, particularly in California, where the Asian American population was concentrated, threatening the stronghold that white students had historically maintained at the top undergraduate universities. At Berkeley, Professor Wang accused the university of instituting racist and reactionary policies, stating, "The university, as far as I can see, each year uses different kinds of mechanisms to affect the enrollment [of Asian Americans]...so UC Berkeley will not be over-run with a so-called Asian invasion."[16]

The policy change that was most suspect to the task force at Berkeley was the imposition of a minimum verbal test score of 400 (out of a possible score of 800) on the college entrance exam known as the SAT. The Asian Task Force alleged that the imposition of a minimum verbal test score had a foreseeable and intended disparate impact on immigrant applicants. Previously no minimum verbal score had been required, and applicants to Berkeley gained admission with high cumulative math *and* verbal scores. Recently emigrated Asian students tended to score low on the verbal section of the SAT but scored high in the math section, yielding a competitive cumulative score that won them admission. Because Asians made up 80 percent of the immigrant student population, the imposition of a minimum verbal score disproportionately affected Asian applicants.[17]

University officials denied charges of such a policy, and steered attention away from the issue of discrimination and toward the issue of over-representation of Asian Americans in the student population. In a 1986 interview with the *San Diego Union Tribune,* University of California President David Gardner stated that there were proportionately more Asians at the university than in the general population of the state of California. He then suggested that Asians had been admitted at the expense of the "truly" underrepresented and tied Asian admissions to African American and Latino admissions. He concluded by saying that whites were underrepresented at Berkeley. In the course of the interview, President Gardner implied that not only were Asians not victims of intentional discrimination, but they were threatening the enrollment of "real" underrepresented students.[18]

In tying Asian admissions to affirmative action, President Gardner confused the issue. As at the law school, with the exception of underrepresented students such as Filipinos, who had more difficulty gaining entrance to the university, Asian Americans were no longer considered under an affirmative action program. Thus, for the most part, the admission of Asian Americans did not affect the admission of other minority students who, due to the competitiveness of Berkeley, were unable to gain admission with test scores and grades that were relatively lower than those of other applicants. Asian Americans instead competed directly with white students, and it was these students, not underrepresented minorities, who were threatened.[19]

Sumi Cho, an Asian American joint-degree law student at Boalt (class of 1990) and doctoral student in the Ethnic Studies Department (class of 1992), was particularly concerned by the evasion of the issue of discrimination against Asians.[20] She had been active on campus since 1980 when she first arrived at Berkeley as an undergraduate, and had spent her years in graduate school involved in the Graduate Assembly, which lobbied the central administration to be more assertive about affirmative action in the graduate programs. Just when she thought the Graduate Assembly was starting to see some results, the administration took a disappointing step backward, undermining affirmative action policies by using them to explain away the drop in Asian undergraduate admissions and turning to the "merit" argument. Cho knew this was a dangerous argument to adopt. It ignored the inequities of traditional, numbers-based criteria; moreover, it built resentment between Asian and other minority students who were working together to make Berkeley a more welcoming and supportive environment for diverse students. Cho and other students concerned with this issue tried to expose university tactics and demonstrate how Asian admissions had very little to do with minority admissions and much more to do with white admissions.

In 1987, Cho was elected chair of the Graduate Assembly and spoke out publicly against the discrimination against Asian students. She stated, "Here at the university it is the survival of the fittest—until it seems that Asians may in fact be the fittest." Cho accused university officials of laying blame for the discrepancy between white and Asian admission rates on affirmative action. "The most vile thing the university is doing is using affirmative action as a scapegoat. This is just a tactic of divide and conquer. Affirmative action is a protected category that does not affect the number of Asian or white admissions. Asians are competing with whites for spaces, but the competition is not fair." Asian Task Force member

Henry Der agreed with Cho, observing that many university officials' comments had been laced with an innuendo that African American, Latino, and Native American students "are taking spaces from Asians. But the fact is that Asian applicants are competing with white applicants."[21]

In 1988, following several years of repeated denial that Berkeley had intentionally discriminated against Asian Americans, the "SAT 400 memo" surfaced in a State Assembly hearing on Asian undergraduate admissions. The memo, written by the director of admissions and sent to the vice chancellor at Berkeley, confirmed the allegation that a minimum SAT verbal score of 400 had been imposed to limit Asian admissions. Berkeley Chancellor Ira Michael Heyman was present at the hearing and immediately apologized for "disadvantaging Asians" in the admission process. Attempting to mitigate public embarrassment for the university, Chancellor Heyman apologized publicly to the Asian American community, acknowledging that the policies instituted at Berkeley "indisputably had a disproportionate impact on Asians."[22]

The issue of Asian admissions received national media attention and caught the eye of neoconservatives, who seized upon Asian Americans as the apparently natural allies of whites in opposing affirmative action. As neoconservatives viewed the issue at Berkeley, the problem was not that Asian enrollment was limited vis-à-vis white enrollment, but that Asian *and* white enrollment was limited vis-à-vis African American, Latino, and to a lesser extent, Native American enrollment. To neoconservatives, the bottom line was clear: the consequence of affirmative action was that better-qualified whites and Asians were losing to blacks and Latinos in the zero-sum game of admissions. In Asian Americans, neoconservatives had found their "model minority," who gained admission to the university without the aid of affirmative action and proved that the playing field was even. Thus, in the eyes of neoconservatives, the continued use of "preferential policies" for underrepresented minority students was nothing short of discrimination against whites and Asians.[23]

In early 1988, James Gibney, a neoconservative pundit writing for the *New Republic,* emphasized the zero-sum relationship between Asian admissions and affirmative action. He wrote, "If Asians are underrepresented based on their grades and test scores, it is largely because of affirmative action for other minority groups. And if blacks and Hispanics are underrepresented based on their fraction of the population, it is increasingly because of the statistical over-achievement of Asians.... [T]he blame can no longer be placed solely on favoritism toward whites."[24] By drawing Asian Americans into the admissions debate, Gibney effectively extracted the issue of embedded preferences for whites and gave credence to the idea that whites are "victims" of "preferential policies."

Given the neoconservative rhetoric of the 1980s, it came as no surprise that white students began to view themselves as "victims," squeezed between Asian American achievement and preferential policies for minorities, especially blacks. Many white students, while insecure about competing against Asian Americans in higher education, were openly angry about what they perceived as underachievement among their black peers. Despite the fact that blacks had always constituted a relatively small proportion of freshman enrollment at the highly selective schools, many whites, and some Asians too, begrudged the presence of blacks in higher education. A complaint often heard among whites was that less-qualified blacks were accepted, while better-qualified whites were rejected.[25]

By the mid-1980s, white grumbling about black students was punctuated by an alarming "new racism," a wave of harassment, verbal insults, and incidents of outright racial violence.[26] The 1988 academic year alone was cause for concern. Arsonists set the first black fraternity ablaze at the University of Mississippi. A fraternity at the University of Wisconsin at Madison held a mock "slave auction." Freshman pranksters at Stanford caricatured blacks on a defaced poster of Beethoven. A swastika, along with the words "white power," was found on the door of the Afro-American center at Yale. And a writer for the *Dartmouth Review* described a black professor as a "used brillo pad." At some campuses, the verbal insults were backed by organized white student campaigns against affirmative action that argued that individual merit should be the only criterion used in admissions. These arguments were buttressed by neoconservative claims that the universities had abandoned excellence to accommodate diversity.

In 1990, racial tensions on the Berkeley campus reached an all-time high. The 1990 undergraduate admissions process at Berkeley produced a more racially diverse freshman class than ever before. The percentage of blacks admitted was 11.4 percent, Asians constituted 27.8 percent, and Latinos, 21.4 percent. Together these three minority groups filled 60 percent of the spaces in the entering class. White enrollment, at an all-time low, sank to 32 percent of the class.[27] For some white conservative faculty, the decline in white enrollment was an outrage. Some professors, believing that the administration was "giving away" the university to minority concerns and hence turning its back on white interests, registered strong discontent with affirmative action policies.[28]

In this same year, Dr. Chang-Lin Tien, a well-liked professor, was appointed chancellor at Berkeley. In the wake of the public acknowledgment that Berkeley had "disadvantaged" Asians, the appointment of Chancellor Tien was seen as a positive step in repairing the rift between the Asian community and the University of California. Chancellor Tien was the first Asian American and only the second person of color to head a campus at the University of California.[29] In contrast to the rhetoric of neoconservatives, Chancellor Tien championed diversity and considered it part of the excellence of a university. An ardent supporter of affirmative action, upon his appointment, Chancellor Tien stated, "We must diversify at all levels — undergraduate, graduate, faculty, staff, and campus life in general."[30] He was far from being the Asian ally that neoconservatives hoped would join them in the fight to oppose race-conscious policies.

Nevertheless, neoconservatives seized on Berkeley as an example of how affirmative action discriminated against whites and Asians, and how it compromised the stature of the university. Dinesh D'Souza, a prominent neoconservative pundit, stated in a 1991 article in the *New Republic,* "Each year state schools such as Berkeley... turn away hundreds of white and Asian-American applicants with straight A's and impressive extracurriculars, while accepting students from underrepresented groups with poor to mediocre academic and other credentials." D'Souza asserted that, as a result of affirmative action, blacks and other preferred minorities were misplaced at Berkeley and at other top campuses, and could not succeed, dropping out at an extremely high rate. Furthermore, he argued, classroom pressures on misplaced students, compounded by the social dislocation that many of them felt in the new campus environment, were "at the root of the serious racial troubles on the American campus." Blaming racial tension on campus on blacks and Latinos, D'Souza justified the racial hostility of whites. He stated, "Many white students who are generally sympathetic to the minority cause become weary and irritated by the extent of preferential treatment and double standards involving minority groups on campus. Indeed, racial incidents frequently suggest such embitterment."[31]

In an essay countering claims made by D'Souza and other neoconservatives concerning Berkeley, Chancellor Tien articulated the importance of using affirmative action to enroll a diverse student body from a racially diverse population.[32] "[E]xcellence in higher education," he stated, "is impossible without equity." Given the sweeping demographic transformation occurring in California and across the country, Tien contended,

[The] ethical, educational, economic, and political realities of this decade demand that we strive to diversify.... [If we] fail to serve any ethnic or cultural groups, the problem is far greater than limiting educational opportunities for a portion of the population. The lack of a college education in the twenty-first century will effectively shut people out of the social and economic mainstream. In short, if we fall down on the job, we will set in motion the forces that lead to a form of apartheid almost as pervasive and insidious as the strictest segregation in South Africa.[33]

Chancellor Tien addressed what he referred to as "the common myths about affirmative action," which were all asserted by D'Souza. One myth was that academic quality at Berkeley had declined as a consequence of making room for minority students. However, Tien remarked that the reverse was true: "[A]ll segments of our freshman class are stronger than their counterparts of a decade ago."[34] As was the case at Boalt, the university had become more competitive over the years, and the qualifications of African American, Latino, and Native American applicants as well as those of white and Asian American applicants had increased, though a sizeable gap in SAT scores and high school grades continued to exist between them.

An additional myth was that once admitted, a diverse student population would not succeed. Tien rebutted this argument, stating that this was not the case at Berkeley. Over the years, the graduation rates for all ethnic groups had improved significantly.[35] In the 1940s when the university was virtually all white, the graduation rate had been less than 50 percent. In the 1970s, as Berkeley began to diversify its students and become more competitive, the graduation rate jumped to 60 percent. And in the 1980s, the graduation rate had jumped to 70 percent, disproving the argument that academic quality had declined as a result of an increasingly racially diverse student body.[36]

The final myth addressed by Tien was that minority students were the cause of racial tension on campus. Tien acknowledged that the racial transformation of the student body brought with it a challenge to build bridges across differences. But he viewed that challenge as necessary to eradicating entrenched prejudice and discrimination, not as a problem caused by minority students that justified racial hostility. Rather, the problem called for a greater commitment from the university to make the campus a more comfortable place for all students. Tien stated, "Deep-seated social change—especially when it involves affirmative action—touches off many reverberations. We know that while some students gain self-esteem and a sense of cultural identity at Berkeley, others report that they never had close interactions with students from different racial or ethnic groups. We need to make the same kind of commitment to minimizing racial isolation as we have to increasing racial diversity."[37]

Students, like people across the country, had difficulty discussing issues of race and often retreated into their own cultural social groups, making it that much harder to close the communication and understanding gaps between races. This led Chancellor Tien to commission a report on multiculturalism on campus. A team of social scientists at Berkeley, headed by African American sociology professor Troy Duster, conducted a two-year study of campus relations known as the Diversity Project (1990).[38] Through a series of intensive interviews, the researchers developed a rich and complicated portrait of campus culture at Berkeley, drawn directly from the students. Upon analyzing race relations on campus, the researchers suggested ways to facilitate a deeper discussion and understanding of racial issues.

Not surprisingly, the study found that different groups of students experienced conflicts about race in different ways. Minority students complained of a "subtle racism" and feelings of being "ignored or excluded," particularly in mixed racial settings such as the classroom, sporting events, and social gatherings. These students blamed not only whites, but sometimes other minorities. White students related the discomfort of being white in a highly racialized campus climate. Many expressed fear and dismay at being labeled "racist" or "oppressor." And both minority and white students expressed anger, resentment, alienation, and an inability to describe their racial experiences at Berkeley, leading Professor Duster to suggest that language about race and racism had not kept pace with the panoply of student experiences.

Duster concluded that a new language was needed to discuss race.[39] The problem, according to Duster, was not simply that there was a heightened awareness of race, as neoconservatives would have it, but that students lacked both the language and institutional structures to grapple with their experiences and feelings. In his view, the tensions on campus were not a signal that diversity was not working, as neoconservatives claimed, but that students were undergoing an important but difficult learning process. In an article published in *Mother Jones,* discussing the findings of the Diversity Project, Duster wrote,

Berkeley's students are grappling with one of the most difficult situations in the world: ethnic and racial turf. They are doing this, however modestly, over relatively safe issues such as what kind of music gets played or who sits where in the lunchroom.

Perhaps they will learn how to handle conflict, how to divvy up scarce resources, how to adjust, fight, retreat, compromise, and ultimately get along in a future that will no longer be dominated by a single group spouting its own values as the ideal homogenized reality for everyone else.

If our students learn even a small bit of this, they will be far better prepared than students tucked safely away in anachronistic single-culture enclaves. And what they learn may make a difference not just for their personal futures, but for a world struggling with issues of nationalism, race, and ethnicity. [40]

Duster and his research team suggested strategies to foster interaction between and discussion among different racial groups about their experiences at Berkeley. Echoing the comments of Chancellor Tien, the findings maintained that universities ought to start thinking of ways to help students cope with their racial experiences.

Along these lines, race theorists Michael Omi and Howard Winant asserted, in *Racial Formation in the United States,* that the absence of a clear "common sense" understanding of what racism means has become a significant obstacle to efforts aimed at challenging it: "In classroom discussions of racism, white and non-white students tend to talk past one another. Whites tend to locate racism in color consciousness and find its absence in color-blindness. In so doing, they see the affirmation of difference and racial identity among racially defined minority students as racist. Non-white students, by contrast, see racism as a system of power, and correspondingly they cannot be racist because they lack power."[41]

Omi and Winant contended that there were two concepts of race, one in which members of racial minorities, especially blacks, saw the centrality of race in history and everyday experience, and another in which whites saw race as "a peripheral, nonessential reality." The gap between these views inhibited a common understanding of why affirmative action was necessary.

The gap of understanding described by Duster and Omi and Winant also existed at Boalt, inhibiting a consensus on the continuing necessity of race-conscious policies. Jesse Choper, the dean of the law school, who had been appointed in 1982 after Sanford Kadish retired from the post, reflected the views of many white students and faculty. In an interview with the student newspaper, the *Cross Examiner,* Dean Choper remarked, "There are a lot of epithets being tossed around." "Racism," he said, "is an abused word. What does it mean?" Articulating a limited perception of racism as the intentional action of an individual, Choper stated, "I don't think there are many people who are deliberately against people because of race or ethnicity."[42]

Locating racism in race-conscious policies and racially identified organizations, a white law student wrote an article in the same newspaper attacking student-of-color organizations and an Academic Support Program (ASP) designed for, but not limited to, minority students. The student wrote, "Many of the organizations which justifiably decry racism are, however unintentionally, serving to fortify and perpetuate the existing situation.... [W]hatever the advantages of such organizations, the reality is that their very existence serves to perpetuate separatism."[43] Responding to this attack, the director of the Academic Support Program at Boalt, Evangeline Nichols, wrote an editorial describing the role of the ASP and student-of-color organizations. She stated that these organizations "serve to empower formerly and presently disempowered people. They provide support and promote the interests of groups whose perspectives have only recently been acknowledged as legitimate by the dominant society. They are places where differing views can be voiced and validated." With respect to the ASP, she emphasized that the program did not exclude nonminorities; however, it was designed to ensure that students, particularly minority students, who had not had an opportunity to develop their academic potential, were getting the most out of their legal education.[44]

The white student who attacked race consciousness at Boalt suggested that a hypothetical "Caucasian Law Students" organization would be no different from a student-of-color organization, but would meet with allegations of racism were it proposed. Referring to minority organizations, he stated, "I fail to see how any group, which patently defines its membership based solely on ethnic origin is not subject to the same criticism."[45] Pointing out that student-of-color organizations are not restricted by race, Nichols observed that a Caucasian Law Students organization "would be redundant; the law school itself constitutes a Caucasian Law Students Association. Mainstream/white perspectives are voiced and validated every day in class and in the hallways by professors and fellow students." Responding directly to the student's assertion that minority groups were responsible for divisions along racial lines, she added, "Continued divisiveness and separation are not caused by the existence of self-help organizations and programs per se. A more plausible explanation is that 25 years of efforts to attain legal equality have not eradicated the effects of hundreds of years of oppression and discrimination based on race."[46]

The issue of affirmative action was heating up at Boalt, and the validity of race-conscious admissions policies and race-based organizations and programs was being called into question. But the focal point of the affirmative action debate at the law school lay in the controversy over faculty hiring practices. Prior to the appointment of Chancellor Tien, three law school professors, including former Dean Kadish, and twenty-six other senior university faculty members sent a memorandum to the search committee outlining various concerns the next chancellor needed to address. Most notable on the list was a concern that faculty affirmative action programs had turned into "racial and gender preferences... of persons who are not fully competitive on traditional, widely accepted criteria." The letter suggested that this situation threatened the academic reputation of the campus.[47]

When interviewed about his views on the hiring criteria at Boalt specifically, Professor Kadish restated his position, which had not changed since he was dean in the late 1970s and early 1980s. He told the law student who interviewed him that he did not see the "traditional standards" of determining scholarship changing in order to incorporate diversity criteria. The student interviewer expressed frustration and wrote in the *Cross Examiner,* "[T]he same old obstacles are placed before people of color; just different names are given to them. At one time it was called segregation, now it's referred to as academic excellence."[48] By 1988, "traditional standards" had not produced any additional minority or female tenured faculty since 1978, when students protested the lack of diversity and called for concrete action, and the administration had responded that in time, traditional hiring criteria would yield more diversity.[49] A handful of minority and female professors had been hired to teach courses at the law school, but none had been granted tenure. Boalt had a bad record in the hiring of a diverse faculty and was not alone.

Nationally, full-time law teachers of color made up only 5.4 percent and women comprised only 23 percent of the total number of full-time law professors in the country. The spurious "pool argument"—that there was no diverse pool of qualified law school graduates from which to hire—was not credible, given that in 1988, people of color and women represented 11.8 percent and 42 percent respectively of all enrolled law students. At Boalt, the discrepancy between student and faculty diversity was particularly stark. As of 1986, there was but one tenured male faculty member of color, and two full-time and one part-time tenured white women out of approximately forty-five tenured faculty, while students of color and females comprised 25 percent and 40 percent of Boalt students respectively.[50]

In a 1986 article critical of law schools for their failure to increase faculty diversity, particularly with regard to racial diversity, New York University law professor Derrick Bell noted that the modest but measurable growth of minority faculty, from virtually none to two hundred in the nation's law schools since 1970, had stagnated and was now in decline.[51]

Moreover, minority faculty continued to suffer the same debilitating work tensions, isolation, and alienation reported by their predecessors, and continued to be "token presences on their campuses, assuming the multiple burdens of counselor to minority students, liaison to the minority community, and consultant on race to administration and colleagues, while working to establish themselves as effective teachers, productive scholars and congenial colleagues." Bell, who was among the first African Americans to be hired as a law professor, lamented this lack of progress. He wrote, "Those of us who accepted teaching positions in white law schools back in the early 1970s, saw ourselves as pioneers, creating exciting new careers for ourselves, and opening up previously closed opportunities.... We realized that the challenges would be great, the chances for failure numerous, and the strain and stress enormous. But we had been chosen, and we were determined to overcome. Now, we realize that the initiation period never ended."[52]

Bell observed that most law school deans and faculty acknowledged the inadequacy of the token one or two minorities on their faculty, but claimed they simply could not find qualified minority candidates. But, Bell asserted, the record too clearly showed that most law schools did not aggressively search for minority candidates until pressure from minority students and liberal white students and faculty made such a search politic, if not essential. "When undertaken with vigorous commitment, able persons are located, recruited, and hired," he stated. Bell surmised that what was at play in the failure to increase faculty diversity was not a lack of potential candidates but a faculty conception of law schools as "white schools," which led faculty to resist hiring beyond a certain number of even the most qualified teachers of color. The same could be said of the faculty conception of law schools as "male schools," leading faculty to resist the hiring of "too many" women despite their being qualified. To overcome this obstacle, Bell recommended that law faculty "sit down, determine how many teachers of color [and how many women teachers] they and their schools [could] accept or tolerate, and then work out a time schedule... for locating and recruiting that number of minority [and female] teachers."[53]

At Boalt, the faculty established no such hiring goals or time schedules, and the perennial lack of diversity on the faculty angered many students. Following the denial of tenure to two popular, white, female law professors, students reconvened the Coalition for a Diverse Faculty and organized for action.[54] The first female professor denied tenure was Marjorie Shultz, in 1985. Shultz was widely considered to be the best teacher in the school—she had won the Berkeley Distinguished Teaching Award in 1983—and had written several articles, including one on marriage and contracts for her tenure review. However, taking a narrow view of scholarship, an influential faculty member on her tenure review committee told Shultz that her tenure article topic did not contribute much to scholarship since, "we already have one article on marriage contracts," referring to an article that had recently been written by a sociology professor but had been published in a law journal. Another professor on the tenure committee told Shultz, "the whole topic bores and irritates me." Despite this criticism, Shultz's article was published in the prestigious *California Law Review*. She wrote a subsequent article on a related topic, which was published in the acclaimed *Yale Law Journal*. Nevertheless, in 1985, the tenure committee voted to deny tenure.[55]

Though she was denied tenure because her review committee viewed her scholarship as not meeting the standards of excellence at Boalt, Professor Shultz suspected that there was more to her denial than the dubious conclusion that her scholarship was inadequate. Put simply, she was not one of the boys. In almost every respect she was different from the majority of her colleagues. Apart from being female on a predominantly male faculty, Shultz had earned a law degree from Boalt itself, and not an ivy-league school.[56] In addition, she had come to the law from a strong social justice background and not a purely academic background, which led a professor who interviewed her for her initial teaching job at Boalt and asked what issues concerned her and brought her to law school to remark, "[W]hat you are really interested in is politics, not law." Finally, apart from differing in personal and professional style from her colleagues and having a better rapport with her students, Shultz was among the most liberal of the faculty and was outspoken on issues of curriculum reform, student role in governance, and faculty accountability.[57]

Shultz appealed her decision to the Berkeley campus administration, but the law school fought hard to terminate her. Berkeley administrators compromised. Appeasing the Boalt faculty, they turned down the appeal, but recognizing that Shultz's termination would be a great loss to the university, they offered her a permanent lectureship.[58] This was not an ideal solution for Shultz but her financial options were limited, and she accepted the position. She remained a permanent lecturer for four years until, in an odd turn of events, the faculty suddenly voted to grant her tenure after the campus Privilege and Tenure Committee, considering the grievance of a second popular, white, female professor—Eleanor Swift— who had been denied tenure, found evidence sufficient to justify a full hearing on whether she was discriminated against on the basis of sex.

Professor Swift was two years behind Shultz in the tenure cycle, and was denied tenure in 1987. Like Shultz, she was regarded as one of the best teachers at the law school. The denial of her tenure coupled with the earlier denial of Shultz's tenure brought human faces to the struggle for diversity and propelled the CDF into a focal organizational role at the law school. In the fall of 1987, the CDF highlighted the lack of progress over the decades in diversifying the law faculty, publicizing widely and graphically the appalling racial and gender caste system that had seen but one tenured faculty member of color between 1967 and 1987, and had increased the number of tenured, white, female faculty from one to two full-time and one part-time over the same twenty-year period.[59]

On March 22, 1988, almost ten years to the day after the last wide-scale student protest calling for concrete action to diversify the faculty, the CDF organized a general boycott of law school classes in an attempt to highlight what its members viewed as the systematic exclusion of minorities and women from tenured faculty positions at the law school. Among its proposals, the CDF called for more emphasis on teaching excellence in tenure decisions, more objective decision making by ranking tenure candidates on a point system, redefinition of appropriate legal scholarship, and inclusion of students in the hiring process. In the week prior to the boycott, the CDF collected more than three hundred student signatures in support of its position.[60]

Students had met with Dean Jesse Choper over the previous two years in an effort to bring about change, but they felt Choper had ignored student calls for action and refused to open up the hiring process to students. After failed attempts at negotiation, the coalition felt it was time for direct action. The chair of the CDF stated in the campus newspaper, the *Daily Californian,* that although "staying out of class is to the detriment of our studies, it is necessary to express our interest. Boalt's tradition of hostility towards anybody not in the mainstream is unacceptable." A majority of law students honored the boycott, and twenty-eight students marched to the dean's office and presented a written demand that the dean convene an emergency meeting of the faculty within three weeks to address student concerns about the lack of tenured women and minority faculty.[61]

Dean Choper told the students he could not accede to the demand immediately because any public all-faculty meeting would have to be approved by a vote of the entire faculty during one of their regular closed sessions. "I have no authority to call a public meeting of the faculty," he said. "Only the entire faculty can do that. I serve at the pleasure of the faculty." A member of the campus student government, the ASUC, who was observing the situation, disagreed. "As dean, he has the power to call a public meeting if he wanted to." Choper remarked, "Calling a public meeting would be counter-productive...[and] would inevitably end up like a circus." After occupying the dean's office for seven hours, the twenty-eight students were arrested while chanting "Jesse, Jesse, tell us why you won't diversify."[62]

In the fall of 1988, following a year of blistering embarrassment from the publicizing of the egregious lack of diversity on the law school faculty, Boalt made an unprecedented four diversity hires (including an African American male and female, a Latino male, and a white female) out of five total hires. Among them was Boalt's first critical race theorist, Angela Harris, as well as feminist scholar Reva Siegel, outspoken CDF ally Bryan Ford, and the first Latino ever hired at Boalt, Dan Rodriguez. In that same year, the faculty granted tenure to its first Latina law professor, Rachel Moran, who had been hired in 1983.

Adding to the pressure to diversify at Boalt was the threat of a pending lawsuit from Professor Eleanor Swift, who had been denied tenure in 1987 and had filed a grievance with the university alleging sexual discrimination.[63] In the fall of 1988, Swift held a press conference to announce that the Berkeley Privilege and Tenure Committee, to whom she had appealed her tenure denial, had made an unprecedented prima facie finding that there was evidence sufficient to justify a full hearing on whether there had been sexual discrimination in her case. Two weeks later the Boalt faculty abruptly voted to reverse its denial of tenure to Marjorie Shultz.[64]

Building on a successful year of activism at Boalt, in the spring of 1989, a group of students helped organize a nationwide strike to protest the lack of minority and women faculty in American law schools. Renee Saucedo (class of 1990), a second-year Latina law student at Boalt, was instrumental in organizing the strike and saw the fight to increase faculty diversity as fundamental to creating a school atmosphere that was hospitable to and supportive of minority students. She had immigrated from Mexico and had worked hard to get to law school, but had never really felt welcome at Boalt, recalling one instance in which a white student told her, "It's thanks to you that my friend did not get into Boalt." Saucedo was proud to be a product of affirmative action, and at the law school she advocated for increased faculty diversity. The more representative the institution became, she reasoned, the more welcome minority students would feel and the more relevant the law school curriculum would become for all students training to become lawyers in an increasingly diverse state. This was the next step in the march toward racial equality at Boalt and other law schools across the country.[65]

The strike, which took place on April 6, 1989, was the first of its kind. Approximately thirty-five schools participated, including Harvard, Stanford, Yale, Columbia, Northwestern, UC Davis, and UCLA. The strike received national media attention and put pressure on law schools across the country to diversify their faculties. In the first hiring year (1989–90) following the strike, the percentage of full-time law faculty of color shot up to 8.7 percent, a 61 percent jump in one year. To illustrate, there were 273 full-time law faculty of color in 1988–89 out of 5,075. The following year there were 451 out of 5,202—a total increase of 178 additional faculty of color. The subsequent year (1990–91), the percentage of full-time faculty of color increased to 10 percent, or 662 of 6,638 law faculty. Within two years of the nationwide strike, the percentage of people of color teaching in law schools had increased by 85 percent.[66]

At Boalt, the 1989 national strike was honored by 87 percent of the student body.[67] Again, a group of students, mostly from the CDF, occupied the dean's office. Though the four diversity hires and one tenure approval that year were a welcome improvement, students wanted an assurance from the dean that more such faculty would be hired and granted tenure without requiring a media campaign directed at the law school. In an opinion piece written in the *Cross Examiner,* an African American student articulated the value of a diverse faculty. He stated,

Diversity is not valuable simply to provide students and faculty the opportunity to say that there are a certain number of women and minorities teaching at the law school. It is valuable because it gives each of us, from disparate cultural, economic and social backgrounds an opportunity to be fully educated. Both individually and collectively, we benefit from diversity by having a chance to learn from the unique experiences and perspectives of others. If it can be said that there is value in learning through the perspective of a white, upper middle class male (and I think that it can) then mutual respect demands that we also recognize the value of learning through the perspectives of others who don't fit that mold.[68]

Protesting students asked for a sign of good faith that the dean and the faculty would actively pursue diversity in the law school. Though people of color comprised 47 percent of the population in California, they still only comprised 27 percent of the student body and 6 percent of faculty at Boalt.[69] The students asserted that the administration could demonstrate good faith by creating a student participatory role in a policymaking process that addressed diversity. The dean responded to the strike and to student concerns by ordering the arrest of the forty-six students who occupied his office.[70]

Members of the CDF returned to Dean Choper's office several weeks later to discuss their concern that the dean was not adequately addressing the issue of diversity. One student wrote in the *Cross Examiner*, "Boalt must diversify its faculty if it is to survive and remain relevant into the twenty-first century.... Law must expand to embrace every view and... Boalt should be at the forefront, not dragging behind."[71] Protesting students sought one thing: the formation of a student-faculty committee to consider issues of diversity at the law school. Six students who entered Choper's office on May 1 and eight more who entered on May 2 to discuss faculty hiring were cited and released. On May 3, some progress appeared possible. Choper had at first refused to consider forming a committee, citing lack of faculty support, but later in the day he reconsidered his position and agreed to poll the faculty to see if there was sufficient support to put the issue on the agenda of the next faculty meeting.[72] After supposedly consulting with the faculty, Choper reported that the faculty was not interested.[73]

However, at the regularly scheduled faculty meeting on May 12, Professor Robert Berring, who supported efforts to increase diversity at the law school, moved for the formation of a student-faculty committee along the lines proposed by the CDF. Berring was a young, white, liberal faculty member who did not share the hesitance of his older and more conservative peers to discuss issues of diversity. He grew up in a Catholic, working-class environment in Ohio, where "good people" were racist and anti-Semitic, but attended Harvard in the late 1960s at the height of the student movements and believed in the promise of equality. In the early 1970s, he came to Boalt for law school and was a part of the student efforts to make the law school more representative and more relevant. He was now frustrated by the short shrift that diversity was getting at the law school, and took it upon himself as a faculty member to move the issue forward.[74]

Several professors supported Berring's motion and expressed discontent that in the dean's alleged polling they had not been consulted at all. When consulting on sensitive issues, the dean typically contacted only the older, more established, and generally more conservative members of the faculty. Consequently, most policy decisions were made by the dean and his inner circle of advisors. This fact did not sit well with the younger and more liberal faculty, who supported the formation of a committee to consider issues of diversity at the law school. Over the opposition of the dean, the faculty in attendance voted 21–4 to form the committee proposed by the CDF.[75]

The issue of diversity engendered antagonism among both faculty and students. In an article in the *Cross Examiner*, a student who was opposed to race-conscious policies questioned the legitimacy of affirmative action programs, using the language of "merit" advanced by neoconservatives. The student commented, "By increasing the importance we attach to race and gender in admissions and hiring, we necessarily decrease the importance we give other, more conventional criteria, such as intelligence, teaching ability, and academic performance. This is the real price of affirmative action." The student continued, "Affirmative action is often justified as a method of ending discrimination. But it is doomed to failure in this respect, for it operates through discrimination.... Affirmative action discriminates in favor of some—and against others—solely on the basis of race. By definition, then, it can never hope to end discrimination."[76]

Another student responded, contesting the "use of race is racism" argument in the faculty hiring context, and observed that this argument "assumes that in the absence of race or gender consideration, hiring consideration would be made with objective standards of merit." However, this had proven not to be the case at Boalt, leading another student to state that the "anti-diversity rhetoric that calls for a color-blind society is simply empty when placed in the context of late 20th century America."[77] In the course of this debate, in August 1989, Chancellor Heyman awarded tenure to Eleanor Swift. He did so in light of a review of her record by an outside, blue-ribbon committee that found she had met the standards under which the last six men had received tenure at Boalt.[78]

By 1990, sustained student activism had fostered deep resentment among more conservative students and faculty. The CDF defended its tactics as necessary to call attention to the chronic lack of diversity on the Boalt faculty. One supporter of student activism stated in the law school newspaper that the previous student strikes and resulting publicity "were highly successful from the standpoint of bringing public scrutiny to bear on [Boalt]. And even though they made many people 'uncomfortable' they were also quite successful in stimulating discussion about diversity among students." But student activism had undoubtedly contributed to the rising tension that pervaded relations at the law school. The student writing in the *Cross Examiner* noted that the "atmosphere at Boalt has clearly changed. Feelings of frustration, distrust, and even resentment now characterize students' attitudes toward one another. Furthermore, anecdotal evidence suggests unprecedented antagonism between many faculty [members] and student activists," adding that "unless something productive occurs, the atmosphere at Boalt will further degenerate into bitter acrimony."[79]

One potential vehicle for constructive discussion of these issues failed to materialize when the proposed student-faculty committee never got off the ground.[80] Though the faculty voted to form a committee, the committee was given no power to affect the issues it was formed to address. Student voices remained unheard, and meaningful student participation remained unrealized. In a law school forum to discuss student participation in the faculty hiring process, many students and faculty agreed that student participation was important. Professor Robert Cole felt especially strongly about the issue of student participation in the governance of the law school and, until recently, had boycotted faculty meetings for more than a decade to register his protest that, among other things, students had an inadequate role in policy formation at the law school. At the forum, he stated that student participation was essential for several reasons. First, "it creates accountability by including people in the decision-making process with interests different from those of [the] traditionally represented." Second, "the variety of input expands the competence and quality of those decisions." Third, "it sends the message, especially to potential new hires, that Boalt values students and demands high-quality teaching." And fourth, "it promotes harmony on campus."[81]

The concern for student participation expressed by Professor Cole and others was not just about increasing the number of women and minorities at the law school. It was also about making the law school more relevant and more responsive to a diverse student body who needed to be trained to serve the interests and needs of a diverse population. However, the view that the law school should be more relevant and more responsive was not shared by everyone, least of all, it appeared, by Dean Choper. His vision of the law school seemed to run counter to the view that a public law school had a responsibility to the public. In his view, the primary role of the law school was the pursuit of academic excellence, and this was achieved irrespective of the diversity of the law school. To the extent that students and faculty of color did not fare well when measured by traditional standards of excellence, they compromised this primary role. In contrast to the view taken by Dean Edward Halbach, who had led the formalization of an affirmative action program in the late 1960s, Dean Choper seemed to view diversity not as an asset but as a hindrance to the pursuit of excellence.[82]

In February 1990, Dean Choper spoke to the Berkeley Community Law Center as part of an ongoing series of BCLC forums on public service. During his talk, Choper discussed at length his vision of the law school. The forum was an ironic place for Choper to discuss his vision, since the legal clinic appeared to be in many ways inconsistent with his vision. BCLC, like other legal clinics before it, had been started by students to respond to the unmet legal needs of the poor and disenfranchised in the community and to fulfill the student need for greater relevance in a legal education often disconnected from reality.[83] Choper voiced support for the BCLC, saying that an ideal legal education would require at least a semester of clinical work. But he said the law school should not directly fund the BCLC or other clinical programs because they were not integral to the mission of the law school.[84]

As reported by the *Cross Examiner*, Choper stated that the mission of "the great law schools" such as Boalt was primarily to provide an institution for faculty members to pursue legal research and law reform. Any teaching obligation was distinctly secondary. He said that in the United States a legal institution cannot get government funding without taking in students, and he compared this situation unfavorably to other countries which supported centers devoted purely to legal research. Choper went on to say that Boalt had minimal obligations to train its students. The obligations that the law school had, he stated, were limited to legal research and analysis. He commented that Boalt students were sufficiently intelligent to figure out the law for themselves and that as long as the school did not "damage" them, it fulfilled its teaching role.[85]

One student pointed out that even if the law school had no obligation to fund skills training, clinics such as BCLC served the additional function of fostering commitment to public service work, which students would carry with them into their professional careers. Choper responded that it was not the job of the law school to promote either "patriotism or anti-patriotism" or "brotherhood," but to encourage instead "value-neutral legal scholarship." Nor did he think the law school had any duty to provide legal services to members of the local community who could not afford private attorneys. In his view, Boalt had no more obligation to support such efforts than had "a local drug store." A student reporting on the dean's talk, stated, "The Dean's vision is as clear as it is radical; law schools should be hermetic research institutions with minimal teaching responsibilities and virtually no duty to community."[86]

The dean's comments did not help to ease the tension at the law school and further exacerbated student activists' feelings that their concerns were being ignored by the administration. Believing that the administration only responded to students when they applied public pressure, on the first day of November 1990, members of the CDF once again protested administrative and faculty inaction, and once again fifteen students were arrested for staging a sit-in. A first-year student observing the sit-in registered his great distaste for the protest, commenting that the noise, arrests, and general disruption caused by the "activities" crossed the line between acceptable and unacceptable protest. He feared that his education was going to be compromised as the faculty lost "respect" for students. He asked a member of the Boalt Hall Student Association (BHSA) what he was going to do about the protests. The BHSA member, who supported the protests, wrote his response in an editorial:

Every day at this school people from disadvantaged communities are discriminated against by Boalt Hall. The way classes are taught, the way scholarship is evaluated, and yes, the way professors are hired, all contribute to this. The dominant pedagogy presumes that legal analysis is to be taught without discussing conflicts in individual values or cultural background. Rather, the law is supposed to be "objective" without expressing specific cultural, political, or class viewpoints. Students are taught to appeal to supposedly neutral criteria—efficiency, the need for certainty, the reasonable man—as the type of argument that is acceptable....

The implications of this mode of teaching for students not of the "privileged" background are clear. They must assimilate to the dominant norm if they are to be accepted. They must leave their personal background, their culture, their identity behind. While this experience can be alienating to everyone, the middle class white male doesn't have as much of a problem—the absence of a racial viewpoint in our society is the white viewpoint, the absence of a gender viewpoint is male.[87]

The BHSA member asked rhetorically, "So are the CDF's tactics acceptable? Placed in context I have to think yes." He asserted that its tactics sent a strong message to the faculty that business as usual could not be tolerated. "Another report, another 6 months, another committee will not do. Some display of good faith is essential." Directing his comments to the first-year student who had complained to him about the protests, the BHSA member concluded:

As for the student who feels oppressed by the CDF's infusion of confrontation into the atmosphere, I have no answer but to plead that you open your eyes. Recognize that you don't change an entrenched social structure like a law school faculty with good etiquette. Recognize that the faculty who don't understand the pain that prompts the CDF's protests never really respected students in the first place. And recognize that the CDF has not created the conflict at Boalt. They have just made it visible. If that makes some people uncomfortable then that's the whole point.[88]

Following the protest, Professor Robert Berring distributed a memo to the faculty, which was published in its entirety in the *Cross Examiner*.[89]

Berring stated that the recent student protest followed by a meeting of the student-faculty committee on diversity, known as the Diversity Committee, had provoked him to write the memo. "In good conscience," he wrote, "I am unable to remain silent any longer." Berring explained that the Diversity Committee had led a tenuous existence. Originally constituted in response to student demands, the committee was a place to channel student concerns, a place to refer issues raised by the CDF. But he pointed out that the committee had never had any power. In fact, it had "never been sure that it could do anything other than serve as a place to siphon off student energy." Legitimizing student frustration with the faculty, Berring stated that when students had shown themselves willing to talk, the faculty had met them with distrust and delay. "They find it disingenuous at best that we have never directly discussed their demands as a faculty....They contend that the faculty is not discussing the issues. They are right."

Professor Berring wrote that until the faculty was willing to face directly the full range of questions repeatedly raised by students, "until we are ready to talk seriously about them, we can make no progress." Then he addressed a more fundamental problem within the faculty: the faculty was not talking about anything at all. He observed that the faculty "appears to be losing the ability to discuss anything other than the matters forced upon us by tenure and appointment deadlines. We have a long-standing tradition of avoiding conflict on the faculty, a highly valued sense of informality that is proving counterproductive. Instead of fostering dialogue it has paralyzed us. We avoid any matters that might expose differences of viewpoints." Berring asked rhetorically, "Are we too tired, too timid, to face difficult issues? Conviviality is important, but we must confront problems, not hide from them. As a faculty we are adrift."

Referring to the dean's practice of consulting only with older and more conservative members of the faculty, Berring commented that communication about important events was carried out in informal networks that excluded those who were not part of the established loop. "We seem to be losing a whole generation, maybe two, from the faculty, who feel that their ideas are not welcome, that their commitment and possible contributions can only be valuable if they meet the senior faculty's definition of what is valuable at Boalt. We have been unwilling to face the conflict that would attend incorporating new people with new ideas into the school structure." Consequently, he surmised that the faculty had been so successful in avoiding difficult issues that, "we seem to have lost our identity."

Berring asserted that the faculty should now direct its attention to the question of diversity and the standards used in hiring and promoting faculty. He condemned the unwillingness on the part of the administration and the faculty to see inequities produced by "neutral" standards:

At faculty meetings the Dean and other faculty simply state that our hiring and tenuring process has always been free from racist or sexist motives. And yet, in the past three years two of our tenure decisions have been overturned, one by subsequent faculty action, and one by a blind panel of outside reviewers.... Three years ago the Chancellor publicly censured us for moving too slowly in the area of faculty diversity; last year the [American Association of Law Schools] found evidence of possible sexism in our promotion policies.... Could it be that our standards are so rooted in sexist and racist institutions of the past that we cannot even see the problem?... We have never... questioned ourselves. Instead we view each question as an attack.

Berring then turned to faculty-student relations and expressed his concern for how far relations with students had deteriorated. He admonished the faculty for allowing distrust to infect both sides of the relationship, and lamented the treatment of students. Pointing specifically to the dean's talk at the Berkeley Community Law Center, he said the talk "was an indictment of us on its face." He asserted,

The students are an integral part of our enterprise. Our relationship with them is a crucial element of what this institution should be about. Waiting for the "problem" class to graduate will not work; there is no problem class, there are only problems. This is a public law school, not a private research institute.... We cannot solve these problems if we will not face them. The longer we wait, the more painful the solution will be. If we care about the institution we should be preparing for its future, not hiding from it.

Two weeks after the CDF held its protest and Professor Berring distributed his memo, another forum on faculty diversity was held in Booth Auditorium, which filled to near capacity. Students questioned the dean's commitment to diversity. Dean Choper stated that "it's not a question of commitment," and using the pool argument, he stated that "regardless of race, or ethnic background, or gender, there are a very limited number of people who possess the peculiar qualities that make for outstanding academics." He stressed, "I think we're doing all that we can." In the forum, Berring questioned the "peculiar qualities" to which the dean referred and noted that the definition included in it some implicit definitions of "what is quality" and allowed for some very subjective judgments of what really mattered about a person and what he or she could contribute. Berring criticized the "old boys network" syndrome of looking at people "who look a lot like themselves." He suggested, "I think it may be time to take a serious look at some of those implicit standards."[90]

Dean Choper reiterated his vision of a "great law school" and maintained that research universities had a relatively limited purpose that did not include being diverse. "I think there are institutions where it is important they be representative. I am not convinced that the University of California ought to be like the California legislature, ... [or that] this institution, like political and decision making institutions in society, ought to represent [the population]."[91] The dean's statement left no doubt that diversity was not on his list of priorities. It thus seemed doubtful that the dean would actively pursue a race-conscious faculty hiring policy or do more than defend the law school's existing race-conscious student admissions policy.

By 1990, neoconservatives had seized control of the affirmative action debate, effectively advocating a color-blind and merit-based distribution of privileges. The understanding of historical admissions and hiring criteria as including embedded preferences and structural discrimination, and necessitating affirmative action to offset such preferences and discrimination, was giving way. In its stead, neoconservatives fostered a belief that admissions and hiring criteria were based on objective standards of merit and that the continued use of affirmative action therefore tipped the scale in an otherwise even competition. This belief was fueled in large part by the emergence of Asian Americans, most of whom no longer needed affirmative action to compete. In the eyes of the neoconservatives, they proved that the playing field was fair.[92]

Using Asian Americans as a vehicle to attack affirmative action, Republican Congressman Dana Rohrabacher, from Long Beach, California, mounted a legislative initiative in 1989 to examine discrimination against Asians in undergraduate admissions. Although Rohrabacher's bill (HR 147) carried no legal punch or remedy for discrimination, it was a highly symbolic show of Republican Party interest in Asian admissions. The main backers of the bill, conservative Republicans, were quick to link the problem of discrimination against Asians with what they saw as a lowering of standards for other students. Though Rohrabacher denied that the bill was a direct attack on affirmative action, it appeared to some organizations, such as the Japanese American Citizens League (JACL), to be a veiled attack on affirmative action policies. Though Japanese Americans were no longer assisted by affirmative action, and the JACL might have presumably opposed it, the organization was just emerging from a long battle for reparations for Japanese who were interned during the war. The JACL was not quick to forget how Asians had been treated historically in this country and was aware of how they were now being used to justify the status quo. The organization refused to back the bill, as did the Organization of Chinese Americans.[93]

Though Congressman Rohrabacher was unsuccessful in garnering broad support for his bill, he saw another opportunity to attack affirmative action when an Asian applicant to Boalt contacted him about a possible ceiling on Asian American admissions. The applicant had been put on a waiting list identified to the applicant as the Asian American waiting list.[94] Rohrabacher forwarded the complaint to the Office for Civil Rights (OCR) of the U.S. Department of Education, which opened an investigation at Boalt. The law school confirmed that it maintained waiting lists for various ethnic groups, but denied they were used to establish racial quotas. Rather, the separate waiting lists were used to achieve racial diversity in each entering class. After an extensive investigation of the law school's admissions practices, OCR and Boalt entered into a voluntary agreement in which OCR did not formally find any violation of antidiscrimination statutes or regulations, and the law school agreed to stop separating the waiting list by ethnicity.[95]

The conclusion of the investigation in 1992 coincided with Dean Jesse Choper's stepping down. In his place, the faculty proposed and Chancellor Tien appointed Professor Herma Hill Kay to become the first woman ever to head the law school. Kay was accustomed to breaking new ground. Among her many firsts, she was the first woman to head the Faculty Senate on the Berkeley campus and the first woman chosen to receive a Berkeley Campus Distinguished Teaching Award. Kay was also acknowledged as an outstanding scholar in family law and an author of no-fault divorce legislation adopted in California and other states. Kay's excellent credentials, however, were only part of her qualification for the position as dean. Of greater importance for the law school was her ability to build bridges and bring peace.[96]

In the previous decade, Boalt had witnessed increasing tension between and among students and faculty over the issue of diversity and the related issue of student participation in the formation of policy at the law school. This tension had been exacerbated by Dean Choper's lack of commitment to actively increase diversity on the faculty and to address student concerns. In contrast to the previous administration, Dean Kay seemed to bring with her a greater commitment to both increasing diversity and including students in the decision-making process at the law school.

In her first act as dean, Kay created the Admissions Policy Task Force to strengthen the rationale underlying the affirmative action policy at Boalt and, in doing so, protect the admissions policy against further legal attacks. She appointed twelve members to the task force, including four students. In 1993, after a year of work, the task force, chaired by Professor Rachel Moran, issued a report that reviewed the admissions history of the law school and the pedagogical evidence relevant to the admission of a diverse student body. The report used the principle of "critical mass" to assert that meaningful diversity was only possible if a significant number of minority students were admitted. The report stated, "Tokenism is the enemy of diversity. For groups previously excluded from access to legal education, feelings of alienation and isolation not only retard academic achievement but also silence the very voices that are the building blocks of a diverse law school. A critical mass of these students is necessary to achieve a truly diverse student body that contributes to the robust exchange of ideas."[97]

The idea of "critical mass" was not new to the faculty, but it had not been further developed by former Dean Choper. In 1973, the faculty had recognized the value of enrolling a critical mass of minority students to enhance the quality of the student body and, concomitantly, the prestige of the law school. In a political climate more welcoming and supportive of diversity than the present one, the Admissions Committee in 1973 had written a memo to the law school community, reporting on the affirmative action program, stating,

The thing which distinguishes the best law schools from others is at least as much the quality of their students as anything else. An important ingredient in the quality of the student body is its diversity in background, interests and enthusiasms. National law schools like Boalt have long sought diversity in geographical origin and undergraduate experience. Increasingly Boalt Hall has been receiving applications from people who have had broadening experiences after completion of their undergraduate education and we have tended to favor applicants who can bring to school special competencies in related disciplines or experiences which can enrich the intellectual life of the law school.

The Committee on the whole feels that a similar kind of enrichment of the law school community has taken place with the special admissions program, which has brought to the school a significant number of students who come from other than white backgrounds. Particularly with minority students there is also a critical mass problem; unless there is more than token representation, the school does not get the full measure of the benefit from the distinctive perspective of racial or cultural groups.[98]

The task force affirmed the previously held belief that a diverse student body contributed to the quality of education at Boalt and that a critical mass of previously underrepresented groups was essential to ensuring "equal educational opportunity and the robust exchange of ideas." The task force supported this belief with empirical studies that demonstrated how the alienation and isolation of a token number of minority students could prevent the realization of a truly diverse student body. The report cited one study in which a Latina student explained the feeling of being alienated and isolated from a predominantly white student body:

I still can't believe to this day that this happened.... We had to discuss our paper topics in class. [I told them my topic was the] lack of Latino representation at [this university].... Once that was said, the whole class was quiet, like I said something that was taboo. I felt uncomfortable being the only Latino person there, and there was only one other multiracial person in the room.... A guy says, "What do you propose we do, lower academic standards?"[99]

The report also included the statement of another participant in the same study who described how hard it was being "the only one": "[Besides the social scene,] the other thing I find very hard is being the only black person in class.... When class is over with, I try to hang around and get to know the kids in my class, but I'm the only black there and I feel like I should go back to my room."[100] The task force report cited other studies finding the same feelings of alienation and isolation for Asians, particularly those who had recently immigrated to the United States, and for women who studied in academic fields or institutions that were male-dominated. In light of these studies, the task force recommended the adoption of a new admissions policy that strengthened the rationale for the affirmative action program based on the principle of "critical mass."[101]

On May 6, 1993, the faculty adopted such a policy, replacing its former policy, which had been adopted in 1978 following the *Bakke* case. The new policy was noteworthy in its departure from the neoconservative rhetoric used by former Deans Kadish and Choper, pitting diversity against excellence. In a conciliatory tone, the faculty policy began, "Boalt Hall is committed to maintaining the academic excellence *and* broad diversity that characterize its student body." The policy continued,

The School seeks to enroll students whose quality of mind, background, and experience suggest that they have the capacity to distinguish themselves in the study of law and to make a contribution to the learning environment of the School, the legal profession, legal scholarship, the formulation of public policy, and other law-related activities.

In making decisions, the School gives *greatest* weight to numerical indicators... yet numbers alone are not dispositive. Weight is also given to non-numerical indicators such as recommendations, graduate training, special academic distinctions or honors, difficulty of the academic program successfully completed, obstacles or disadvantages overcome, marked success in nonacademic endeavors, work experience, and such other factors as may appear in the file of an individual applicant.

Among the factors that are considered in evaluating an applicant's potential to contribute to the learning environment is the diversity of background and experiences that the applicant brings to the Law School. Using this balanced review process, the Law School considers both numerical and non-numerical factors for all applicants.[102]

The policy went on to describe the past success of the twin pursuits of excellence and diversity, and stated, "Historically, Boalt Hall has been a leader in attracting a diverse student body with outstanding academic credentials." The policy pointed out that from 1977 to 1992, the median grade point average for entering classes ranged from 3.6 to 3.7, and the median LSAT scores ranged from the 91st to the 97th percentile. During that same period, the policy stated, "Boalt Hall classes boasted 5–13% African Americans, 4–15% Asian Americans and Pacific Islander Americans, 8–14% Chicanos and Latinos, and 32–49% women."

The pursuit of excellence and diversity had been made possible by affirmative action, and the policy recommitted the law school to a race-conscious admissions program. Grounding the legality of affirmative action in the *Bakke* decision, the policy articulated the pedagogical value of diversity at Boalt. The policy stated that a law school "must train lawyers to analyze and interpret the law, to develop policies affecting a broad range of people, and to advance arguments persuasively in a wide range of forums. Were a law school [to have]...prepared its graduates to discuss legal issues only with persons similar to themselves [it] would have failed in its mission." Given the importance of diversity to the educational mission of the law school, the policy directed the Admissions Committee to continue to admit, as it had done since the inception of the affirmative action program at Boalt, a "critical mass of students from traditionally underrepresented backgrounds."

Though the new admissions policy fortified the affirmative action program at Boalt against further legal attacks, it could do nothing to protect the program from future political attacks. By 1993, it appeared that the country had come full circle to an understanding of racial equality that preceded the civil rights movement. In returning to a place of blissful ignorance, the merit argument made sense in the debate over affirmative action. No longer, did it seem, were Americans interested in understanding the breadth and depth of racism; instead they were engaged in a full retreat from race.[103]

The country had undergone an identifiable shift in racial politics following the Los Angeles riots, which were sparked by the acquittal of white police officers who had brutally beaten a black man named Rodney King. The shift that took place was not the riot itself, nor was it the Republican analysis that placed the blame on the minority poor or the welfare policies which had supposedly taught them irresponsibility and dependency. The shift was rather the Democratic retreat from race and the party's limited but real adoption of Republican racial politics, with their support of "universal" policies and their rejection of "race-specific" policies.[104]

In 1992, the Democratic Party had sought to win back white voters who had handed the Republicans the presidency in the three previous elections. To dismiss charges of catering to minorities, presidential candidate Bill Clinton adopted the racially coded rhetoric of "personal responsibility" and "family values" which was so successfully used by the right. Clinton and other Democrats chose to remain silent on any explicit discussion of race and its overall meaning for politics. In so doing they fostered a deliberate neglect of racial issues and downplayed the continuing significance of race in American society. It was but a small distance from the Democratic "universal" position to the Republican "color-blind" position.[105] The retreat from race helped deliver the presidency to Clinton, but it also exposed affirmative action programs to a new wave of attacks. Neoconservatives no longer needed to win the legal argument that affirmative action was "unconstitutional." They now only needed to win the political argument that it was "unfair."

In the coming years, campus affirmative action policies would once again come under scrutiny. Many students, faculty, and administrators would continue to assert that affirmative action was necessary to achieve excellence and diversity in higher education. But this time, where before there had been additional support from prominent Democrats, a demonstrable silence would fall. In this silence, neoconservatives would launch an aggressive political campaign to dismantle affirmative action throughout the state of California. The campaign would prove successful. But at the University of California, and at Boalt in particular, the outcome would prove disastrous, dismantling thirty years of racial progress in higher education.

CHAPTER 3

Dismantling Diversity

In 1993, two San Francisco Bay Area academics—Glynn Custred and Thomas Wood—introduced a ballot initiative that in one vote promised to eliminate affirmative action throughout the state of California. Custred and Wood viewed affirmative action as both unfair and contrary to their own interests. Custred was a white anthropology professor at California State University at Hayward who was upset by, among other things, the hiring and firing practices employed by his university to create and maintain racial diversity on the faculty. Consideration of race had been a factor in a number of hiring decisions and had also threatened to override the seniority system in determining which professors should be laid off in a budget crunch. Custred felt it was unfair that as a senior, white male professor he might be asked to leave, while a junior, female or minority professor might be allowed to stay in order to maintain a diverse teaching staff. His distaste for affirmative action prompted him to help start the California chapter of the National Association of Scholars, which billed itself as "the only American academic organization dedicated to the restoration of intellectual substance, individual merit, and academic freedom in the university." Through this organization, Custred met Thomas Wood.[1]

Also frustrated with affirmative action hiring policies, Wood blamed these policies directly for his difficulty in finding a job as a white university professor. After working outside of academia for several years, Wood had applied for a position at San Francisco State University as a professor of religious philosophy but was turned down, he felt, because the position was earmarked for a minority candidate.[2] He thought it unfair that race should be taken into consideration in the university hiring process, or for that matter, any process where opportunities were at stake. Wood and Custred shared their concerns and together decided to take action. They had seen previous attempts to unravel race-conscious policies—legal challenges, federal investigations, and legislative bills—fall flat. They knew that though there were many opponents of affirmative action policies, on the whole, courts, federal agencies, and legislatures were still not prepared to declare such policies unconstitutional or prohibit their use. So they turned to the initiative process, which allowed ordinary citizens to enact a law and even an amendment to the state constitution by bringing an issue of concern to the voters.

The initiative process—adopted into the state constitution in 1911— had been designed to give citizens a way to bypass the government and enact new laws with a popular vote. However, the day when ordinary citizens could successfully propose an initiative appeared to be long gone. The initiative process had come to be used more often by well-organized political and economic entities, particularly on the right, and by incumbent politicians from the governor on down, than by "the people." It was still "the people" who voted on the initiatives, but interest groups, backed by media consultants, direct mail specialists, pollsters, and others, usually financed the costly signature drives required to get measures on the ballot and the advertising campaigns that put them over.[3]

Custred and Wood were not prominent or wealthy men, nor were they part of political or economic organizations interested in placing an anti–affirmative action measure on the ballot. They were ordinary men who thought that if they wrote a legally sound and politically viable initiative on affirmative action, they would be able to get the backing necessary to mount an initiative campaign. They spoke with countless constitutional law professors and political consultants to develop the language of an initiative. A look at the polls told them that voters disliked quotas and preferences, but distinguished these from affirmative action policies, which they still tended to support. So without using the words "affirmative action" Custred and Wood wrote their initiative—the California Civil Rights Initiative (CCRI)—which amended the state constitution and prohibited affirmative action in public education, employment, and contracting.[4]

In October 1993, the authors filed their initiative with the state attorney general in time to coincide with a newfound interest in the prohibition of affirmative action in the state legislature. Assemblyman Bernie Richter, a Republican from Chico, a rural district in California, had proposed Assembly Bill 47, which mirrored CCRI in barring the state from taking race or gender into account in education, employment, and contracting. The bill was unlikely to get out of committee, but Custred and Wood hoped that interest in it would generate the interest and the support they needed to get their initiative off the ground. Interest in the bill was tenuous and did not build the momentum they had hoped for.[5] The proposed legislation, however, did draw out opponents of affirmative action and gave Custred and Wood an opportunity to meet Ward Connerly, who would do more than anyone else for CCRI.

Ward Connerly was an African American businessman from Sacramento and a regent of the University of California who adamantly opposed affirmative action. Though he was black, he claimed Indian, Irish, and French Creole blood. Originally from Louisiana, Connerly had grown up in Sacramento under the wings of his grandmother, who was fair-skinned and, according to family members, barely "tolerated black people." A cousin of Connerly once told a *New York Times* reporter doing a story on Ward that his grandmother "thought she was better than black people," and that this had rubbed off on the young Connerly.[6] The cousin stated that growing up, "Ward always disliked being a child of color. He [thought he was] white." Nevertheless, graduating from Sacramento State University in 1962, Connerly knew his dark skin was an impediment to getting a job in the private sector. He had done well in school, had become student body president, and had held a full-time job during college. But as Connerly later reflected, "Back in the sixties if you were black and you graduated from college, you felt the [only] option available was government." So Connerly went to work in the public sector at the state Department of Housing and Community Development, where he met Pete Wilson, the aspiring politician who was then the head of the new Assembly Committee on Urban Affairs and Housing in the state legislature.[7]

In many ways, Pete Wilson was the antithesis of Ward Connerly. Originally from Illinois, Wilson had attended private schools, graduated from Yale University, and gone on to enroll at Boalt Hall Law School. It was an era when competition to get into Boalt was minimal for white men from good schools, and Wilson enjoyed the privilege of his circumstances. He was an indifferent student and it took him four tries to pass the state bar exam, though this hardly mattered to his political career. Coming out of law school, he ran for a seat in the State Assembly and won. As the head of the Assembly Committee on Urban Affairs and Housing, Wilson heard about Connerly, an up-and-comer, and recruited him to work for the assembly committee as its chief consultant. Though the two men came from different worlds, they took a liking to each other and "became bound by a friendship made more powerful by the promise that each held."[8]

Wilson soon left the assembly and went on to become the mayor of San Diego, then a senator in the United States Congress, and finally the governor of California. During this time, Connerly left the public sector and started Connerly and Associates, which consulted for local governments that needed to meet changes in planning laws put into place by Wilson when he was in the assembly. Connerly's business thrived, and he supported Wilson's political ascent with generous campaign contributions. As governor, Wilson did not forget his friend, and when it came time to make appointments to the Board of Regents of the University of California, Wilson named Connerly to fill one of the seats. He did so, however, under pressure to diversify the regents. Wilson had wanted to appoint another longtime friend who was white to the post, but Wilson's critics promised a revolt, arguing that the appointment of another white millionaire would not broaden the board's outlook. Wilson also faced the constraint of a 1974 revision of the state constitution that required the Board of Regents to reflect California's "economic, cultural, and social diversity... including minorities and women." As of 1993, the board's eighteen appointees—out of a total of twenty-six board members—included twelve white men, four women, two Latinos, one Asian American, and one African American.[9]

In a move to appease his critics and diversify the regents, Wilson appointed Connerly. Lydia Chavez, in her book *The Color Bind,* noted the irony of the race-conscious appointment. "In a sense," Chavez wrote, "the Connerly appointment reflected Supreme Court Justice Powell's recommendations on affirmative action in the *Bakke* case. Connerly was entirely qualified—he had proven himself a capable businessman—but race was among the many factors that Wilson considered." The irony lay in the views of the new regent, who opposed the race-conscious practices that had led to his appointment and, previously, had helped his company win public contracts as a minority-owned firm.[10] As a regent, Connerly was outspoken about his views on affirmative action and questioned the continued use of race-conscious policies at the University of California. In August 1994, he focused his attention on the issue when he was approached by two white parents, Jerry and Ellen Cook, who believed that their son had been kept out of medical school by race-conscious admissions practices that let in less-qualified minority students. Connerly examined the admissions process and stated that he was shocked to find out what a "huge" gap existed between the grade point averages and test scores of university applicants from different ethnic groups.[11] The new regent did not like what he saw and was firmly decided about race-conscious policies when he attended the State Assembly judiciary committee hearing on Bernie Richter's bill eliminating affirmative action in the public sector.

Speaking in support of AB 47, Connerly told the standing-room only audience, which included Glynn Custred and Thomas Wood, that "[t]here was a time when affirmative action had a value.... There was discrimination in all sectors of California and we needed some sort of shock treatment." But, he asserted, "The time has come to take off the training wheels." Despite Connerly's support and the support of other opponents of affirmative action, Richter's bill failed to make it out of committee. Nevertheless, Custred and Wood were impressed with Connerly and introduced themselves as the authors of an initiative in which Connerly might be interested. Connerly was indeed interested and promised to keep in touch with the two men. The California Civil Rights Initiative had not attracted the support necessary to get off the ground, and the short-lived campaign was over for the time being, but another race-based initiative—Proposition 187—was gaining momentum and cutting the electoral path for a reincarnated CCRI to follow.[12]

Proposition 187, otherwise known as the "Save Our State" or "SOS" initiative, was written to curb illegal immigration, denying undocumented children access to public schools and excluding illegal aliens from virtually all other public services, including health care. Most of the provisions of the initiative were considered unconstitutional, but supporters of 187 did not care. At a time when the economy was suffering from a recession and many whites blamed immigrants—particularly those from Mexico—for drawing down public resources, supporters of 187 wanted to send a strong message to immigrants that they were not welcome. Because the demographics of the state were also changing and immigrants threatened to tip the racial balance, the xenophobic and exclusionary overtones of 187 had additional appeal to many white voters.[13]

The vote on 187 coincided with the gubernatorial election in which Pete Wilson was running for a second term. Trailing behind his opponent Kathleen Brown, Wilson made Proposition 187 his issue and appealed directly to white voters. He ran campaign ads showing shadowy figures, presumably illegal aliens, running across a road while a narrator said eerily, "They keep coming." The ad was a covert, though hardly subtle, assault on all of California's ethnic minorities, despite Wilson's vehement assertion that he was concerned only with illegal immigrants.[14] He became the point man for the campaign, spending $2 million on commercials supporting 187, and he wagered his success at the ballot box on the success of the initiative. On the day of election, the governor's political instincts proved correct. He won almost as resoundingly as Proposition 187—Wilson won with 55.2 percent of the vote, and Proposition 187 won with 58.9 percent of the vote. The *Los Angeles Times* described Wilson's landslide victory as "one of the most dramatic comebacks in California political history." And the paper noted its consequences: the victory thrust Wilson "firmly into the ranks of possible Republican contenders for the White House in 1996."[15]

The victory also demonstrated that California was fertile political ground for racial wedge issues—issues that could split whites (particularly white males) away from the Democrats and send them to the Republicans. White men had voted 63 to 37 percent in favor of Proposition 187—nearly the same proportions in which they voted for Wilson.[16] In addition, the victory demonstrated the advantage of taking a racially divisive issue directly to the voters. Though the population in California was changing rapidly, and in a few years the state would no longer have a majority racial or ethnic population, the voting population remained overwhelmingly white, and to a lesser extent male. The consequences of these demographics were clear. If proponents of a racially divisive initiative could successfully place a measure favorable to whites on the ballot, voting demographics would be on their side. This boded well for Custred and Wood, who sought once again to bring their initiative to life.

The success of Proposition 187 gave the California Civil Rights Initiative a boost. Custred and Wood had set up an office on Martin Luther King Jr. Way in Berkeley and, until the passage of 187, had received few phone calls from people who could help turn the idea of an initiative into a reality. But this changed in the aftermath of the election. On December 27, 1994, the *Washington Post* published an article drawing national attention to the changes taking place in California: "California voters gave the nation a jolt from the right last month when they passed Proposition 187.... Now the state could be on the verge of doing it again. Conservatives hope to place [an] anti-affirmative action measure ... on the ballot." Wood told the reporter from the *Post*, "The tide has turned: there is an anti-affirmative action issue coming down the pike in California that is going to make 187 look like kindergarten." After the *Post* article, Custred and Wood were contacted by a group of Republican men who helped them put together a campaign team to try, for the second time, to get the CCRI off the ground. However, no one on the team had fund-raising experience or the connections necessary to raise the kind of money required to make the campaign viable. What money the team was able to raise helped to keep the CCRI afloat, but much of it went to salaries and legal and consulting fees, and the initiative still seemed like a long shot. Few donors felt it was urgent to support a state measure when affirmative action was quickly becoming a part of the national debate and a state measure might duplicate possible federal efforts or be overtaken by the decisions of an increasingly conservative Supreme Court.[17]

In January 1995, Ward Connerly put the issue of affirmative action at the top of the news when he called for a "review" of affirmative action at the University of California.[18] He used the term "review" euphemistically to signal the beginning of an aggressive campaign to eliminate race-based policies at the university. Describing affirmative action as "unfair," he told the regents, "I want something in place that's fair." As Lydia Chavez recounted, "The impact of a successful black man publicly questioning affirmative action in the name of fairness was powerful.... [I]f a black regent had lost faith in affirmative action, how could others keep the faith?"[19]

For minority students at Boalt Hall, the question was not about faith, but about reality. For many of these students, affirmative action *was* about fairness. It was about giving traditionally underrepresented students a chance to pursue a legal education and correcting for embedded preferences that worked to their disadvantage. It was also about welcoming and supporting diversity within the law school and in the larger society. Without affirmative action, Boalt would be a different place, and many minority students understood that they would not be included at the prestigious public law school. Shortly after Connerly called for a review of affirmative action, minority students at Boalt received hate mail, foreshadowing the demise of race-inclusive policies and race-sensitive attitudes. On February 11, 1995, around the time when fall-semester grades were posted, a first-year law student discovered the following message (uncorrected for grammar and punctuation) in her box and the boxes of fourteen other students of color:

Rejoice you cry baby Niggers it's affirmative action month. A town hall meeting will not save you the wetbacks or the chinks. Your failures are hereditary and can't be corrected by these liberals. Look around Boalt Hall besides the few hand picked affirmative action professors this is a quality law school. Clinton nomination of Foster another unqualified monkey is similar to your existence here at Boalt a failure. When I see you in class it bugs the hell out of me because you are taking the seat of someone qualified. You belong at Coolie High Law don't you forget!

This was the second of two flyers distributed to first-year minority students. The first had been distributed the previous semester, on December 13, 1994, the first day of fall exams, and read, "AFFIRMATIVE ACTION SUCKS!!!! DON'T FLUNK OUT!!!!" on one side, and on the other side, next to a photocopy of an article reporting the resignation of former Surgeon General Jocelyn Elders, it read, "CLINTON AND TIEN AGREE: MONKEES BELONG IN THE JUNGLE HASTA LA VISTA SAYONARA SANS BLAGUE RESPONDEZ SIL VOUS PLAIT."

Appalled by, but not unfamiliar with, these hateful comments, the black student group at Boalt Hall, the Law Students of African Descent, responded:

We are both angered and disappointed, but unfortunately not surprised, by this hateful gesture. Beyond hurting the sensibilities of those targeted by it, hate speech creates a hostile environment where students of color do not feel safe or comfortable in the larger community. Despite the challenges such an affront creates, we want the entire student body to know that this type of cowardly act will not deter us from striving to excel. We will not apologize for being here and we certainly are not leaving (without JDs). We will not, however, isolate ourselves from other people at Boalt who understand the value of our diverse environment.

We abhor the note as a cruel and demeaning attack, but recognize that it tangentially references issues which elicit strong opinions within the Boalt community. Affirmative Action and diversity in faculty hiring are currently debatable topics throughout the state and the nation. We do not oppose civil and respectful discourse on these matters; as a group, we seek to promote tolerance and inclusion. We will continue to advocate the atmosphere of openness promised to us all at Boalt. We request that all like-minded individuals stand together against those who would interject hate into our community.

The administration and faculty did not immediately respond, and minority students were upset by what they viewed as an attempt by the administration to cover up the incident; not until minority students brought the hate mail to the attention of the press did the administration and faculty publicly condemn the incident. Echoing the 1993 admissions policy, administrators and faculty issued a statement that read, "We reaffirm our commitment to keeping Boalt Hall a place where diversity and excellence are understood to be consistent, and are consistently honored." Minority students felt betrayed by the law school, which did little more than issue this public statement, and felt more alienated at Boalt. One African American student commented, "The first year of law school is already difficult, and there is a lot of pressure on you as a minority to do well and prove yourself, and then to receive hate mail like that is a real blow to your self esteem."[20] A Latino student added, "You feel like the odds are stacked against you because there are a limited number of you there and there are so few faculty who look like you and so little support for minorities in general. Something like this just compounds the feeling of isolation."[21]

The truth was that at Boalt, despite the new leadership of Dean Kay, minority students continued to feel marginalized. Though Boalt endeavored to enroll a "critical mass" of minority students, their number still fell short of their representation in the population, and long-standing concerns about more relevant coursework, more faculty diversity, and a more supportive environment remained largely unresolved. In fact, in the spring of 1993, Latino law students at area law schools had conducted an analysis of how different law schools fared in their commitment to diversity. The students convened at Boalt to announce their findings as part of a rally for diversity. In their analysis, Boalt was rated mediocre, and Latino students pointed to problems and suggested areas of improvement. Dean Kay appeared before the crowd and rebutted student assertions that Boalt had fallen short on its commitment to diversity. The students at the rally were dismayed that the dean, whom they considered to be a pioneer of civil rights, did not seem to recognize the problems they had identified.[22]

Kay left students to continue with their rally and stepped onto the grassy field in front of the courtyard, to practice throwing a baseball in preparation for the following day, when she would throw the opening pitch at the Oakland A's baseball game. A photographer who had come to cover the rally snapped a picture of the dean practicing her pitches against the backdrop of frustrated students. The scene seemed symbolic of the dean's treatment of minority student concerns.[23] Unlike former Dean Choper, Kay was the first to pursue diversity at the law school. But much like him, she believed Boalt was doing all that it could on the issue. This was perhaps a practical view. The faculty remained mostly white, male, and conservative, and Dean Kay knew from more than thirty years of experience that the faculty, which made all major decisions at the law school, would only move so far and so fast on issues of diversity.

In February 1995, two weeks after the hate mail incident at Boalt, the state Republican Party held its semiannual convention, pushing California one step closer to deciding how it would distribute opportunity in the state. At the convention, Governor Wilson sought to use affirmative action, as he had used illegal immigration, to create a racial wedge issue that would fuel his political career. Though he had promised his supporters he would not run for president, Wilson had presidential aspirations and believed that the successful dismantling of affirmative action in California would deliver him into national prominence. Abandoning his previous support of affirmative action, Wilson publicly endorsed the California Civil Rights Initiative and asked all Californians "to once again send East from California a message about fairness. . . . I ask you to join me in changing the law to restore fairness, to make real again that American dream." The state Republican Party endorsed a resolution in support of the CCRI, leaving Democrats to respond if they so chose. But they did not.[24]

California was a must-win state in the 1996 presidential election, and President Clinton understood the demographics of the voting population—it was predominantly white and male. Affirmative action was quickly becoming a Republican cause, and already Speaker of the House Newt Gingrich and all the leading Republican presidential aspirants, including longtime affirmative action supporter Senator Bob Dole, had endorsed the CCRI.[25] President Clinton responded by steering a middle course, attempting to address the concerns of frustrated whites whose votes he needed to win the election while not offending minorities, who constituted his traditional support base. He refrained from unequivocally supporting affirmative action and instead, in February, called for a review of all federal affirmative action programs. Seeing how vulnerable Clinton was to the divisive issue, Republicans pushed it even further. They had less to lose and everything to gain in opposing affirmative action; they sought the white vote and had no minority support base that they worried about losing.

Senator Dole, the Republican front-runner in the upcoming primaries, asked the research staff at the Library of Congress to compile a summary of all the affirmative action programs operated by the federal government so that he, as well as President Clinton, could review them. In March, attacking affirmative action on the Senate floor, Dole declared, "Race-preferential policies, no matter how well-intentioned, demean individual accomplishment. They ignore individual character. And they are absolutely poisonous to race relations in our great country." In that same month, the bipartisan Glass Ceiling Commission that had been created at the suggestion of Dole as part of the Civil Rights Act of 1991 completed its review of racial progress in America. The commission stated, "Before one can even look at the glass ceiling, one must get through the front door and into the building. The fact is large numbers of minorities and women of all races and ethnicities are nowhere near the front door." Nevertheless, affirmative action programs—the only programs in place to correct for persistent and pervasive racial and gender inequities—were under attack.[26]

In California, Governor Wilson and Ward Connerly kept affirmative action in the news. Governor Wilson, having embraced affirmative action as his new target, issued a series of executive orders ending those state affirmative action programs that were subject to his sole discretion. With unnerving zeal, he also filed suit against his own state to end affirmative action programs that he had once supported.[27] In a similar vein, Ward Connerly declared, "We need to give affirmative action, as a system of preferences, a decent burial." He stated ominously, "[T]he digging should start at the University of California."[28] Two weeks later, UC President Jack Peltason, who had replaced former President David Gardner, issued a report concluding that the elimination of affirmative action would mean sharp decreases in the numbers of African American and Latino students attending the university. The report found that the consideration of socioeconomic factors—an often-suggested replacement for the considerations of race—would not mitigate this result.[29] Connerly responded that he was dubious about claims that black admissions would drop so dramatically. Expressing his resolve, he stated, "I don't think this information is going to detract me from the path I'm on."

At Boalt, the architects of the affirmative action program at the law school expressed their support for its continuation. In an interview discussing the origins of affirmative action at Boalt, Professor Jan Vetter, who had served on the law school's first affirmative action Admissions Committee and had helped defend affirmative action in the *Bakke* case, commented, "We thought [it] was a good idea [then]. We still do."[30] Vetter had joined the faculty just as affirmative action was being put into place and throughout his time at the law school had stayed heavily involved in the admissions process. Affirmative action was something he believed in.[31]

In the course of his life, Vetter had come to realize the necessity and value of race-inclusive policies. He had started his education as a white child in a segregated school system in Kansas City, Missouri. Indicative of the times, however, he was unaware of the segregation and was not cognizant of the substantial black population in the city. His only contact with a black person in his early childhood was with the maid of his house and her child. He subsequently moved to Los Angeles and attended a predominantly white but somewhat integrated high school, where he came to know several Japanese and Latino students as well as one African American student through basketball and other activities. In high school, Vetter began to understand how opportunities in this country were distributed unevenly by race and thought this unfair. Like many of his white peers, he held hopes and expectations for gradual improvement as older and less enlightened generations passed on. But he recalled that at the time, in the late 1940s and early 1950s, though there was some consciousness of race, it was not a highly salient matter for most whites, and there was still a "fair amount of stereotyping and an enormous amount of naivete."[32]

However, little more than a decade later, in 1965, riots broke out in Watts—a mostly black section of the city close to downtown Los Angeles, where Vetter was then practicing law—shocking many, including Vetter, out of their naïveté. Vetter remembered, "Along with a lot of white people in Los Angeles who had no significant relations with the city's black residents, I had the notion that Los Angeles, and Watts specifically, was not like, for example, the South Side of Chicago or Harlem, and that Watts was a happier place and that relations between blacks and whites were better in Los Angeles than in those places or in the South." Looking back on the incident, Vetter reflected, "It seems to me that the shock of the Watts riots and the riots that followed in many other cities over the next few years had a great deal to do with creating the climate of opinion in which affirmative action was more or less spontaneously and simultaneously developed in higher education across the country."

In affirmative action, Vetter saw hope. His first exposure to affirmative action was not at Boalt as a new professor of law in the late 1960s, but in the army, in the late 1950s. At that time, the army was the most integrated institution in America, and this was so because of a conscious policy of racial inclusion. Vetter found the army to be very democratizing and very diverse. Certainly there were still instances of discrimination, but "people who were expected to get along, got along." They lived, worked, and drank together, and, in the process of interacting, they learned to respect one another and found common ground. At Boalt, affirmative action had resulted in the admission of minority students who would not have otherwise been admitted. To Vetter, this was important for two reasons. First, the admission of minority students had produced minority lawyers who represented the school well in every sector of the legal profession. Second, paralleling his experience in the army, the admission of minority students had forced people of different races to interact and had fostered varying degrees of cross-cultural awareness, understanding, and friendship. Getting below a superficial level was hard, but in Vetter's mind, it was a necessary prerequisite to building a healthy multicultural society. Relations between the races had improved over the years, but in 1995 there was still a long way to go.

Joe Jaramillo (class of 1995), a third-year student at Boalt, felt the same.[33] Jaramillo was a Chicano[34] student who grew up in a racially mixed neighborhood and went to a racially mixed high school in Vallejo, a medium-sized, working-class city in the San Francisco Bay Area. He came from a world where people of different races appreciated one another. But when he enrolled at UC Davis as an undergraduate student, he discovered that this was not always true in other places. At Davis he was surprised to find, for example, that Chicano literature was belittled and devalued at the university. He took this personally and became involved in multicultural issues, joining in student efforts to get the university to require an ethnic studies course so that students would be exposed to cultures other than their own. Jaramillo reasoned that students could not appreciate differences between people if they did not even understand those differences, and perhaps an ethnic studies course would help. Apart from courses, Jaramillo thought it was important to interact with students of different racial backgrounds, and this he was able to do, first at Davis and then at Boalt, where he found his classmates to be quite diverse.

At Boalt, Jaramillo met for the first time students who were Bolivian, Nicaraguan, Taiwanese, Vietnamese, and Native American. This diversity was meaningful to him. He valued getting to know students from different cultural backgrounds, to learn where their families came from and what sort of things formed their ideas and beliefs. Interacting with these students destroyed certain stereotypes he had and gave him a better sense of how different people viewed the world. In this exchange of thoughts and experiences, Jaramillo also shared his background, and gave his classmates insight into the views and values of a Chicano from Vallejo. Through their interactions, Jaramillo and his classmates learned not only about their differences, but also about their similarities, their shared interests in sports and music, as well as their interests in politics and the law.

Jaramillo was concerned about the path that Ward Connerly was on — it steered too close to home. Jaramillo was a product of affirmative action and knew that without it he would not be at Boalt. He had been involved with the admissions process at the law school and knew that traditional admissions criteria were not finely tuned to select the people who would succeed and to keep out the people who would not. More important, he knew that the consideration of traditional criteria alone, without the additional consideration of race, would preclude many minorities from entering the law school, making Boalt a far less diverse place. The cross-cultural interaction he valued so much as a student would no longer be possible.

Professor Jan Vetter was also worried about the direction in which Ward Connerly was headed. Vetter thought that at the University of California the only way affirmative action could be effectively challenged was if a black regent led the charge.[35] Affirmative action had been under attack for some time, but its critics were mostly white neoconservatives who could be accused of ulterior, racially self-serving motives. However, as a black man, Connerly brought legitimacy to the view that affirmative action was wrong. His role in opposing affirmative action was pivotal, and its effect on others could not be underestimated. Professor Vetter watched with great interest and deep concern as the events of the summer began to unfold.

On May 18, the regents held a hearing to review the affirmative action programs employed at the university, and particularly at the law schools. Dean Herma Hill Kay was invited to speak and stated her unequivocal support for affirmative action. She remarked, "The need to diversify the legal profession is not a vague liberal ideal: it is an essential component of the administration of justice. The legal profession must not be the preserve of only one segment of our society. Instead, we must confront the reality that if we are to remain a government under law in a multicultural society, the concept of justice must be one that is shared by all our citizens."[36]

The dean forewarned the regents that if Boalt were to admit students only by reference to their LSAT scores and undergraduate grades, the numbers of underrepresented minorities—African Americans, Latinos, and Native Americans—would fall precipitously. She noted that had the entering class of 1994 been admitted solely on the basis of numerical indices, the numbers of underrepresented minorities would have dropped from 66 to 9, and the total percentage of minority students, including Asians, would have been reduced from 40 percent to 14 percent.[37] Drawing from the Boalt admissions policy, she added, "These numbers are insufficient to create a critical mass of minority students who can help sustain the robust exchange of ideas necessary for a diverse education in the law."[38] Dean Kay echoed the testimony of all other university administrators and officials who came before the regents that day. She, like they, argued for affirmative action programs that had proven to be effective in increasing diversity and maintaining excellence at the University of California.

Although the hearing was held during final exams, a group of dedicated students from across California attended the hearing at the Mount

Laurel campus in San Francisco to voice their support for affirmative action. Though not on the program, they demanded to be allowed to address the regents but were kept from doing so by police in riot gear. One student from the Santa Barbara campus stated, "To bring forth a proposal like this, you are basically implying that racism no longer exists in this society. I will tell you racism is not gone." Another student—the chair of the University of California Students Association—stated, "We have students from every single UC campus here. We care very much about this issue. We hope you listen to us."[39]

Turning a deaf ear to students and ignoring statements made by administrators, Connerly released a proposal on July 5 to abolish all race-based admissions and announced his plans to bring a vote to the full Board of Regents on July 20.[40] The next week, President Peltason sent a letter to Connerly stating it would be a "grave mistake" to dump UC affirmative action programs. He wrote, "We are a public institution in the most demographically diverse state in the union. Our affirmative action and other diversity programs, more than any other single factor, have helped us prepare California for its future. Any action now to dismantle our diversity programs would be premature and against the best interests of the University and California."[41]

The letter was backed by the university's vice presidents and by chancellors of all nine campuses. They unanimously urged, in the strongest possible terms, the continuation of affirmation action policies at the university. In a separate statement, which President Peltason also signed, they declared, "California cannot afford the economic and social consequences of failure to foster leadership for the 21st century. Such leadership must be able to negotiate the complexities of a global economy and multicultural world. Cultivating a campus community of diverse ethnicities, ideas, cultures, talents, races, interests and values must remain at the center of the University's obligation to the state and the nation. The University must remain committed to a diverse and rigorous intellectual environment."[42]

In the weeks leading up to the vote, national events focused attention on the drama unfolding in California. In June, the U.S. Supreme Court struck a heavy blow against affirmative action. In a case called *Adarand Constructors v. Pena*, the Court struck down a program that set aside a portion of highway construction contracts for minority firms, declaring that all racial classifications by federal agencies were inherently suspect and presumptively invalid, and were subject to strict scrutiny.[43] The Court did not declare all affirmative action programs to be unconstitutional, but it raised the bar of legal scrutiny. The Court had come to the decision with a five-to-four vote, and two of the justices—Scalia and Thomas—concluded that racial classifications were per se unconstitutional. The country as well as the Court seemed divided on the issue of affirmative action, and a change in policy in California threatened to tip the balance of public sentiment against affirmative action.

The *Adarand* decision gave President Clinton cover to pursue his middle course, and the day before the regents' vote, he concluded his five-month review of affirmative action. On the evening of July 19, Clinton delivered a nationally publicized speech in which he declared that "[a]ffirmative action has been good for America," and that instead of ending it, the country needed to mend it.[44] Affirmative action would be a front-page story the following day, and the vote to overturn it at the University of California—the country's premier public university—was not to be missed. By the time night fell in California, every major newspaper and network was in San Francisco, preparing for the meeting that would take place at the Mount Laurel campus the next day.

It appeared that Ward Connerly and Governor Wilson would carry the day. They had made repeated statements in the press that they had the votes to eliminate affirmative action at the university. Behind the scenes, it was believed that Governor Wilson had met and carried on phone conversations with a majority of the board members, seeking assurances from some and pressuring others to vote for the proposal. Governor Wilson had a lot riding on the vote. Passage of the proposal would likely give him the notoriety he needed to become a national contender in the presidential race. To Wilson, the proposal to end race-conscious programs at the university was not so much about good public policy as it was about good political strategy. The governor did not want any surprises on the day of the regents' meeting, and he made sure that the votes were counted and in the bag.

As the vote approached, Joe Jaramillo felt compelled to call Ward Connerly.[45] The vote seemed strategically timed to take place during the summer when students were out of school and less able to organize against the proposal. Students had really only become aware of the proposal in late spring and had not had time to mobilize an effective opposition. School was now over, and Jaramillo was worried that student voices were not being heard. In the middle of studying for the bar exam, Jaramillo called the office of Connerly and Associates in Sacramento and asked to speak to Ward Connerly. At the very most, Jaramillo hoped to get Connerly to reconsider his proposal. At the very least, Jaramillo wanted him to know that his proposal was affecting real students like himself and that if it passed it would shut out others like him.

When Connerly picked up the phone, Jaramillo began to make his case. He explained that he and his Chinese American friend in law school were prime examples of why affirmative action worked. His friend was someone who did well on standardized tests, had scored in the 95th percentile on the LSAT, and was admitted without affirmative action. Jaramillo had scored in the 79th percentile on the LSAT, and was admitted with affirmative action. Nevertheless, Jaramillo earned higher grades than his friend, who had been predicted to outperform him. The bottom line was that the lower standardized test scores of underrepresented minorities did not say anything about their ability to succeed at the university. Connerly disagreed. He stated that he worked in public contracting, and had seen what happens with racial preferences—unqualified people get the contracts—and the same thing appeared to be happening at the university. The conversation turned argumentative, devolving into a shouting match, and ended with Connerly yelling an expletive at Jaramillo and hanging up.

On July 20, the day of the vote, Ward Connerly and Governor Wilson marched into the regents' meeting confident that they would prevail. At the meeting, a number of public officials and civil rights leaders spoke before the regents, many urging them to delay their vote until the issue had been considered further. California State Senator Tom Hayden, who had been a civil rights and antiwar activist leader in the 1960s, warned the regents against a "Darwinian rationing of seats." Reverend Jesse Jackson urged the regents to reject outright the proposal to eliminate affirmative action, and in a moving statement explained, "I remember what it was like to live in a colorblind society—I was invisible." Calling for the continuation of race-conscious policies, Jackson stated, "In a color-caring society, each of our unique experiences would come into play, broadening our collective lives to bring compassion into a national dialogue on overcoming race and gender inequality."[46]

Despite vocal opposition to the proposal and multiple pleas to delay the vote, the bitterly divided regents proceeded with the roll call. They would first decide on affirmative action in hiring and promotion and then on admissions. On the issue of hiring and promotion, the regents voted 15–10 to end affirmative action. Of the appointed regents, only two white regents—Roy Brophy, a Sacramento real estate developer, and William Bagley, a San Francisco attorney—voted against the proposal. The other appointees who voted "no" included Ed Gomez, a Latino student regent, Alice Gonzalez, a Latina and former state employee, and Tom Sayles, a black executive appointed by Wilson in 1994. The remaining "no" votes came from UC President Jack Peltason and the four Democrats, who held their seats on the board by virtue of being elected officials.[47]

The regents next turned to the issue of admissions and, with a vote of 14–10, ended affirmative action at the university.[48] The resolution they adopted—Special Policy 1 (SP-1)—stated, "[T]he University of California shall not use race, religion, sex, color, ethnicity, or national origin as criteria for admissions to the University."[49] With their vote, the regents dismantled the most effective means the university had ever had to increase racial diversity in the student body. Affirmative action policies that had been well reasoned and fine-tuned over the years were all at once and with very little consideration eliminated. Schools such as Boalt, which had adopted and implemented race-conscious policies to address racial inequalities and educational necessities, were left in a precarious position without a means to ensure diversity at their schools.

The vote to end affirmative action provoked an angry response. Amid police in riot gear, more than five hundred protesters just outside the meeting listened in disbelief as the results were announced. After the vote, Regent Roy Brophy, who had voted against ending affirmative action stated angrily, "The votes that came out were not based on what's good for the university. We didn't listen to the chancellors; we didn't listen to the faculty. We simply believed the best way to cure a sore throat was to cut the baby's head off."[50] Jesse Jackson charged the governor and the regents with "ramrod[ding] the academic community." He stated, "They didn't just run over students, they ran over the President of the university, the chancellors, the faculty, and others."[51]

The decision to end affirmative action, and the manner in which that decision was made, frustrated many in the faculty. Boalt Professor Robert Cole, who was particularly concerned with issues of governance, remarked, "This was very much a top-down decision that came out of the blue. There was inadequate consultation, and what there was took place too close to the decision making." Furthermore, he added, "It was a complete violation of the implicit rules of governance here, that the regents are not going to make decisions like this and certainly not without much more consultation." Cole concluded, "The whole thing was like a coup."[52] Indeed, it appeared that way. After Connerly called for a review of affirmative action in January, every piece of information and every administrator who spoke before the regents had made clear that affirmative action was working at the university and that without it, problems would ensue. Nevertheless, affirmative action had been eliminated a short six months after it was called into review.

Following the vote, Lieutenant Governor Gray Davis, a Democrat who had supported the continuation of affirmative action, stated, "[This is a] sad day for California."[53] But not everyone felt that way. On the Berkeley campus, an undergraduate student applauded the regents' decision and told a news reporter, "I think it is good affirmative action was started 30 years ago. Thirty years is one generation. I think that is enough time for minorities...to make it...without help."[54] Homer Mason, one of the early African American law students who had helped implement affirmative action at Boalt, read these comments and responded, "People who say that thirty years is enough forget about the long history of oppression in this country." He added, "We should be working toward policies of inclusion not exclusion. The regents' vote shows a lack of interest, care, or concern about minority students. In taking away affirmative action the regents have taken away hope for a number of talented and hardworking students, who still face discrimination and for whom opportunities are still hard to come by."[55]

Summing up the significance of the vote, one journalist wrote, "[The] vote places the [University of California] in the middle of the national debate over the future of racial preferences."[56] Wilson's ratings, which had been lagging in the national polls, shot up five points, and four days after the regents' meeting, he enjoyed his biggest fund-raiser yet.[57] On that same day, Senator Bob Dole held a press conference in Washington to announce that he and a congressman from Florida had just proposed legislation to abolish all federal affirmative action programs.[58] This new infusion of interest encouraged the authors of the California Civil Rights Initiative. With fresh financing within reach, Glynn Custred and Thomas Wood filed the CCRI for the second time with the state attorney general.

By the end of August, New Hampshire voters were watching television commercials boasting that Pete Wilson "was the first to outlaw affirmative action quotas in state hiring and end preferences for college admissions." Polls showed that voters responded favorably to the ads, and affirmative action promised to deliver Wilson into the running for the Republican presidential nomination. But Governor Wilson faced troubles at home. He had promised his financial backers that he would not run for the presidency, and many of his supporters refused to support his presidential bid. They needed him in California, if for nothing more than to prevent a Democratic lieutenant governor from becoming governor. This lack of support proved fatal, and in September, Wilson withdrew from the race.[59]

About that time the political pendulum began to swing when affirmative action programs received the public support of General Colin Powell—the first black chairman of the Joint Chiefs of Staff—who was more popular than either President Clinton or Senator Dole, the probable contenders for the presidency. Powell was not running for president, but both political parties courted him, and the media hung on his every word. Countering the rhetoric of neoconservatives directly, Powell told the press, "We should not deceive ourselves into thinking the playing field is equal. We should not deceive ourselves that we are a color-blind society." When asked about racial preferences, Powell said that the nation was "full of preferences" and added that the very politicians "who scream about quotas and preferences" are the ones who vote to give preferences to their corporate supporters.[60]

At Berkeley, students returned to school angered by the action of the regents and began to organize to put pressure on the regents to reverse their decision. At Boalt, students started a new group called Boalt Students for Affirmative Action (BSAA). Daniel Tellalian (class of 1998), a second-year Puerto Rican law and business student, was one of its founders. Over the summer, Tellalian had watched in disbelief as the regents dismantled affirmative action. He considered SP-1 to be an affront to minorities; it was blind to the educational inequities that persisted in California and negated the value of racial diversity in higher education. Moreover, it perpetuated a feeling of resentment against minorities that had begun with the passage of Proposition 187. With its racist overtones, Proposition 187 had been a wake-up call for Tellalian that minority rights were in danger. While participating in public protests against the ballot measure, he had been told, "Go home, this is our country." This had hurt him, but not as much as the hate mail he and other minority students received in their first year of law school. Tellalian had grown up in Los Angeles as one of a few Latino students in an overwhelmingly black elementary school and one of a few minorities in an overwhelmingly white high school, so he knew well the feeling of racial isolation. But it was not until he arrived at Boalt that he felt truly unwanted. He had been shocked by the hate mail and viewed it as a reflection of things getting worse. To him, the passage of SP-1 was a confirmation that hard-won advances in civil rights were tenuous at best. When he returned to school in the fall, Tellalian was determined to do what he could to respond to the attacks on racial and ethnic minorities in California.

Through BSAA, Tellalian and a small but committed group of law students met to learn how the regents had come to their decision. Tellalian reflected, "We learned that the regents were political appointees of the governor, that they were overwhelmingly wealthy business interests and friends of Governor Wilson. In addition, they had little or no educational experience, which led us to believe that Wilson had forced them to act over the summer with little research or recollection. Subsequent information confirmed these suspicions."[61] BSAA sought to educate the law school community about what had happened over the summer and worked to build momentum to pressure the regents to reconsider their decision. Students distributed flyers explaining why affirmative action was still necessary and why the "color-blind" rhetoric of neoconservatives was inconsistent with reality. They also tried to sway Dean Kay to stand up to the regents' decision, but she refused to protest on any level. Though she did not agree with the decision and felt the regents did not understand what they were doing when they eliminated race-conscious policies, she felt compelled to comply with SP-1.[62]

In early October, BSAA held a forum for the Berkeley community and invited civil rights activists and attorneys to speak on the politics of affirmative action. One speaker at the forum stated, "Berkeley is ground zero in the battle to preserve affirmative action." The eyes of the nation had turned to Berkeley to see how the most academically competitive as well as most politically active campus at the University of California would handle the dismantling of affirmative action. If there was going to be an organized protest, it would most likely originate at Berkeley. The California Civil Rights Initiative was coming down the pike—it would appear on the November 1996 ballot if the proponents were able to collect enough signatures—but there were already rumors that some of the regents were having second thoughts about eliminating affirmative action at the university. If students, faculty, and administrators who supported race-conscious programs could influence the regents to reconsider their decision, a reversal of policy might keep the CCRI from winning a majority of votes. In a compelling appeal, another speaker at the BSAA forum remarked, "Sometimes there is only one place to be. This is it. If students here stand up and refuse to be a mirror for society's racism and prejudice, but [instead are] a model [of resistance], other students will follow. You have two semesters, folks."[63]

On October 12, thousands of UC Berkeley students boycotted classes and gathered on Sproul Plaza as part of a full day of protest to restore the university's affirmative action policies. BSAA rallied students at the law school to join the protest, which had been organized by undergraduate students. Law students, several hundred strong, marched through the hallways of Boalt chanting, "Open it up, or shut it down!" and, "Qualified, here to stay, join the fight or get out of the way!" The mass of students then marched down to Sproul Plaza, carrying a large banner that read "BOALT STUDENTS FOR AFFIRMATIVE ACTION." As the students entered the plaza, they were greeted by a roar. In the plaza, Jesse Jackson spoke to a crowd of five thousand, stating, "We must choose affirmative action and inclusion over negative action and exclusion." Following the rally, the protesters marched into the city of Berkeley, chanting loudly, disrupting traffic, and drawing support in the form of applause and car horns sounded in rhythm to the chanting of students. Linked arm in arm, students marched toward the Bay Bridge, intending to cross into San Francisco. When students arrived at the entrance to the bridge, they were met by police, who blocked the entrance and ended the protest.[64]

State officials reacted to the rally with skepticism, saying the demonstration would have little effect on current policies. Ward Connerly commented, "I would characterize it as a protest that fizzled," and pointed to the fact that rally attendance was very small in proportion to the number of people affected by the decision.[65] Daniel Tellalian, who had helped organize the protest, thought differently. Defined in terms of the protests of the late 1960s—when tens of thousands of students took to the streets—the October protest was small. But in the context of the 1990s— when few students felt passionately enough about anything to take a public stand—the protest was significant. Tellalian reflected, "I think much was accomplished. We showed the regents the faces of the people they affected—that of both underrepresented minorities who would be shut out by their policy and of white and Asian students who would suffer from the lack of diversity at the university." Tellalian added that at a time when the fate of affirmative action was by no means settled, the voices of five thousand protesting students were an important demonstration of opposition to race-exclusive policies.[66]

Admittedly, however, it was hard to sustain that kind of pressure on the regents. The core activists, such as Tellalian, had worked hard in the early part of the semester organizing students, educating the community, and putting together the protest, and by the second half of the semester they were exhausted. Though, when asked, the majority of students said they supported affirmative action, the greater student body was still not willing to miss a class or a television show or a party to defend affirmative action. In addition, many white students did not view the issue of affirmative action as affecting them directly and remained on the sidelines of the debate. One such freshman, who had not joined the October protest, stated in the *Daily Californian,* "I'm paying for my entire education. I'm not going to miss any classes. Not all of us have something to gain. I'm paying $25–$50 for this one session."[67] Minority students shouldered much of the burden of sustaining opposition to anti–affirmative action measures, but they alone were not enough to influence the regents.

Student efforts were supplemented, however, by faculty activism. Following the October 12 protest, the Berkeley campus faculty voted to ask the regents to rescind their July decision. In an emotional speech before the faculty, sociology professor Jerome Karabel asked rhetorically, "Is it acceptable for the governor to drag perhaps the greatest public university in the country into the lowest depths of political primaries," referring to Wilson's failed presidential bid. Karabel continued, "The Regents circumvented the University President, the Chancellors and the Academic Senates. We need to communicate very clearly this is not acceptable."[68] Over the course of the next month, faculty at all nine campuses passed similar resolutions and the UC Academic Senate voted 124–2 to call on the regents to rescind their vote.[69] Activism at the Berkeley campus and other campuses across California had a demonstrable effect on the regents, some of whom were now rumored to be preparing proposals to amend or rescind SP-1.

This was not good news for the CCRI campaign, which was having trouble qualifying for the ballot, and needed all the momentum it could get. The campaign had 150 days, until February 21, 1996, to collect a number of signatures equaling 8 percent of the last gubernatorial vote—693,230 signatures—to place the measure on the ballot. But the drive to get signatures was riddled with problems. The campaign had no volunteer base, which meant having to build one from scratch, which took time and energy. The campaign was also conducting a paid petition drive, but even that was having trouble. The signature-gathering firms with which the campaign had contracted for seventy cents a signature were finding that women and ethnic minorities—who made up the bulk of their workforce—were refusing to collect signatures for a measure that ran against their own interests.[70]

Finally, the campaign was running out of money, and just before Halloween, the CCRI went public with the news that the campaign was broke, and if it was to be saved, the people "who talked the talk would also have to walk the walk." The campaign had only collected 200,000 signatures and in so doing had spent $500,000. Campaign managers estimated that they needed an additional $1 million to pay people to collect the remaining signatures.[71] Republicans across the state responded with financial contributions, and within a few days the campaign was back on its feet. Several weeks later, the CCRI announced that Ward Connerly had become the new chairman of the campaign. Connerly told reporters that he decided to chair the initiative campaign because he feared the regents' decision would be rescinded.[72]

Connerly was a great asset to the campaign. Not only was he an effective speaker, astute politician, and impressive fund-raiser, but he had direct access to Governor Wilson, who offered his mailing list of small donors, asked state legislators to have their staff collect signatures, and even called on donors himself. For the first time, money was not a problem for the campaign. Less than a month after Connerly had taken over, Wilson raised more than $500,000—the bulk of which came from the Republican Party—and the campaign was able to attract more enthusiastic signature gatherers by paying more than $1 a signature. Connerly's color was also an asset to the campaign. "To be blunt, the fact that he was black was very important," stated one of the CCRI campaign managers. "It's like using affirmative action to defeat affirmative action." The campaign manager admitted "It's slightly unprincipled." But the fact of the matter was that it worked.[73]

At the regents' meeting in January 1996, several regents expressed concern about SP-1.[74] The regents had passed the resolution with only a brief discussion of the consequences of their policy, and they now understood there to be no effective substitute for the consideration of race in the admission of a diverse student body. The Task Force on Admissions Criteria found that, regardless of what other factors were considered, under a "race-blind" admissions policy the university would become less diverse. Two proposals were therefore put forth at the end of the meeting. One was to rescind SP-1 and the other was to change it from binding to advisory until the regents had undertaken a full evaluation of their policy. Discussion of the proposals was tabled for the next meeting in March. In the interim, Connerly announced that the CCRI campaign had raised the necessary money and collected the necessary signatures to place its initiative on the November ballot. At the subsequent regents' meeting, Connerly convinced the regents to postpone consideration of the proposals to rescind or amend SP-1 until after the November election, when voters would decide for themselves whether or not to allow race-conscious policies in public education, contracting, and hiring. If the CCRI passed, then any further discussion of SP-1 would be moot.[75]

Connerly, however, was not content to rely on the ballot initiative to eliminate all remaining forms of affirmative action. He announced that he and Governor Wilson were drafting a resolution for consideration by the regents that would ban race and gender preferences in financial aid and outreach programs at the university.[76] But as Connerly and Wilson continued their campaign to strip opportunities from those who needed them most, they reinforced the opportunities of those who needed them least. In March, the newspapers reported that the governor and some of the regents, including Ward Connerly, regularly used their positions to get students with well-connected parents into the University of California.[77]

To Richard Russell, an African American who was a regent by virtue of his elected position as vice president of the Alumni Association of the University of California and who had opposed SP-1 (though at the time of the passage of SP-1, he was only a regent designate and had no vote), this was outrageous. Russell resented the hypocrisy of regents who on the one hand said that race did not matter and on the other hand lobbied for white students in the admissions process. Russell did not buy into the "color-blind" rhetoric. His children had only recently been called "niggers" by neighbors, and he knew from his own experience that race still mattered. In his view the regents were failing to represent the entire student population. How could they when they called blacks and Latinos "unqualified" and stood up for the "rights" of whites and Asians. In what way were they advocates for underrepresented minorities at the university? To Russell, they were clearly not. "For Ward Connerly to hand deliver applications to Chancellor Tien and call the Chancellor if the applications are not acted on favorably, undermines his whole argument of equality of opportunity."[78]

In Russell's mind, the hypocritical actions of the regents compromised the integrity of the whole board, which had assumed the responsibility of deciding how scarce and precious seats at the university should be distributed.[79]

By April 1996, the Boalt faculty was engaged in a reevaluation of the school's admissions policy to bring it into compliance with SP-1 before the next admissions cycle began in the fall. The regents had decided that affirmative action would first be eliminated at all graduate and professional schools, and in the following year would be eliminated at all undergraduate schools. This meant that Boalt would be among the first schools to admit an entering class under a "color-blind" policy and among the first to feel the effects of the regents' decision. The law school faculty still claimed to be committed to diversity, but without being able to consider race, it was unclear how diversity would be achieved. With the exception of a few professors, the faculty seemed unable to respond to the regents' resolution. A task force appointed by Dean Kay determined that admitting students "primarily" on the basis of their predictive index scores would yield, in the worst-case scenario, eight underrepresented minority students—a far cry from the sixty-six underrepresented minority students enrolled the year before, in 1995.[80] Despite this ominous warning of what the continued heavy reliance on index scores would mean for the diversity of the law school in a "race-blind" context, the Boalt faculty voted to adopt only a nominal change in their admissions policy. In addition to removing the consideration of race in the admissions process and agreeing to send two hundred more files to be read by the Admissions Committee, the faculty voted to lessen the weight of numerical indicators from "greatest" to "substantial" weight, without further clarification.[81]

Days prior to the adoption of this revised policy, Professor Marjorie Shultz—who had survived a tenure battle tinged with sexual discrimination in the late 1980s—distributed a memo dated April 22, 1996, to the faculty, which challenged the complacency of such minimal action in the face of impending doom: "Our current system of admissions intends to identify the most qualified applicants. But, in my view, it does not. Our policy lacks accuracy, efficacy, and legitimacy with regard to that task.... [W]e are in danger of entrenching those serious shortcomings in our revised policy as well."[82]

She pointed to the heavy reliance on numerical indices of qualification and questioned whether these indicators were accurate and useful for the purpose of identifying promising students. With respect to the LSAT, she noted that the Law School Admission Council—the administrator of the LSAT—emphasized that scores were only approximate and that "use of scores within the same range...to distinguish the ability of students is INVALID." "Yet," she continued, "Boalt does just this." Critical of this practice, Shultz wrote, "Numbers have an appealing concreteness. They tempt us to resolve indecision, to save time, and to satisfy our sense of fiduciary obligation by giving them great weight, but it is weight that they simply cannot bear." She pointed to the limitations of numerical indicators, stating that though they reflect success in test taking in particular and school in general, they do not predict "outstanding competency in and contribution to the profession and to society." By using traditional numerical indicators to determine who should be admitted, she added, "We also inescapably choose who will have access to a scarce and coveted public resource and to the status, income, influence, etc. that they often produce."[83]

"What then should we do?" she asked: "Assigning heavy weight to numerical indicators has the advantage of comfort... [c]omfort in the reaffirmation of our own worth. Comfort in relieving us of large amounts of work in an apparently neutral and apparently precise, and therefore satisfactory, fashion. But, our comfort is too costly. Our precision is too chimerical. Our rectitude is misplaced." Shultz rejected the argument that better alternatives to the present system were implausible. She urged the faculty to try to design a better system and to "recognize the disjunction between our means and our ends." "If we need additional incentive, we need only contemplate the untenable prospect of having an overwhelmingly white class selected by a system that is traditional but grossly lacking in justification." In the end, the faculty chose not to consider alternative designs and instead nominally changed the weight accorded to numerical indicators, clearing the way for the full force of SP-1 to take effect for the admitted class of 1997. This decision would prove disastrous for diversity at the law school and would draw strong criticism from all quarters.

In May 1996, Richard Delgado, a University of Colorado law professor who had graduated from Boalt in 1974 and had been invited back to speak at graduation, faced his audience in the Greek Theatre. He told the departing students that his class at Boalt had been the first to experience a fully diversified student body, and he noted with regret the fact that their class was likely to be the last. Delgado explained that in preparation for his commencement speech he had asked administrators at Boalt to tell him where his fellow students of color and female colleagues had wound up. Had they all flunked out, failed to pass the bar, or assimilated quietly into obscure corners of the corporate kingdom, as predicted by the nay-sayers? Not at all, he answered. Every one of them had passed the bar exam and gone on to do quite well. They had started their own companies and their own law firms; served as state court judges and in the U.S. Congress; acted as legal counsel for large corporations as well as state and federal agencies; headed public interest and civil rights organizations; and taught law students as professors around the country. After listing the successes of each of his classmates, Delgado commented, "[D]etractors of affirmative action warn that we are in danger of sacrificing quality. Well, you certainly could not tell it from that list." Delgado concluded his speech by lauding the rich diversity at Boalt, and inviting the graduating students who had experienced such diversity to join him in supporting affirmative action.[84]

In a commencement address on the other side of the country, at Bowie State College in Maryland, General Colin Powell also spoke up for affirmative action. In defense of race-inclusive policies, he remarked, "There are those who rail against affirmative action. They rail against affirmative action preferences, while they have lived an entire life of preference."[85] Powell continued his defense of affirmative action several months later at the Republican National Convention in San Diego, where, in his keynote address, he called on the party to become more inclusive: "Let the Party of Lincoln be in the forefront, leading the crusade, not only to cut off and kill discrimination, but to open every avenue of educational and economic opportunity to those who are still denied access because of their race, ethnic background, or gender."[86] Powell received a standing ovation at the conclusion of his speech. He had made clear his support for affirmative action, and in so doing, had made clear his opposition to the CCRI.

But it would take more than a speech from General Powell to combat the comfortable lead that the CCRI enjoyed. Polls showed that 70 percent of voters supported the initiative. This support, however, did not translate into support to end affirmative action. Tellingly, when voters were asked whether they favored "affirmative action," 50 percent said yes. When a qualifying clause was added, and voters were asked whether they supported "affirmative action programs to ensure equal opportunities for minorities," support rose to 61 percent. These responses indicated that the majority of voters supported affirmative action, particularly when it was employed "to ensure equal opportunity." But these responses also indicated that the majority of voters did not make the connection between the CCRI and the weakening or ending of affirmative action. In fact, only 41 percent of voters understood that "if passed, CCRI will end affirmative action in California."[87]

Custred and Wood, the authors of the CCRI, had been aware of this from the start and for this very reason had not included the words "affirmative action" in the language of the initiative. Now Ward Connerly, as the spokesman for the campaign, was careful not to associate these words with the CCRI. He told the press that the initiative was "an attack on preferences," and not "an attack on affirmative action." Pointing to the language of the initiative, he stated, "You will not find the words *affirmative action* in it anywhere."[88] This put opponents of the CCRI in the awkward position of explaining that the initiative was in fact an attack on affirmative action. A loose coalition of civil rights organizations formed an opposition campaign to get their message out, but they faced a number of obstacles, not the least of which was the Democratic Party. More than anything else the opposition campaign needed visibility, which President Clinton could provide them in opposing the CCRI. However, in a disheartening move, Clinton campaign strategists tacitly agreed with CCRI strategists early in the presidential campaign that Clinton would not support the opposition, financially or otherwise, if the initiative proponents did not draw the president into the debate by emphasizing his support of affirmative action. Articulating the priorities of the Democratic Party, Don Fowler, who was head of the Democratic National Committee, had told party executives as early as February 1995, that the party's main goal was to get President Clinton reelected and was "not to go down with the sinking ship of affirmative action." Subsequently, President Clinton actively refrained from publicly opposing the CCRI, even though he privately assured the opposition camp that he would "actively oppose this measure."[89]

Without the support of President Clinton and the Democratic Party, CCRI opponents turned to corporations who were sympathetic to their cause, but Governor Wilson preempted them by sending letters to corporate executives warning them not to contribute to the other side. He reminded potential contributors of how much business they did with the state or how heavily regulated they were. One corporate executive told an opposition fund-raiser, "The Governor is a moral pygmy, but he can cost me $250 million."[90] As a result, corporate sponsors were hesitant to step forward, and the opposition campaign was left to rely largely on individual donations. Opposition fund-raising efforts were no match for those of the CCRI, which enjoyed the support of state and national Republican leaders. Governor Wilson and Newt Gingrich, for example, pitched big contributors on the idea that to give to the CCRI campaign was to help all Republican candidates. It worked, and with money in its coffers, the CCRI was able to keep the opponents at bay.

As school began at Berkeley in the fall of 1996, the attention of student activists turned to the impending November election. Though affirmative action had already been eliminated in admissions at the university, the proposed CCRI would go one step further and prohibit race-conscious outreach, recruitment, and scholarships, making it even more difficult for the university to enroll a diverse student body. Beyond the University of California, the CCRI would also prohibit affirmative action at the California State University and all other public institutions of education, as well as prohibit race-conscious programs in the areas of public contracting and hiring. Berkeley student activists joined the opposition campaign, which was now being driven by Californians for Justice (CFJ), a statewide grassroots organization based in Oakland. CFJ had been formed by veteran political activists when the loose opposition coalition of civil rights organizations—divided by geography and by strategy—had started to fall apart. CFJ targeted largely minority and low-income precincts where the voter turnout was traditionally low but could be increased sharply with the help of door-to-door volunteers. With materials translated into Spanish, Tagalog, and several other Asian languages, volunteer precinct walkers registered voters, explained to them the consequences of the CCRI, asked them to vote against the initiative, and gave them posters to put in their windows and bumper stickers to put on their cars. CFJ did not expect to turn the vote completely around, but hoped to build a permanent organization to counter the seemingly endless attacks on people already at the margins of society. As Jan Adams, the cofounder of CFJ, pointed out, "We have the demographics on our side. If we bring the people who are not in the electorate into it, we can have an impact."[91]

At Berkeley, student activists hoped—though it was a long shot—that if the CCRI failed at the ballot box, the loss would provide valuable momentum to convince the regents to reconsider their decision to eliminate affirmative action at the University of California. Beyond volunteering for CFJ, student activists did what they could where they could. At the law school, Boalt Students for Affirmative Action held educational forums on the CCRI and sponsored debates on the ballot measure. BSAA also formulated its own arguments in support of affirmative action, addressing head-on the arguments used against affirmative action in a one-page summary (table 3), which students distributed on the Berkeley campus.

As the November vote drew near, proponents of the CCRI fashioned themselves as civil rights advocates and billed their initiative as a return to the ideals of the civil rights movement. In the ballot pamphlet distributed to voters, they drew direct analogies to the Civil Rights Act of 1964, stating, "A generation ago, we did it right. We passed civil rights laws to prohibit discrimination. But special interests hijacked the Civil Rights Movement. Instead of equality, governments imposed quotas, preferences, and set-asides." Using the terms "quotas, preferences, and set-asides" to describe affirmative action programs, CCRI proponents characterized such programs as unfair. Without distinguishing between state-sanctioned, race-exclusive programs of the past and state-sanctioned, race-inclusive programs of the present, proponents characterized all such programs as discriminatory.

They turned a blind eye to history, ignoring the tenets of the civil rights movement of equality not only in the law but also as a result. Even

TABLE 3. Arguments Opposing and Responses Supporting Affirmative Action

Arguments Opposing Race-Conscious Admissions Policies	Responses Supporting Race-Conscious Admissions Policies
They undermine the notion of merit.	"Merit" is what someone says it is. The problem with merit now is that it is defined by dominant social groups. Its use excludes non-dominant groups. The "merit" system used in law school admissions does not capture a student's potential for success, either in law school, on the bar exam, or in the legal profession.
They give unfair preferences based on skin color.	We, too, disfavor unjustifiable and arbitrary preferences. The preferences now in place (both subtle and overt) give preferences to Whites. Preferences, which accumulate over time rather than being limited to one particular act, also flow to those with privileged economic backgrounds. Recognizing racial background is not a "preference," it is an acknowledgement of social reality. It is an acknowledgement that people's experiences and identities are still shaped by their own—and others'—perceptions of race.
They stigmatize members of racialized minority groups portraying them as in need of assistance.	The "social stigma" argument presents a no-win situation. Here's the choice: Whites can stigmatize non-whites for being in institutions of higher education where affirmative action is in place, or can stigmatize them for being absent from those institutions. The problem again is the insistence on seeing affirmative action as "assistance for the needy" rather than as adjustment for accumulated social inequality.
They promote racism by fostering resentment among White Americans.	Racialized animosity and misunderstanding is only fostered by segregation. Unless different groups of people interact with one another as peers and equals, they cannot gain insight into each other's experiences and views. Also, we need to ask why we are measuring the value of a social policy by the perceptions of one social group. Since when is a "public good" something that simply makes Whites happy?
Affirmative action hasn't achieved its goals.	These policies have served intended goals: Affirmative action has dramatically increased the number of women and minorities who have made their way into higher education and employment. Affirmative action was not intended to undo racism directly, but to undo racism's most pernicious effect: segregation.

SOURCE: Boalt Students for Affirmative Action, 1996.

more egregious, proponents of the initiative invoked the image of Martin Luther King Jr., producing a campaign ad that contained footage of King's historic "I Have a Dream" speech.[92] Coretta Scott King and her son, Dexter Scott King, urged television stations not to air the ad. The Kings stated, "Martin Luther King Jr.'s words... clearly indicated that he supported affirmative action. Those who suggest that he did not support affirmative action are misrepresenting his beliefs and indeed his life's work." Ward Connerly responded that the ad was "an accurate reflection of Dr. King's words. I don't think it's rocket science to look at Dr. King's words and the proposition and say it's basically the same concept." However, history suggested otherwise, and wanting to avoid unnecessary controversy in the final weeks of the campaign, the state Republican Party, which had funded the ad, decided to pull it.

The final days of the campaign became a war of messages, proponents of the CCRI asserting that the initiative was synonymous with the Civil Rights Act of 1964, and opponents arguing that the initiative ran counter to the act and to the very goals of the civil rights movement. With the help of Governor Wilson and the Republican Party, the CCRI campaign raised a substantial amount of money, enabling the proponents to distribute their message widely and drown out the message of their opponents. On Halloween, President Clinton spoke at a rally in Jack London Square in downtown Oakland. His victory in California was already assured. Standing in front of a mostly black crowd in which a lot of CFJ posters were visible, Clinton broke his silence and stated publicly, for the first time, his opposition to the CCRI.[93] But his support was too little too late. On November 4, Californians went to the polls, and 54.6 percent of the electorate voted for the CCRI. Identified on the ballot as Proposition 209, the initiative read, "The State shall not discriminate against, or grant preferential treatment to, any individual or group on the basis of race, sex, color, ethnicity, or national origin in the operation of public employment, public education, or public contracting."

As the polls closed that day, proponents of the initiative gathered in a large ballroom at the Hyatt Regency in Sacramento to celebrate. In a room full of white men in suits, Ward Connerly claimed victory.[94] He stated, "Many people who went to the polls were voting not just to end preferences, but voting to end this obsessive concern about race."[95] Tellingly, white males, who had made up a majority of those voting at the polls, overwhelmingly approved the initiative.[96] In communities of color, however, Proposition 209 was soundly rejected: 76 percent of Latinos opposed Proposition 209, as did 74 percent of African Americans and

61 percent of Asian Americans.[97] Aileen Hernandez, a former member of the U.S. Equal Employment Opportunity Commission who had campaigned against 209, questioned the intent of the electorate. She commented, "This initiative was drafted in such a deceptive way that a lot of people were unaware of what they were voting for."[98] Indeed, a *Los Angeles Times* exit poll showed as much. Asked whether they supported affirmative action programs "designed to help women and minorities get better jobs and education," 54 percent of the voters exiting the polls had said yes and 46 had said no—nearly the reverse of the 209 vote.[99]

Twelve hours after the polls closed, the American Civil Liberties Union (ACLU), in conjunction with other civil rights organizations, filed a lawsuit in federal court in San Francisco and, pending trial, asked for an immediate order blocking Proposition 209. The ACLU asserted that the prohibition on governmental entities' taking voluntary action to remedy discrimination through the use of constitutionally permissible affirmative action programs was unconstitutional. In late December, Judge Thelton Henderson, chief U.S. District Court judge for the Northern District of California, granted the injunction, finding that the plaintiffs were likely to prevail in their case at trial. Judge Henderson (class of 1962) was one of the few African Americans who had graduated from Boalt prior to the implementation of affirmative action. He graduated at a time when there had never been an African American federal judge, and young African American law school graduates like himself could not realistically hope to be interviewed by a large law firm, let alone aspire to become federal judges. He knew how far the country had come and how far it had yet to go, and he knew what was at stake in the 209 case. In his written opinion, he stated, "It is not for this or any other court to lightly upset the expectations of the voters. At the same time, our system of democracy teaches that the will of the people, important as it is, does not reign absolute but must be kept in harmony with our Constitution."[100]

Proponents of 209 appealed the ruling and awaited a decision that would issue in April 1997. In the interim, riding the momentum of his November victory, Ward Connerly created the American Civil Rights Institute, a national organization based in Sacramento which was formed to target and dismantle affirmative action programs around the country.[101] In January 1997, on Martin Luther King Jr.'s birthday, Connerly once again invoked the image of the civil rights leader and formally launched a national campaign against affirmative action, infuriating civil rights activists. Connerly stated, "We do no disrespect to [King] by acknowledging what he wanted this nation to become, and we're going to fight to get the nation back on the journey that Dr. King laid out." King's son, Martin Luther King Jr. III, told the press he was "appalled at the audacity of Ward Connerly," describing him as a "demagogue." Connerly's campaign targeted Washington, Oregon, Colorado, and Florida for ballot initiative efforts similar to Proposition 209 in California. Seeking high moral ground by unabashedly aligning the civil rights movement with his own effort to dismantle affirmative action, Connerly remarked, "The Civil Rights Movement has lost its way since King's death in 1968, and has come to champion racial divisions and racial favoritism rather than uncompromising equality."[102]

In California, Connerly attempted to take the dismantling of affirmative action at the University of California one step further. In March, he asserted that SP-1 did not go far enough and pushed for a name-blind policy so administrators would not be swayed by ethnic-sounding surnames.[103] Admissions officers, he contended, might not be able to avoid the temptation to give preference to students on the basis of race, ethnicity, or gender as long as names were available to provide clues. University administrators called Connerly's proposal "overkill." One administrator stated, "It's unrealistic to expect applications to be completely free of any reference to race or gender, particularly because applicants are required to write essays about themselves." The UCLA admissions director responded quizzically, "We tell students to write a personal statement about who they are as human beings, but we're going to take their names off so they're just a number?" Regent Richard Russell exclaimed angrily, "What's the point? Why don't we just ban blacks and Latinos." Despite Connerly's enthusiasm for the proposal, it lost steam due mostly to its impracticability.

By the beginning of March 1997, the admissions process was in full swing at Boalt. As one of the first schools to implement a "race-blind" admissions policy, the law school was already having problems with the policy. In the application to law school, Boalt had invited students to include in their personal statements instances of obstacles that they had overcome. During an Admissions Committee meeting, a student member of the committee inquired whether an applicant's individual experience of racial discrimination, as described in the applicant's personal statement, could be considered as a "plus" factor in making a decision on that file. A faculty member responded that such experience could not be considered without substantiation beyond the personal statement. Such consideration, he said, would come too close to considering "race as a criterion" and would violate SP-1. Furthermore, the *San Francisco Chronicle* had reported that "Boalt invites applicants to write an essay about how they might contribute to the school's diversity—racial or otherwise." But the faculty member stated in the Admissions Committee meeting that the description in the article was incorrect and that applicant essays discussing "racial diversity" or "racial adversity" could not be considered favorably by the Admissions Committee.[104]

In addition, some faculty members of the Admissions Committee were giving greater weight to more traditional undergraduate majors that tended to favor white applicants and disfavor minority applicants. In one instance, a faculty member described an applicant who had majored in classics as the ideal applicant to Boalt. In contrast, he described an applicant who had majored in African American studies as a less ideal applicant, asserting that such a major was less rigorous and would not have prepared the student as well for the successful completion of law school.[105] This attitude and the likely results of a race-blind admissions process at the University of California, and at Boalt in particular, prompted the Mexican American Legal Defense and Educational Fund (MALDEF)—with the help of their new attorney, Joe Jaramillo, who had graduated from Boalt two years earlier—and other civil rights organizations to file a complaint with the Office for Civil Rights at the U.S. Department of Education. The complaint alleged that the admissions criteria used by the University of California, following its implementation of resolution SP-1, had resulted in the discriminatory treatment of minority applicants to graduate programs. The complaint stated, "As implemented, resolution SP-1 has operated to eliminate consideration of admission factors that have acted to ameliorate the discriminatory impact of graduate admissions against minorities [and women]. UC's concomitant failure to mitigate in any fashion the effect of the remaining criteria that have an adverse disparate impact on minority and women applicants has resulted in a pronounced discriminatory impact on such applicants."[106]

In the complaint, MALDEF asked the Office for Civil Rights to "undertake an immediate investigation and take appropriate action to enjoin, prevent, and sanction the [university]" from further discriminating against minority and women applicants. The complaint singled out Boalt in its accusation of discriminatory admissions practices, highlighting the fact that officials at Boalt had projected the decline in enrollment of underrepresented minorities from a consistent enrollment of approximately 25 percent (60–70 students) over the past several years to an estimated 4 percent (8–12 students) as a result of SP-1. These projections, MALDEF charged, "[demonstrate] how UC graduate program admission criteria, in the absence of any ameliorative criteria have operated and will continue to operate cumulatively to exclude qualified minority and female applicants to graduate programs."[107]

The complaint pointed to three factors contributing to the cumulative discriminatory effect. The first of these was the improper weighting of standardized test scores. Recognizing the potential for cultural bias and the limited predictive validity of these tests, MALDEF noted that the producers of these tests themselves cautioned against relying too heavily on the scores:

[T]he Educational Testing Service, which designs many of the tests utilized in evaluating applicants to UC graduate programs, cautions that, with respect to minority students, "[s]pecial care is required in interpreting the scores of students who may have an educational and cultural experience somewhat different from that of the traditional majority."

Yet, UC admission officials may no longer take special care in interpreting these scores because resolution SP-1 deprives them of their ability to consider an applicant's racial [or] ethnic... background. The practice of according increasing weight on standardized test scores without considering any criteria which would ameliorate the discriminatory effect of such scores results in a disparate impact on qualified minority and female applicants.[108]

The second factor contributing to a discriminatory effect was the adjustment of undergraduate grade point averages. At schools such as Boalt, an applicant's UGPA was adjusted based on the LSAT percentile for all test-takers from the applicant's university with the applicant's UGPA and on the grading patterns at the university. The effect of this practice was to adjust downward UGPAs from universities with high minority enrollment. Because minority students tended to score lower on the LSAT, the LSAT percentile for test-takers from a university with high minority enrollment tended to be lower, and consequently, the earned UGPAs of students from that university were adjusted downward. Thus, an earned UGPA of 3.4 was adjusted upward to a 3.6 for students attending Harvard and adjusted downward to a 3.2 for students attending Howard.[109]

The third factor contributing to a discriminatory effect was the consideration of "whole person" characteristics that carved out of consideration any experiences that might have arisen from an applicant's race or ethnicity. "Such a system," stated the complaint, "excludes many of the most challenging or enriching life experiences of... minority applicants, and, at the same time, continues to grant full weight to the life experiences of other applicants." This disparate impact, the complaint continued, is exacerbated by the fact that many of the remaining "whole person" criteria—for example, parental alumni status, professional background, and institutional interest—significantly favor white applicants.[110]

Finding enough evidence to warrant an examination of admissions practices at the University of California, and at the law schools in particular, the Office for Civil Rights (OCR) decided to open an investigation into the admissions practices at the Boalt, UC Davis, and UCLA law schools. If the OCR found the admissions practices at Boalt or any other law school in violation of federal antidiscrimination laws, then the federal government could withhold $1 billion in federal funds from the University of California. Such a move, however, would take enormous political will, which Democratic leaders from the president on down had not exhibited on the issue of affirmative action. Nevertheless, the investigation would be valuable in learning more about the admissions practices at Boalt and other graduate schools. In addition, the investigation focused media attention on Boalt and brought greater scrutiny to bear on admissions practices that were charged to be not only unjust as a matter of public policy, but also illegal as a matter of law.[111]

In early April, a three-judge panel of the U.S. Court of Appeals for the Ninth Circuit overturned Judge Henderson's preliminary injunction in the 209 case. Prior to the appellate court ruling, Governor Wilson, Republican lawmakers, and conservative talk-show hosts had vilified Judge Henderson—the only African American ever to hold his post—and condemned his opinion, an opinion which Henderson defended as a "sound bit of legal reasoning" firmly anchored in case law. For months after his decision, Henderson had come out of his chambers to find FBI agents wearing white gloves, carefully handling plastic bags with envelopes inside that contained death threats. In addition, conservatives in Washington had called for his impeachment, and demonstrators had marched outside the federal courthouse in San Francisco where Henderson worked.[112] The three appellate court judges who reviewed Henderson's decision were all Republican appointees and were considered among the most conservative judges on the Ninth Circuit. In overturning Henderson's opinion, the judges wrote, "A system which permits one judge to block with the stroke of a pen what 4,736,180 state residents voted to enact as law tests the integrity of our constitutional democracy."[113] The opponents of 209 appealed to the entire Ninth Circuit and waited to hear whether it would review the case *en banc*.

In May, one month after the appellate court ruling, nine students at Boalt held a press conference, releasing a report that they had prepared entitled "New Directions in Diversity." Expecting the worst from the admissions process and frustrated that Boalt had done little to mitigate the impact of race-blind admissions, the students had spent the semester researching alternatives to the present admissions system. Their suggestions were aimed at getting the administration to respond to the impending admissions crisis and to keep the worst from happening. In their report, students wrote, "Boalt must pay critical attention to the assumptions that underlie its allocation of places at the law school." The report detailed the steps involved in the admissions decisions, and demonstrated how minor, sometimes arbitrary differences in LSAT scores and undergraduate grade point averages could lead to big differences in the likelihood of admission. The authors concluded that the excessive reliance on numerical indicators was "misguided." They stated,

[G]iven the imprecise nature of these indicators, their inability to capture an applicant's full range of qualifications and aptitude, and their potential class, race, and gender bias, we find Boalt's reliance on them to be improper and unjustifiable. By looking primarily to these numerical factors to make its admissions decisions, Boalt does little more than reinforce embedded preferences and existing disparities in the access to resources and information.[114]

The authors made four recommendations to mitigate the inequities in Boalt's current admissions policies. First, they called for greater consideration of non-numerical indices that describe an applicant's ability to succeed in law school. Second, they recommended incorporating alumni interviews to identify attributes such as speaking skills and other interpersonal skills that an exam score or an essay cannot capture. Third, they called for greater outreach to underrepresented communities, where students face particular disadvantages in getting to law school. Finally, they recommended considering race in the admissions decision, not as a criterion in itself, but rather as a measure of experiential diversity, acknowledging the experiences of applicants that may relate to their race.

The report was well received by civil rights leaders, campus professors, and some state and federal legislators, who also urged Boalt to do more. Supporting a reevaluation of the traditional criteria used to determine admissions, U.S. Congressman Ronald Dellums commented, "Those of us who reject the assault on affirmative action do so because we believe such programs remain required to root out the continued inequality that is perpetuated by privilege and discrimination. While more subtle perhaps than in previous eras, such forces continue to skew and thereby discredit, the very criteria upon which some opponents of affirmative action would solely base admissions decisions."[115]

Several days later, Dean Kay announced the outcome of the law school's "race-blind" admissions process. The results were stunning. From the previous year, the number of African Americans admitted to Boalt had dropped 81 percent (from 75 to 14), the number of Native Americans 78 percent (from 9 to 2), and the number of Latinos 50 percent (from 78 to 39).[116] In total, the number of underrepresented minorities admitted to the law school had dropped 66 percent (from 162 to 55), unraveling much of the progress made over the previous thirty years in increasing racial diversity in the student body at Boalt.[117] The other law schools at the University of California had not fared well either. At UCLA, the number of African Americans admitted to the law school had dropped 80 percent, the number of Native Americans 60 percent, and the number of Latinos 32 percent. At Davis, the number of African Americans had dropped 26 percent and the number of Latinos 28 percent. Unexpectedly, the number of Asian Americans (who generally are not considered "underrepresented") had also declined at Davis, dropping 21 percent. Though the number of underrepresented minorities had fallen at all of the law schools, they had fallen most drastically at Boalt. These were just the admission numbers; the numbers of those who enrolled were likely to be less.[118]

Dean Kay stated to the press that while the school had expected underrepresented minority admissions to plummet following the ban on affirmative action, officials were still stunned by the severity of the drop. "It is quite shocking," Kay said.[119] She added, "This dramatic decline is precisely what we feared would result from the elimination of affirmative action at Boalt. When I testified before the Board of Regents in May of 1995, I opposed the proposed resolution banning affirmative action in admissions and explained that such a resolution would make an enormous difference in the composition of our student body." Kay stated, "The students and faculty at Boalt have obtained great educational benefit from the racial diversity of our student body. Moreover, our minority graduates have made significant contributions to the legal profession." The dean concluded, "I deeply regret that Boalt's offers of admission to minority applicants have dropped so sharply. We must do everything we can to encourage those students of color who are admitted to Boalt Hall to accept our offers of admission."

While the dean and other administrators lamented the decline in the numbers of underrepresented minorities admitted to law school, Ward Connerly welcomed the drop as the public unmasking of an "artificially engineered system of preferences that has been propping up the university." He stated, "For so long, we've operated out of a sense of political correctness. Let's raise the standards and hold [minorities] to the standards. Let the chips fall where they may." Connerly called for "tough love" for minority students. He remarked, "We can't keep blaming institutional racism. They're going to have to study. They're going to have to give up basketball after school. They're going to have to stop ridiculing other blacks who want to put an emphasis on education, and stop calling them nerds."[120] Jennifer Nelson, the executive director of the American Civil Rights Institute—the organization started by Ward Connerly—added, "These minority kids are going to have to say 'I have to earn my place. I have to go home and hit the books.'"[121]

Leslie Brown was one of the African American students who had applied to Boalt but was denied admission. Contrary to Ward Connerly's perception of who was being kept out of the University of California, Leslie had not played basketball, she had never ridiculed blacks for studying too hard, and she had never called them nerds. In fact, she had always done well in school and graduated from Brown University with a computer science degree. She had earned a B average and scored in the 93rd percentile on the LSAT. In addition, she had worked as a software consultant for almost ten years before applying to law school. She was accepted to three other California law schools—Hastings, Davis, and Santa Clara—but chose to go to Colorado, where she won a full scholarship. In the coming year, she would do well in law school and would apply to Boalt again as a transfer student, to be closer to her ailing father.[122] She would be admitted to the school that had once denied her, and would excel at Boalt, dispelling the myth promulgated by Ward Connerly that black students "are not as competitive to be lawyers."[123]

In June, Dean Kay announced that not one of the fourteen black students admitted to Boalt had decided to enroll. This turn of events prompted the dean to call the numbers "a total wipeout." Richard Russell, one of three blacks on the twenty-six-member Board of Regents, put it another way: "It's obvious that the re-segregation of higher education has begun." Kay commented that if she were a black student weighing whether to attend Boalt, "I would certainly be very concerned about my ability to flourish here." "We've already had some Caucasian students withdraw from our waiting list because they prefer to go to a school with a more diverse student body," said Kay, who added that she feared the education of the students who enrolled in the fall would suffer. "Their training will be deficient in that they will no longer have the ability to engage in debate and dialogues with members of disadvantaged groups who were here formerly," she said.[124]

In the newspaper, prominent black attorneys voiced their concern. Ray Marshall, one of the few black partners in San Francisco's major law firms, who would soon become president (1998–99) of the California Bar Association, viewed the drastic decline in minority admissions as a major setback to integrating the nation's overwhelmingly white legal profession. "I've been there, done that, I know what the history's been," said Marshall. To Marshall and others, the need for diversity went beyond employment goals to the practice of law itself. "The law, in large part, is how different people see the same set of facts," remarked Krystal Denley, an associate at McCutcheon Doyle, the law firm at which Marshall was a partner. "It hurts the profession as it hurts society if many viewpoints are not expressed."[125] Judge Thelton Henderson, one of two African Americans in the Boalt class of 1962, expressed his belief that the drop in minority enrollment would hurt not only the classroom but also the courts: "Justice requires representation and views that reflect all of society. You don't get that with one kind of lawyer or with one kind of judge with one background.... We will all be shortchanged."[126]

Robert Harris, a vice president of PG&E, who was educated in a segregated, two-room school and picked cotton in Arkadelphia, Arkansas, as a child, shared these same sentiments. Harris (class of 1972) had enrolled at Boalt twenty-eight years earlier with nine other black students. He commented, "More than a quarter of a century later, to have only one person of African-American descent in the class clearly shows something is fundamentally wrong." The African American to whom he referred had deferred enrollment from the previous year. Harris urged Dean Kay, who had once taught him family law, to do more. "I would like to believe that my former professors at Boalt are astute enough to devise some means to ensure diversity is a reality at that school," he said. "That's what they teach us at law school." Dean Kay replied that she was "happy to work with anyone who has good ideas for us." But she also said that, without lifting the ban on the use of race, "it's not clear to me what that would produce. The problem is our inability to make offers of admission to students under an affirmative action program."[127]

In early July, National Public Radio aired a segment on *All Things Considered* about the decline in minority enrollment at Boalt Hall.[128] Dean Kay stated that Boalt had done everything it could to attract the minority students who had been offered admission. But a Latino student, Michael Miramontes, who had been admitted to Boalt and had chosen to go to Harvard, held a different view. Miramontes said he declined Boalt because it expressed so little interest after accepting him. "Three different folks from Harvard called me.... I got calls from the admissions folks at Georgetown and Cornell. And at Columbia... I've talked to probably two or three of their folks. And I didn't get any of that, except for the one call from Andrea [Guerrero] who called me and... tried to persuade me to look at Boalt seriously." Having been newly elected as co-chair of La Raza Law Students Association at the end of my first year, I worked with members of La Raza and other student-of-color organizations to encourage minority students to come to Boalt. We did this despite feeling undermined by the administration, which refrained from giving us the names of newly admitted minority students until the last days of the semester, when we were entering final exams. In the NPR segment, Dean Kay explained that administrators felt constrained by the affirmative action ban not to reach out to minority students, fearing such actions might be viewed as a violation of the ban. They had been so cautious, the reporter remarked, that they delayed releasing the names of the incoming class until many newly admitted students had already made commitments elsewhere.

At the close of the summer, the dean reported that Boalt would enroll one black student, who had been admitted the previous year but had deferred enrollment for one year. In the *Washington Post*, Henry Ramsey Jr., a retired judge and former dean of Howard Law School who had been one of the first African Americans to graduate from Boalt (class of 1963) and the second ever to become a professor at the law school, wrote an opinion in which he posed the question, "Are we returning to the early 1960s?"[129] Ramsey had entered Boalt Hall in 1960, as the only black student in his class. He criticized the regents for adopting a "mean-spirited and fatally flawed policy... that has caused the dramatic and drastic reduction in legal educational opportunities for California's minority students." Rejecting the use of test scores and grade point averages as surrogates for merit, he stated, "[W]e should not accept admissions policies that, however unintended, deny black Americans and other people of color the educational opportunities that are absolutely essential for positions of leadership in American society."

As the first day of classes drew near and the realization sank in that Boalt would enroll only one African American, Ward Connerly accused the dean of intentionally trying to keep admitted minorities from enrolling in order to pressure the regents to overturn their ban on affirmative action. "I don't have any proof of it, but I believe [it] deep in my soul," he said. "Kay should have been more assertive in trying to persuade the 14 to come."[130]

"It's odd that Ward Connerly has accused her of sabotaging the process," said Marvin Peguese (class of 1998), one of the students who wrote the "New Directions in Diversity" report. "We feel the Dean's been overly cautious in enforcing SP-1. Her heart is in the right place. But the political and legal fallout has made her timid." "It hasn't been easy," Dean Kay conceded. "To have to preside over the dismantling of policies that have a great deal of benefit is personally quite painful."[131]

CHAPTER 4

Reaching for Answers

The arrival of the entering class at Boalt Hall in August 1997 promised to attract national media attention. For the first time in thirty years, the law school had admitted students without reference to their race, resulting in the admission of only 55 underrepresented minority students, down from 162 the previous year. Of these 55 students, only 7—all Latinos—had chosen to enroll. Not since 1968, the first year of affirmative action, had only 7 newly admitted underrepresented minority students matriculated to Boalt.[1] The media ensured that the significance of this parallel would be noticed. Boalt was not the only school to show disastrous results—for example, two of the five medical schools at the University of California had failed to enroll any African Americans at all—but the law school was a national lightning rod. Boalt was one of the premier public law schools in the country and was the most extreme example of the results of "race-blind" admissions.[2] The major newspapers and television networks that had covered the decision of the regents to eliminate affirmative action were sure to be at Boalt on the first day of school to report on its consequences.

Taking advantage of the media attention, Boalt students concerned with the demise of diversity organized an alumni speak-out for the first day of school. They invited Eva Paterson, the executive director of the San Francisco Lawyers' Committee for Civil Rights and an African American graduate from the class of 1975, to lead the event. Paterson had been critical of the regents for adopting SP-1, and of Boalt for exacerbating its effects. Over the summer, when she heard that Boalt had admitted very few underrepresented minority students and that only a small percentage of those students had decided to enroll, she called a public meeting of area attorneys and students to press for action. In early July, more than a hundred law firm partners and associates had crowded into a meeting room with some fifty students at the Bar Association of San Francisco to discuss the dramatic decline in the number of underrepresented minorities.

The attendance of attorneys from almost every major law firm in San Francisco was an impressive show of interest by the legal community, which had a particular concern for diversity. In 1989, the Bar Association of San Francisco established hiring guidelines for member firms in an attempt to increase minority representation.[3] A study conducted three years prior had indicated that law firms consciously or unconsciously discriminated against minority students in the interview process.[4] In the study, top minority students found it harder to get call-back interviews than similarly qualified white students, and among average students, whites had more than double the success rate of minorities in the interview process. As a result, minority representation at law schools was not reflected in law firms. The Bar Association set goals for member firms to use their best efforts to fill 15 percent of all associate or equivalent positions with minority lawyers by 1995, and to increase that number to 25 percent by the year 2000. Member firms were also encouraged to make 5 percent of all partners minorities by 1995 and 10 percent minorities by 2000. But in 1997, many law firms were behind schedule, and with the drop in minority enrollment at Boalt—the leading feeder school for the area—they were concerned that they would not be able to reach the goals set by the Bar Association.

At the meeting in July, participants gave moving testimony of how race-inclusive attitudes and policies had changed their lives. Many in the room, including Paterson, had lived through the transition from segregation to integration. Paterson recalled the humiliation of being turned away from a hotel that had a "vacant" sign in the window; the fear of moving into an all-white neighborhood with a policeman stationed outside her house for protection; and the frustration of being passed over for an award in high school from the Daughters of the American Revolution because she was black. However, as a result of an admissions policy receptive to minority students at Northwestern University, Paterson attended college with a broad array of black students. She had not needed affirmative action to gain admission, but she benefited from the black student community and the black studies courses that race-inclusive policies generated. She excelled at Northwestern and became student body president. After graduating, she applied to Boalt. She scored in the eighty-eighth percentile on the LSAT, but that was not good enough in a highly competitive admissions environment. Like many minority students, however, Paterson was admitted to the law school under affirmative action. She knew personally the difference between a life with and without race-inclusive policies and attitudes, and conveyed to the meeting participants her deep disappointment in the changes taking place at her alma mater.[5]

Other attorneys at the meeting echoed her disappointment and offered their own lived experiences as examples of why race-inclusive policies were important in the march toward racial progress. One African American attorney described what it was like to grow up black in a segregated southern town, to overcome negative racial attitudes and stereotypes, to attend college and then law school despite every obstacle imaginable, and to succeed as a black lawyer in a profession that was overwhelmingly white. It was possible—he had become a partner at one of the city's largest law firms—but it was difficult, and without affirmative action he felt that many blacks would be unable to surmount the entrenched discrimination and embedded preferences that worked against them every step of the way. The attorney's testimony was punctuated by a white attorney who, by coincidence, had grown up in the same segregated southern town and had also found his way to San Francisco where he too had become a partner in a prominent law firm. The white attorney acknowledged the privileges he enjoyed vis-à-vis his black colleague, and condemned the race-exclusive policies of the past and the race-insensitive policies of the present.

At the conclusion of the meeting, the participants set upon a course of action to bring visibility to the loss of diversity at Boalt, in hopes of pressuring the regents and the law schools at the University of California to do what was necessary to prevent the resegregation of legal education. For the national convention of the American Bar Association held in San Francisco that summer, they prepared a statement, which was distributed by law students, declaring that the "dramatic decline in diversity that SP-1 has wrought on California's public law schools affects all members of the legal community and threatens the integrity of a profession committed by the ABA to 'promote full and equal participation... [of] minorities and women.'" The statement further asserted that "diversity is essential... [if we are] to educate... attorneys who will serve the diverse communities of the 21st century."[6] Following the convention, Eva Paterson and a small and diverse group of prominent Boalt alumni met with Dean Kay to press her to do more. They advocated the adoption of student recommendations outlined in the "New Directions in Diversity" report and urged the dean to incorporate alumni interviews as a way of identifying the qualities of an applicant that are not described by traditional numerical criteria but are nevertheless essential to the practice of law. Dean Kay hesitated to support alumni suggestions and told her visitors that her "hands were tied." In a time of crisis, her inaction infuriated the alumni and set the stage for the alumni speak-out.[7]

On the morning of August 18, 1997—the first day of school—Eva Paterson arrived early at Boalt to prepare for the speak-out organized by students. She found a sea of reporters and television crews awaiting a glimpse of the few minority students who had enrolled at Boalt. Eric Brooks—the sole African American entering Boalt Hall that year—was the one the media most wanted to see. Brooks had awoken with a knot in his stomach as he listened to the radio announcer describe the swarm of reporters awaiting his arrival. Boalt had not enrolled so few African Americans since the 1960s, prior to the implementation of affirmative action. Now, with affirmative action gone, Brooks had the dubious distinction of being "the only one."

Brooks was from Bloomington, Indiana, and had always been one of only a few African Americans in school even at Indiana University, where he had attended college. The soft-spoken Brooks was not a political activist, nor was he outspoken about issues of race, but he was well aware of the ways that people of different races were perceived and treated in this country. Over the course of his life he had seen how minorities were depicted in the media and disparaged in conversation, and he knew that white was the best color to be in America. He assumed things were different in the Bay Area, however, and thought of Berkeley as a place where diversity thrived. When applying to law school, Brooks had sought a more diverse environment and had submitted an application to Boalt.[8]

He was admitted in 1996, but deferred enrollment for one year so he could accompany his wife to Boston for a job. Brooks looked forward to coming to Boalt and being a part of a racially diverse community. But as fate would have it, his entering class would mark the radical decline in the number of underrepresented minority students at the law school. In 1997, only 14 African American students were admitted, and none had chosen to come, some stating that they felt "unwelcome." Boalt admitted 2 Native Americans, but neither had decided to enroll. Of the 38 Latinos admitted to the law school, only 7 had chosen to attend. An additional 7 Latinos had deferred enrollment from the previous year and would be attending the law school with Brooks. In total, Boalt would enroll 15 underrepresented minority students out of a class of approximately 270.

As ready as he would ever be for this first day, Brooks put on his sweater, kissed his wife good-bye, and headed for school. Though he had met with the dean and other Boalt administrators over the summer, and they had assured him he was welcome, he still felt uneasy arriving at Boalt. He entered the law school through a back door, temporarily avoiding the media, and joined his classmates at the first orientation event. He was surprised to see that neither the administrators nor the students discussed the press outside or the lack of diversity inside. When the orientation event ended, Assistant Dean Lujuana Treadwell directed Brooks to a room full of reporters, where he had previously arranged to give a prepared statement, in hopes of appeasing the media and finding peace. With every eye in the room on him, twenty-seven-year-old Eric Brooks stepped up to the microphone and stated,

I was greatly surprised and disappointed when I learned that I was the only African American matriculating into the program this year. When choosing a law school, I placed a high value on the diversity of the student body, and contemplated going to school elsewhere after hearing the news. However, I quickly reminded myself that Berkeley's reputation and ranking, specialized programs, legal aid clinics, affordability and local community still best met my needs. I am confident that my classmates and instructors will treat me without bias and as an individual who has earned the right to attend this prestigious University.[9]

After the statement, Assistant Dean Treadwell led Brooks out of the room to the second-floor courtyard to join other first-year students for lunch. Brooks sat alone. At a table nearby, Norma Aguilar, one of the fourteen Latino students in the first-year class, sat awkwardly with a small group of students who had been discussing anything but the issue of diversity. Though she felt strongly about the matter, she was not sure how others at the table felt.[10]

Aguilar had grown up in a Mexican community outside of Los Angeles. She was the child of immigrants who had not been fortunate enough to receive an education. Neither parent had finished elementary school, but they had worked hard to ensure that their daughter had the opportunity to pursue higher education. Aguilar was grateful to them not only for enabling her to attend school and inspiring her to succeed, but also for instilling pride in who she was. In the application to law school, Boalt had asked applicants to write a personal essay. Aguilar understood that she was not supposed to talk about race but did not understand how to convey who she was without discussing her cultural background. So she wrote in her essay, "I am Mexican." Even if the Admissions Committee did not want to hear it, she felt compelled to tell them. She explained how far she had come in life and how much of her success had been due to her family and her community, which were undeniably Mexican.[11]

To Aguilar, a "race-blind" admissions policy seemed ridiculous. If someone could not understand where she had come from, how could they understand her at all. Despite her candid essay, Aguilar had been admitted to Boalt, but she was uneasy about coming to a place where there were so few students of color. On that first day, she recalled, "When I walked into the law school, I felt everybody around me was white—I didn't see another person of color. Right away, I felt so alone." The lack of diversity was striking, she remembered, "and it was strange that no one was talking about it."[12]

No one except the alumni down below, that is. While first-year students ate lunch in the courtyard above, two hundred protesters and a horde of media gathered in the lower courtyard for the alumni speak-out. Standing before a group of students carrying signs that read "Little Rock Had Nine," Eva Paterson began the event, lamenting, "This is a sad and disgraceful day for the University of California, for the State of California, and for America."[13] For thirty years, Boalt had been one of the most diverse law schools in the country, and now it was quickly becoming one of the least. In one year, the percentage of underrepresented minorities in the entering class had dropped from 21 to 5 percent. Including Asian Americans, the total percentage of minorities had dropped from 35 to 19 percent.

Over the course of an hour, Boalt-trained lawyers rose one by one to condemn the University of California for rolling back affirmative action. Some alumni said they would withhold donations from the university. "We need to send the message loud and clear that our dollars will not go to a university that does not value diversity among its students," declared Renee Saucedo, a 1990 graduate who was now the executive director of the Northern California Coalition for Immigrant Rights. "I feel ashamed of this institution," she stated. Other alumni said they would hire fewer Boalt graduates to join their firms. "We must have a diverse body of lawyers serving our diverse clients," said Leonard Weiss, a 1962 graduate who was a partner in the San Francisco law firm of Steefel Levitt & Weiss. He continued, "If we can't get it from Boalt Hall, we'll go elsewhere."[14]

Alumni stressed that all Boalt students would suffer from the lack of underrepresented minorities. Professor Marjorie Shultz, a 1976 graduate, stated that, while Boalt's new students were very accomplished, "How can [they] be excellent collectively if [they] have experiences that are nar-

rower than the experiences of this population?"[15] In a statement issued
to the press, alumni speakers and student organizers attacked not only
the regents' ban but also the admissions policy at Boalt that had resulted
in a stark decrease in minority students. To prevent that outcome from
happening again, they urged Boalt to "rethink admissions criteria and
qualifications in terms of the skills needed to successfully practice law."
They asserted, "Boalt Hall can do more to halt the re-segregation of the
law school."[16]

Eric Brooks watched the speak-out from afar. "I wanted to be a part of
it, but I knew that if I approached the rally I would be hounded by the
press."[17] Norma Aguilar, free of the watchful eye of the press, attended the
event with Manjari Chawla, a South Asian student who sat with Aguilar
at the lunch table and invited her to go down to the courtyard to listen to
the alumni. Aguilar was relieved to find someone in her class who cared
about what was going on and was interested in talking about it.

Chawla was born an "untouchable" in India and was an avid supporter
of affirmative action. In India, "untouchables" were the lowest group in
the caste system, and historically were not allowed to go to school. Consequently, no one in her family had ever received an education until the
government implemented affirmative action programs, and her father
had the opportunity to attend not only elementary and secondary school,
but also college and medical school, a feat previously not even dreamed
of for an "untouchable." When Chawla was young, her family had immigrated to the United States, where they prospered, free of the caste
system. But they never forgot how they had benefited from affirmative
action, and they supported programs in America that helped others as
they had once been helped.[18]

In the United States, Chawla felt most comfortable in a mixed racial
setting, where differences were more likely to be a subject of curiosity
than a matter of disdain. She worried about the homogenous environment being created at Boalt and already felt uncomfortable. The rally en-
ergized her, but she fell into a state of depression when she returned to
orientation and to discussions devoid of diversity. "I guess it sank in what
it really means to have so few people of color. I realized that this is what
it's going to be like every single day."

Alistair Newbern and Mike Murphy, two white first-year students,
who like Aguilar and Chawla were concerned about the lack of diversity
in the entering class, also attended the rally. Newbern and Murphy had
both applied to Boalt because they were seeking a racially diverse learning environment. When they learned that the law school would be a far

less diverse place than it had been in the past, they both considered not coming. But thinking that they could be agents of change, they each decided to come. Standing in the courtyard reading the sign that said "Little Rock Had Nine," Newbern thought about the great irony of her situation. She was from Arkansas and had attended Little Rock Central High School, which had been forcibly integrated in 1957 by nine black children with the help of the National Guard. Her high school teachers never let her or the other students forget the struggle that had taken place to integrate Central High. Confronted with the fact that there was only one black student in her class, Newbern felt as if she were stepping back in time. She knew how important it was to speak up for inclusion, and she committed herself to do what she could to better the situation. She expected everyone in her class to feel the same, to be outraged, but looking around the lower courtyard, she saw very few first-year students who had come to support the rally.[19]

Standing at Newbern's side, Mike Murphy was sickened by the situation. As an undergraduate, he had attended Oberlin where, through his interaction with minority students, he had become aware of the subtle and not-so-subtle forms of prejudice. He also had become aware of the extent to which white students can choose to engage in efforts to overcome prejudice and discrimination. He recalled a meeting that students of color organized, inviting the whole student body to discuss police mistreatment of minority students. Though many white students condemned the mistreatment, the only one who attended the meeting was Murphy. He found that, more often than not, white students chose not to engage in the difficult issues of race, and their acquiescence perpetuated conscious and unconscious racism. In coming to Boalt, Murphy promised himself that he would not be one of those students who acquiesced.

Earlier that morning, in the first orientation activity of the day, Murphy had sat in an auditorium of mostly white faces and listened to the admissions director expound on the virtues of the entering class. His stomach had turned when the admissions director told the class how smart they were, how high their LSAT scores were, and how proud they should be of themselves. The admissions director overlooked the glaring shortcoming of the class—its almost complete lack of underrepresented minority students—and Murphy decided then to take a stand for diversity, beginning with attending the speak-out.[20]

For some of the students in the entering class who occasionally glanced down at the rally, the lack of diversity was not a cause for concern. A few students told the press that they supported the regents' ban on affir-

mative action, and they did not appear to be troubled by its consequences. Several more expressed mixed feelings. "It creates a conflict for
me," a white student requesting anonymity told the *San Francisco Chronicle.* "I support affirmative action. But the fact is that maybe the change
has opened up a spot for me here."[21]

As the alumni speak-out ended, Eric Brooks walked to his afternoon
orientation activity. On his way, he ran into Eva Paterson. Brooks recalled, "She gave me a big hug and gave me her telephone number and
told me to call her if I ever needed to talk." Paterson was the only other
African American that he saw the entire day. Brooks made his way to his
small-section class meeting, where, in a round of introductions, he introduced himself as "the reason your first day is not as normal as it would
otherwise be." After the meeting, Mike Murphy, who was in the same
section as Brooks, approached Brooks and commended him for his ma-
turity and poise in a difficult situation. He told Brooks he had misgiv-
ings about coming to Boalt but hoped that students could turn the situation around. Murphy was one of the few people who spoke to Brooks
that day and his words were comforting. That night, Brooks watched
himself on the local and national news. "It was unnerving," he said. Reflecting on the day, he remarked, "It was not what I wanted my first day
of law school to be like."[22]

Chancellor Robert Berdahl, who had replaced Chancellor Tien the year
before when Tien had retired, stated to the press that the Berkeley campus
was "on the front lines as a new chapter unfolds." He described the initial
consequences of the regents' ban, namely, the composition of the entering class at Boalt, as "deeply disturbing." The chancellor remarked, "I do
not believe this is in the best interests of our students, whose education is
enhanced in a diverse environment; the employers of California, who desire a diverse workforce; and the citizens of California, who live in the
most diverse state in the union." He called the decline in the number of underrepresented minority students "simply unacceptable."[23]

On that first day of school, Dean Herma Hill Kay reiterated her concerns to the press. Without diversity, she said, "it is more difficult to have
a classroom discussion. It's like the old days, when we didn't have any
women. When we talked about alimony, it was only from the men's point
of view."[24] A "Questions and Answers" pamphlet distributed by Boalt aptly
summarized the significance of enrolling a racially diverse student body:

The legal education of all students is enriched in the presence of a critical mass of
students with diverse experiences and backgrounds, including students from a
wide range of racial and ethnic backgrounds. A racially and ethnically diverse stu-

dent body ensures a robust exchange of ideas with the faculty and throughout the school—inside and outside the classroom, in Boalt Hall student organizations and through the school's nine student-edited law journals. Students training to become lawyers benefit from early exposure to the needs and backgrounds of people from many walks of life, especially people who are traditionally underrepresented or disadvantaged in society. In the absence of such a student body, legal education is diminished in this important dimension.[25]

On the second day of orientation, Eric Brooks arrived at Boalt through the front doors. That day there would be no press conference. Though the throng of media had left Boalt, several reporters and camera crews remained, as they would off and on throughout the year. Brooks thought it strange that in the orientation activities thus far the administration had not mentioned the lack of diversity. The matter of diversity was discussed entirely outside of orientation events. Not until the end of the second day of orientation did any speaker address the question of diversity, and even then the issue was not raised by an administrator, but by an alumnus. By that time, Brooks thought, "It was too late. It looked like the school thought diversity was a non-issue." He said, "If I had not met with the dean and other administrators previously, I would have thought that the school was perfectly happy with the way things were. That must have been how other minority students felt."[26] That was, in fact, exactly how Norma Aguilar felt. "I had applied to Boalt because it was a school that claimed to value diversity. The number of underrepresented minority students certainly did not reflect that, nor did the school's complete silence on the matter."[27] The administration treated diversity, or the lack thereof, as the elephant in the room.

After two days of orientation, first-year classes began. For professors who were used to teaching a racially diverse group of students, the first day was a startling reminder of the consequences of "race-blind" admissions. Reflecting on the first day of her contracts course, Professor Marjorie Shultz wrote,

It's the first day of class...and despite having enjoyed teaching for many years, I realize that today I am uncomfortable....

The faces in front of me...reveal the bright, eager intelligence that I've been fortunate enough to become accustomed to as a professor teaching at this distinguished public law school. But as I survey my nearly 100 students, my unconscious color-comfort meter is blinking.... [S]adness registers as I realize that I'm not seeing the range of students I'm used to teaching in this very diverse state of California....

The racial composition of my class affects more than my comfort. Less diversity will deprive our group of crucial perspectives on the material we will be studying....A few White students, but many students of color, personally, or through chosen group empathy, identity, and concern, articulate the perspectives of poverty, know about the pathologies of the criminal justice system, and distrust the "fairness" and "objectivity" of authority. Many minority students and some Whites as well see intense contradictions in the American Dream and its land-of-the-brave-and-the-free ideology. They hold greater-than-average skepticism about success being merit-based, earned through effort. Market economics is not so frequently their answer of choice....

Whites dominate most conversation in most places, including Boalt. But at Boalt, the (previously) large number of students of color gave me unique and priceless opportunities to better understand my profession, my fields of expertise, and my pedagogical tasks. Once plentiful, that opportunity is now diminished.[28]

First-year students spent the first week adjusting to their new regime, but some could not shake the feeling of being unwelcome. In her first attempt to participate in a criminal law class discussion, Manjari Chawla was interrupted by her professor when she brought up an example of how the race of a minority defendant came into play in the case being discussed.[29] The professor stated he was "uncomfortable with that sort of example," and provided his own example to elucidate the case, ignoring the implications of race. Feeling silenced, Chawla was hesitant to speak in class again. In another class, minority students were taken aback by conservative classmates who made snide comments about student-of-color organizations.[30] Several of these students, who were white, attempted to start a white male fraternity, asserting the need to protect their interests at the law school. In another class, Eric Brooks, feeling very alone, sat quietly toward the back of the room.

In the second week of school, student groups met for the first time. At the first meeting of the Law Students of African Descent (LSAD), a deep sadness pervaded the room. Sonya Enchill, a second-year student and recruitment chair of the organization, looked out at the solemn faces and smiled sympathetically at Brooks. She had "lost all love" for Berkeley. Prior to that year, she had held Berkeley in high regard. It was the place where her immigrant parents—her father from Ghana and her mother from Ireland—met in the 1960s and marched together for civil rights. She attended Berkeley as an undergraduate, where she thrived in the racially diverse environment, and came to Boalt seeking a similar experience. But the university regents and the law school had let her down, dismantling diversity before her very eyes. The first organizational meeting of LSAD began as usual, with announcements, and then everyone welcomed Brooks. Enchill recalled, "Instead of all bombarding him with our attention, one person was appointed to help him out with whatever he needed. Our committee system, which usually functioned in support of the first-years, had no reason to operate. Individual tasks were just picked up by various organization members." She reflected, "It was very depressing. There was a complete and utter lack of morale."[31]

At the first meeting of the Coalition for a Diverse Faculty and Student Body (CDF/SB), anger and frustration pervaded the room. The previous spring, the Coalition for a Diverse Faculty (CDF), which had been virtually defunct, merged with Boalt Students for Affirmative Action (BSAA) to form CDF/SB. At that first meeting, close to 150 students packed into a medium-sized classroom to talk about the admissions fiasco and about what could be done to ensure that it would not happen again. Second-year and third-year student activists, who had witnessed the dismantling of affirmative action, came ready to form a plan to pressure the administration to open its doors to more minority students. First-year students, including Norma Aguilar, Manjari Chawla, Alistair Newbern, and Mike Murphy, who were new to the debate at Boalt, came to ask questions, share concerns, and meet with others who were interested in taking action. Fueled by a collective commitment to better the situation, CDF/SB hit the ground running. In that first meeting, the group became the largest student organization at Boalt. Its singular mission that semester was to increase the diversity of the class that would be admitted the following year.

The group developed a plan to push for changes in the admissions policy. They adopted the student-written "New Directions in Diversity" recommendations and began to seek support from the dean, faculty, alumni, legal employers, and the state legislature. In a newsletter distributed to many of the city's attorneys, I wrote an article advocating the reevaluation of admissions criteria at Boalt and calling on Boalt to "lessen or abolish the weight of criteria with embedded preferences, such as the LSAT, and instead use criteria that address professional skills and community needs." The article emphasized the importance of considering nonnumerical criteria:

"[T]o be a successful lawyer," according to a 1990 Law Services Report, "you need a number of attributes that often don't show up on test scores and transcripts. You need a high degree of motivation. You need the ability to communicate cogently and with conviction. You need stamina. You need the power to recognize crucial points in a mass of acts to assimilate facts quickly."

The repeal of affirmative action measures and their subsequent impact on diversity raise critical questions about the state of education in this country, and ask of us what kind of action we are willing to undertake to ensure a true equality of opportunity.[32]

A group of committed students at Boalt would respond to that question in the course of the year.

Ten days after the start of school, the Ninth Circuit Court of Appeals declined to review the three-judge panel decision made in April, bringing Proposition 209 into full effect. This was a devastating blow. The situation was about to go from bad to worse. Where SP-1 had banned only race-conscious criteria for the admissions decision itself, 209 went one step further, banning race-conscious outreach, scholarships, and academic support programs—more or less the full range of the admissions process. August 28—day one of Proposition 209—marked the thirty-fourth anniversary of the historic March on Washington, when Martin Luther King Jr. delivered his famous "I Have a Dream" speech. Fueled by the Ninth Circuit action, more than ten thousand people walked across the Golden Gate Bridge in a march previously organized by Reverend Jesse Jackson to commemorate King's speech and protest race-insensitive policies in California.[33] Over one hundred Boalt students joined the marchers, including Eric Brooks, who was uplifted by the event. "It was the first time I had seen a broad coalition of support for affirmative action since moving to California that summer."[34] At a rally following the march, Jesse Jackson asked Brooks to join him on stage and asked the crowd to pray for Brooks.

Shortly after the march, opponents of Proposition 209 appealed their case to the U.S. Supreme Court. While waiting for the Court to decide whether it would hear the case, students and alumni urged Boalt to do something to mitigate the effects of 209. Fearful of a lawsuit, the administration refrained from conducting targeted outreach and ceased to administer or even publish information about minority scholarships—actions that would later be reversed.[35] Many students and alumni felt the law school was overcomplying. Some pleaded with the faculty to challenge the anti–affirmative action measures: "You are the best legal minds in the state of California. You should challenge this law which violates the equal protection rights of minority students," stated one alumnus.[36] The faculty did not respond to the call to defend affirmative action as they had done in the 1970s by preparing briefs for the *Bakke* case. Instead, several conservative faculty members submitted an *amicus* brief on behalf of "Law Professors and Law Students for Civil Rights" in support of 209 and in support of the elimination of affirmative action in California.

John Yoo, a young Asian American professor, wrote the bulk of the *amicus* brief. Hired in 1993, Yoo was an up-and-coming star on the faculty. He had attended a predominantly white, private high school and had earned his undergraduate degree at Harvard. While at Harvard, he began to take a position on affirmative action and wrote an opinion piece arguing that marked differences in standardized test scores suggested that affirmative action put people into schools that they were not ready to attend. He felt that "Harvard should not be in the business of bringing students up to speed." Following Harvard, Yoo attended Yale Law School, where he was exposed to and adopted constitutional arguments against affirmative action. He then took a teaching position at Boalt and, after one year, clerked for the highly conservative U.S. Supreme Court justice Clarence Thomas during the time in which the Court wrote its *Adarand* decision and Thomas made clear his abhorrence of race-conscious policies.[37]

Yoo arrived back at Boalt in time to see affirmative action dismantled and to witness the consequences of a "color-blind" admissions policy. However, he did not see the resulting lack of diversity as a problem and felt that the law school was the subject of undue attention. In his view, what was most important to the law school was getting the "best" students—those students with the highest grades and test scores—admitted. He, like other conservative members of the faculty, felt that excellence and diversity were a trade-off and believed that excellence should not be compromised by policies instituted to achieve diversity. Furthermore, he did not agree that Berkeley should be representative of the population of California. In his view, less prestigious campuses and law schools could meet the needs of a diverse population. Though Yoo was considered perhaps the most conservative member of the faculty and many of his views were not shared by other professors, his voice in the void of public faculty support for affirmative action helped give rise to the perception that Boalt no longer believed in affirmative action and no longer valued diversity.

Student-of-color organizations protested the law school's apparent lack of commitment to diversity and, more specifically, the lack of targeted outreach to minority students, but to no avail. Dean Kay and the faculty were hesitant to do anything that might appear to be race-conscious or might subject the law school to attacks from the right.[38] Consequently, student-of-color organizations took it upon themselves to organize their own outreach efforts. Daniel Tellalian, then a fourth-year student in the joint law and business program and the outreach coordinator for La Raza Law Students Association, spearheaded a new group called Students Supporting Students (SSS), which was formed to reach out to potential minority law school applicants. Through SSS, student-of-color organizations planned to coordinate and expand their outreach efforts, drawing on the assistance of committed minority and white law students. Tellalian recalled, "We wanted to reach out to students from the California State University and typically neglected universities which tended to have high minority, low income, and commuter student populations. We knew Boalt would never focus on these folks, so it was incumbent on us to do it."[39]

Between plans for extensive outreach and intensive advocacy, second- and third-year student activists were overwhelmed and needed to bring first-year students up to speed. In the third week of school, student-of-color organizations, CDF/SB, and the Boalt Hall Students Association held a teach-in for first-year students. Well attended, the teach-in provided an opportunity for second-year and third-year students to share institutional memory and for first-year students to ask questions and vent their frustrations. At the end of the teach-in, several first-year students expressed their view that their class ought to make a statement about what was happening to them and to let people know that the lack of diversity was not acceptable.

A small group of students, including Norma Aguilar, Manjari Chawla, and Mike Murphy, wrote a letter for which they sought the signatures of as many first-year students as possible. The first draft was forceful and called for the return of affirmative action policies, but the students could not get many of their more conservative classmates to sign the statement. They removed an explicit position on affirmative action from the letter and were able to procure the signatures of 71 percent of the class (194 students). Directed at the administration, faculty, and regents, and distributed to the press, the letter, dated September 13, read as follows:

Due to the media attention this year's entering class has received regarding affirmative action and diversity, we have decided to speak for ourselves on these topics. We wish to make it clear that we recognize what an honor and privilege it is to attend Boalt Hall. However, many of us chose to attend Boalt *in spite of* our grave disappointment in the lack of diversity evidenced in the Class of 2000.

Although affirmative action programs needed improvement, completely abolishing them without implementing any other sufficient means of achieving diversity has compromised our legal education. The pool of background experiences and perspectives we are exposed to has diminished significantly, limiting our opportunities for intellectual growth. Because as lawyers we will certainly be called upon to work with individuals of many different backgrounds, such interaction is a necessary part of legal education. Clearly, if such a trend in admissions continues, Boalt will not be able to provide such exposure.

Boalt Hall is falling behind prestigious schools who have recognized the importance of diversity and have kept their affirmative action programs intact. In fact, we have already lost many excellent students of color to these other schools. As a public institution which relies on public funds, the University of California at Berkeley has an even greater obligation than its private counterparts to ensure the presence of a student body which reflects the state's heterogeneous population, and to provide lawyers who will serve all facets of our complex society. Even under the new limitations, other UC professional schools have fulfilled this duty with greater success than we have by enacting creative admissions criteria and outreach strategies. Boalt must do the same and more, particularly considering its competitive status....

Our greatest concern is what lies in the future.... We urge you to consider recommendations, such as those outlined in the "New Directions in Diversity" report, which would help the school to maintain a racially and ethnically representative student body while still complying with existing restrictions. Ensure that our class is an aberration, not the norm.

Eric Brooks took comfort in the number of students who signed the letter, but he was disturbed by the strong resistance exhibited by those unwilling to sign. "They seemed happy with the policy and the results; the outcome didn't seem to matter," reflected Brooks.[40] In the press, Ward Connerly rejected the letter, and responded, "If they're so interested in diversity, how many would step forward and say, 'You can have my seat in the interest of diversity.'"[41] Taking his words literally, first-year students would answer Connerly exactly one month later.

On September 19, CDF/SB released a four-page open letter to the Boalt faculty recommending detailed changes to the admissions policy to promote diversity at the law school. CDF/SB issued the recommendations out of a concern that "another year or more will pass without the faculty implementing any substantive changes to the current admissions policy." Students continued to await a report by a faculty task force charged with studying "New Directions in Diversity" and recommending its own solutions to the diversity crisis. In a meeting with the authors of "New Directions" on August 28, newly appointed Associate Dean Robert Cole—the principal author of the task force report—anticipated it would be released within two weeks. But completion of the report took longer than expected, and students became frustrated.

One month after the meeting, student activists launched a comprehensive faculty lobbying campaign around the CDF/SB proposals. The lobbying effort was aimed at educating members of the faculty about the nuts-and-bolts of various exclusionary mechanisms in the current admissions process. Students made specific recommendations, which they urged the faculty to consider and adopt immediately, before the admissions process for the coming year was begun. The recommendations put forward by CDF/SB included the following:

(1) As suggested by the administrators of the LSAT, use banded LSAT scores instead of making fine distinctions between applicants based on insignificant one or two point differentials.

(2) Given its limitation in predicting law-school performance, reduce the weight of the LSAT in the index calculation.

(3) Discontinue the adjustment of undergraduate grade point averages (UGPAs) based on the average LSAT score of all other students from the applicant's college who take the test; this unfairly favors students from wealthier, more exclusive, and predominantly white schools.

(4) Include alumni in the admissions process to better identify and select for the skills needed to succeed in the profession.

(5) Provide training to the Admissions Committee on how to read files, so that readers are aware of the assumptions and judgements they make in reading files and are sensitive to culturally different lived experiences described in essays.

(6) Solicit additional qualitative information from applicants such as socio-economic information as well as information that demonstrates communication skills, interpersonal skills, and leadership skills.[42]

With the support of alumni, members of CDF/SB met with every faculty member in teams of two students and one alumnus, urging the faculty to move quickly to consider and adopt the recommendations. Simultaneously, students contacted state legislators, asking them to set parameters on the interpretation, implementation, and enforcement of anti–affirmative action measures in order to deter overcompliance.

By October, despite a substantial and comprehensive lobbying effort, the faculty still had not yet met to consider student recommendations or any other recommendations concerning admissions. Frustration mounted. In the first week of October, Dean Kay held a town hall meeting and explained that student recommendations would be considered in the Cole Report, which she promised was forthcoming. Student body president Venus McGhee, who was also co-chair of the Native American Law Student Association, asked when the faculty was scheduled to discuss the admissions process for the coming year. She was fed up.

McGhee had been lured to the law school two years earlier by the school's relatively large Native American population. Instead of only one or two students per entering class, Boalt had four to five students. This was important to McGhee who, growing up, had felt isolated and not well understood by whites or other minorities. At Boalt, she benefited from the presence of a significant number of Native American students who supported one another and increased awareness of Native American issues in the larger community. It appeared, however, that future students—should there be any—would not be so lucky. Boalt had enrolled zero Native Americans in the fall, and McGhee expected the faculty to respond to what she viewed as a crisis.[43]

The dean answered that the faculty was not scheduled to discuss the matter. McGhee pressed her to call a special faculty meeting or at least to put the matter on the agenda for the next faculty meeting. Dean Kay refused to commit to either. She reiterated her belief that the faculty could do very little to ameliorate the situation. In exasperation, she pointed to SP-1 and Proposition 209 as the real impediments to maintaining diversity at the law school. "My hands are tied," she repeated. Many students left the meeting even more frustrated, believing that the administration and faculty *could* do something. Anger and sadness set in among student activists who had for seven straight weeks spent their energy advocating changes and reaching out to minority students. Inside the classrooms, lessons proceeded as if nothing out of the ordinary was taking place. The interview season came and went. Beyond the 150 or so students who were involved in advocating change in the admissions policy, the remaining 700 students, and much of the faculty and administration, did not appear to be either troubled by or engaged in the issue.

Feeling that the policy recommendations they had made had gone unheard and that there was no sense of urgency, student activists turned to protest. They chose a day less than one week away: October 13, known as Indigenous Peoples Day in Berkeley and Columbus Day in the rest of the country. One month after Ward Connerly asked who among the predominantly white first-year class would give up their seats to a student of color, a group of first-year students planned a response. They would, on October 13, ask that question of themselves and symbolically give up their seats to visiting students of color. Following this event, student-of-color organizations and CDF/SB would stage a rally followed by a sit-in to demand that the dean and the faculty take action.

The student activists planned meticulously for the day of protest. Organizers selected two morning classes for the "walk-in" and identified sympathetic white students who would give up their seats on the day of the protest. Short on underrepresented minority students, the student-of-color organizations called sister organizations at area law schools such as

Stanford, Davis, Hastings, and Santa Clara. They asked for volunteers to come to Boalt to take the seats offered up by white first-year students. Organizers then identified a diverse group of students to speak at the rally and printed pamphlets to explain why the students were protesting. In addition, students cut green armbands to distribute to supporters of the action and printed gray T-shirts that read on the front, "It's Not a University Without Diversity," and on the back, "Educate Don't Segregate."

On Sunday night—the night before the protests were to begin—organizers held a mandatory meeting for those who would be involved in the sit-in. Nearly one hundred students sat nervously but resolutely around the packed room of La Raza Law Students Association. Several alumni joined them, including protest veteran Renee Saucedo, who brought a soothing force of experience into the room. The organizers asked to see the hands of all those volunteering to sit in. More than fifty people, many more than the organizers had expected, raised their hands. Three were selected to lead the sit-in, and two were selected, myself among them, to negotiate the demands for action with the dean. The students who had not volunteered to sit in divided themselves into three groups: media crew, support crew, and legal observers. The media crew would send press releases in the early morning and conduct interviews with the English-, Spanish-, and Chinese-speaking press. The support crew would provide water and food to the protesters.

Finally, the legal observers would stay with the protesters and, if they were arrested, would record any civil rights violations. Though the protesters had committed themselves to a peaceful and nonviolent course, they were unsure how the dean would react to the sit-in and, more important, how the university police would treat them in the event of an arrest. Van Jones, an attorney from Cop Watch, had been invited to the meeting to instruct the protesters on how to guard against police brutality. He explained the "ladder of force" used by the police, and what action of the protesters would justify what rung of force. He also suggested that if the police escalated force without justification, protesters and support crew should chant "No" to the rung of force being used. Legal observers would be on hand to record any unjustified police action. Jones reminded the group that the university police had, in the past, singled out men of color and used excessive force in the arrest process. The group agreed to make sure that all protesters were free and that no one remained detained before heading home after being released. Hoping for the best but prepared for the worst, the protesters left the meeting to get some sleep.

Students participating in the walk-in arrived at school early the next morning with their "It's Not a University Without Diversity" T-shirts. The walk-in students congregated at the fountain to the west of the school. More than thirty minority students who had come from other law schools to assist in the protest joined them. At this same time, Eric Brooks sat down in class wearing his protest T-shirt. As class began, minority students who had assembled at the fountain made their way into the school and into the classroom. They stood at the back of the room. A white first-year student stood up and asked other white students to join him in volunteering seats to the newly arrived minority students. A number of white students stood up, gave up their seats, and moved to the back of the room.

Minority students took their seats and proceeded to engage in the class discussion. For the first time after almost two months of school, Eric Brooks was not the only black student in the room. Norma Aguilar sat toward the front and looked around, listening to the visiting minority students contribute their perspectives on the law, and thought about how different this class experience was from the experiences she had had thus far.[44] She was uplifted by the demonstration, but was also saddened that her class experience that day was only a protest, and the following day she would still be one of the few Latino students in the room. After twenty minutes of class, having made their point, the minority students walked out of the classroom and asked the first-years to join them at a rally outside.[45] Students proceeded to the rally, which was drawing others out of their classrooms and was surrounded by reporters. After hearing several speakers, the rally participants marched through the school chanting "What do we want? Access! When do we want it? Now!"

In the course of marching through the school, sit-in participants broke away and headed first to the dean's office, which was locked, and then to the registrar's office, a central location in the school, where they issued the following statement:

The passage of SP-1 and...Proposition 209 has had an appalling effect on the state of higher education in California. After decades of struggle toward parity in education, the admissions of African Americans, Native Americans, and Latinos are decreasing to levels that existed during segregation.

Two years ago, the administration predicted that only eight students from underprivileged minority groups would [enroll]. Despite this ominous prediction, the faculty and administration failed to make any significant efforts to ensure diversity...at Boalt Hall....While Little Rock had nine, zero African Americans [who were admitted in 1997] enrolled in the class of 2000. In addition, this "colorblind" class has no Native Americans, seven Latinos and significantly fewer

Southeast Asians. The administration and faculty have yet to respond to this crisis. As each year passes, African Americans, Native Americans, Latinos, and Southeast Asians are being denied access to public education.

We, the students of the University of California Boalt Hall School of Law, recognize not only the importance but also the necessity of racial and ethnic diversity to a quality education. Since anti-affirmative action laws were proposed, law students at Boalt Hall have adamantly voiced concern to the faculty and administration about the retention of diversity at the law school. We find the present situation morally reprehensible. We refuse to accept complicity in the administration and faculty, and condemn their failure to lead.

WE DEMAND that Dean Kay and the Boalt Faculty IMMEDIATELY . . .

(1) Remove the deterring language of SP-1 from the admissions application

(2) Adopt student recommendations to reform the admissions process

(3) Maintain scholarship opportunities targeted at students of color

(4) Maintain targeted outreach to underrepresented minorities

(5) Diversify faculty through targeted outreach, recruitment and retention[46]

The dean stated, "I cannot meet these demands," and reiterated that the Cole Report was forthcoming and would address student concerns. She then left. Renee Saucedo, one of the alumni who had joined the students in protest, stood up and addressed the protesters and the crowd that had gathered around them. "We pay the salaries of this public institution," she said.[47] "We cannot allow them to forget that this school is ours. This school belongs to our children and grandchildren. As alumni and current students we will sit here as long as need be to remind them of that fact." The protesters continued to sit in the registrar's office, chanting "Boalt Hall, Law for All."

In the course of the afternoon, the Alumni Association Board held a regularly scheduled meeting across the courtyard from the protesters. They decided, given the extraordinary circumstances, to discuss the low minority enrollment and to ask the dean what would be done. Troubled by what they heard, they gave the floor to Daniel Tellalian, the chair of Students Supporting Students, who, against the backdrop of chanting protesters, asked the board to help fund a student-based outreach effort. Tellalian recalled,

We had previously gone to Dean Kay for funding for our program and had been turned down. She said that all the money allocated by the regents for student outreach had been paid to a contractor to film a video about Boalt, which would be sent out to people admitted. The video, however, was aimed at recruiting admitted students and not at increasing the numbers of minority applicants.

After Dean Kay had refused our funding, Linda Lye [a second-year student] and I put ourselves on the agenda for the Alumni Association meeting through our student representative. Dean Kay tried to dissuade the Board from hearing us out, stating that Boalt had outreach under control. I wouldn't let it go and presented our program to them. One Board member was moved enough to cut us a $1,500 personal check. The Board committed $7,500 to funding our outreach program.[48]

Tellalian thanked the board, left the room, walked across the courtyard, shared the good news with the protesters, took off his tie, and sat down with his classmates. The sit-in lasted for six more hours before the dean entered the registrar's office with the police and asked the students to leave. The protesters reiterated that they would not leave until they had some assurance that the administration and faculty would address their demands. Cristine Soto, a third-year student and one of the leaders of the protest, said to the dean, "We are getting no support from the administration. We have to get arrested instead of going to class just to get you to listen to us. . . . We're here because this administration has failed us. You have failed us."[49]

At 5:00 in the evening, the dean walked out of the room, and the campus police proceeded to arrest the protesters, who sat in a large circle with locked arms singing "We Who Believe" and "We Shall Not Be Moved," songs from the civil rights movement.[50] Police closed and locked the wide glass doors opening out from the registrar's office into the corridor and the courtyard beyond, leaving only a small side door open. The activity had drawn a large crowd: legal observers, student supporters, friends and family of the protesters, and the media gathered outside the registrar's office. Police dislodged the protesters one by one, handcuffing them and leading them out the side door and down a hallway, where they were arrested, charged, and released. As each protester was pulled from the circle, the remaining protesters closed the gap and continued singing. Supporters outside sang in unison with those inside.

The first to be arrested were women. As each protester was taken away, the energy inside and outside of the registrar's office became more charged. The police moved closer to the circle to dislodge the men. As had been feared, the police escalated their use of force, applying pain holds to the men of color who sat limp in the circle. The police turned protesters onto their bellies, pressed their bodies and faces to the ground with their elbows, knees, and hands, wrenched their arms, and pulled their ears before handcuffing them and leading them out of the room.

The legal observers who remained in the room took copious notes. The protesters inside and the student supporters outside chanted "No pain holds," but the police ignored them. Students on the outside feared for their classmates, but refrained from confronting the police. In two hours of arrests, fifty-three protesters had been charged and released. Legal observers subsequently filed a complaint with the university police. After a review, the police department responded, issuing a letter that stated, "[T]he officers were authorized to use force and used reasonable levels of force to complete their arrests." The letter went on to say, "It is our policy to use pain compliance techniques to accomplish arrests, when necessary. We have found that these can reduce the overall amount of force necessary to obtain compliance or control of an individual."[51]

Having been arrested and released, Norma Aguilar went home exhausted.[52] The day of protest had been long, emotional, and cathartic. Like many student activists, Aguilar had poured herself into advocacy, outreach, and now direct action. "For once," she reflected, "they had to listen to us. For once they couldn't ignore us." Second-year student Sonya Enchill was also arrested and remarked, "I'm proud that I was arrested standing up for something that I believe in." Reflecting on the value of the protest, she added, "It allowed me a release of the anger and disappointment I was feeling from everything in this fight. It also demonstrated that there was still a group of people at Boalt committed to the issue of diversity and it achieved an unprecedented solidarity among those students who had been active in the fight."[53]

Manjari Chawla and other student activists who had relentlessly pressed for changes to the admissions process went to sleep that night feeling, however, that something more needed to be done. "Up to that point," Chawla remembered, "I felt like we could do something. We were such a strong group and we had so much momentum, and even though we were a minority in terms of numbers at the school, I felt that we could make some sort of change." But, she recalled, "From that moment I was sure that nothing more could be done within the school. I could talk to as many people as I wanted, but our efforts were going to have to be much bigger than Boalt."[54]

The day after the protest, criticism of the demonstrations ensued. A first-year student identifying himself as white distributed a letter in student mailboxes in which he criticized the class walk-in. "Active protest is one thing," he said, "disruptive protest is another.... Other than the reporters who covered your action, who were you hoping to influence?"[55] A third-year student who helped organize the walk-in responded in her own letter, which she also distributed in student mailboxes:

THERE ARE NO NATIVE AMERICANS IN THE CLASS OF 2000. THERE IS ONE AFRICAN AMERICAN IN THE CLASS OF 2000. THERE ARE 14 LATINOS IN THE CLASS OF 2000.

However, since school started this semester, first-year classes have gone on as usual, as if the law school was not in a state of crisis....

The point of the protest was *not* to convince [white] first-years that affirmative action should be reinstituted. The protest was directed at the faculty, the Dean and the administration.... Nine weeks had passed and the admissions process for the Class of 2001 had begun. Fearing next year's entering class would be as homogenous as the present one, some students took it upon themselves to let the administration know they would not allow the Class of 2001 to look like the composition of the Class of 2000.

Other first-year students expressed resentment that their morning classes had been interrupted by the walk-in. One referred to the protesters who had been arrested as "academic terrorists."[56] At a town hall meeting, another stated that she had come to Boalt to learn, not to have her classes interrupted by protests. Echoing these sentiments, a second-year law student wrote in an essay critical of the "diversity movement" at Boalt,

I understand that both the law and law schools are not insulated (nor should they be) from politics and current events. But it is my belief that the people of the state of California created Boalt Hall for the study of law, not for the disruptive practices (i.e., walk-outs, walk-ins, sit-ins, sit-outs, etc.) that radicals at Boalt have espoused to make their points about diversity and affirmative action.... I hope that all the hoorah and impetus behind the diversity movement die down, and that we can go back to studying the law at Boalt Hall—as our predecessors once did.[57]

Minority students who participated in the protests viewed these comments as stemming from a sense of entitlement. One student stated, "Those students talked about their precious 20 minutes of class being disturbed, as if Boalt was their school."[58] Norma Aguilar reflected on the remarks made by many white students and thought, "What selfish things to say when whole communities are being excluded from the law school."[59]

In the weekly school bulletin, the dean wrote, "As you all know, demonstrations took place at Boalt on Monday, October 13, that disrupted two classes, and culminated in a sit-in at the Registrar's Office." She continued, "I have received many comments from Boalt students and faculty in the aftermath of those demonstrations. I think it is fair to say that many people who are sympathetic to the protestors' cause were unsympathetic with their chosen methods of communication. University policy does not permit disruption of classes."[60]

There were few words of praise for the protesters in the weeks that followed. However, an editorial written by two third-years in the student newspaper offered welcome words of support:

We had a feeling today that has been largely foreign to us during our time at law school: Pride. Hope-causing, chest-swelling pride. Our pride doesn't stem from the beautiful new someone-owns-every-inch campus. It doesn't stem from our collectively impressive LSAT scores, or from our 98% employment rate after graduation. Nor from our world-class faculty. Our feeling of pride was caused by 53 students and alumni who believed in something so passionately that they were willing to be arrested in order to get someone to listen.

Fifty-three students chose to risk incarceration because they believe that the law school has been slow in trying to preserve diversity at Boalt Hall. The fact that we agree with their concern about diversity only explains part of our pride. Some of the pride comes from seeing students who have passion despite having spent time in the detached-intellect-engaged-ambition halls of a law school. In the last few weeks we have heard discussions of signing bonuses, of the danger of wearing clothes that stand out, or expressing opinions that might not be held by everyone. We have heard about women removing wedding rings in order to increase the chances of getting a call back interview.

In the middle of all this, we saw a group that felt strongly enough about community, diversity, and the value of justice that they were brave enough to break the law. Goofy as it sounds, a group of people linking arms and singing about common goals is enough to make even the grumpiest, most cynical law student blush....

We salute the 53 members of our community who now have rap sheets. They remind us that if you believe you can change the world, you just might.[61]

Many of those who were offended by the protests seemed to confuse the means with the message. Garner Weng, an alumnus of Boalt who published an article about the protests in the *Berkeley Women's Law Journal,* reflected that those denouncing the protests had failed to understand the nature of student actions. He noted that a column in the *San Francisco Daily Journal* had characterized the protesters as offensive and "self-defeating" but had added, "they're right about diversity." Weng commented that, while the support was appreciated, the column missed the point:

Protests are not simply about achieving an end, although they of course seek an end. Protests are also about standing up and yelling when something is wrong and clamoring for everyone else to stand up and yell. They are about generating the morale necessary for all the other actions which may more directly accomplish the end. They are about principle and character.

The student protesters at Boalt Hall are not foolish radicals being arrested for no reason. They are emotional, true, but they are also intelligent, articulate, rational—and under fire. Come tell the woman who is the *first* person in her entire extended family to go to college, let alone law school, that she is likely also to be the *last.* Tell her that although she has excelled in law school and has a bright future—now that she has been given the opportunity—her younger siblings, cousins, and nieces will never get that opportunity. Tell *her* she's just being silly, that there's no urgency, that Regents' Resolution SP-1 and Proposition 209 are not attacks on *her family*.

She is using all she has left in her small, student arsenal—standing up and yelling. Silence is complicity. Instead of criticizing her, you should commend her character.[62]

On October 14, the administration released the Cole Report.[63] Though the administration stated that the release was not timed to respond to the protest, it did ease the tensions in the law school. Working with two other professors and the director of admissions, Associate Dean Cole had written a report over the course of three months, assessing the alternatives available to the law school to increase the enrollment of underrepresented minorities. It paralleled many of the student recommendations.

The Cole Report made some fifty recommendations addressing each stage of the admissions process and included recommendations for changes in the curriculum and for further studies of the definition of "merit" and the use of the LSAT. With respect to outreach and recruitment, the report included the following recommendations that could be acted on by the dean:

(1) Hire as early as possible a full-time Assistant Director of Admissions for Student Recruitment who would among other duties reach out to minority students.

(2) Expand recruitment efforts to include CSU colleges and other institutions with high minority enrollment.

(3) Include an insert in the Admissions Catalog designed to counteract negative impressions that artificially reduce applications and enrollments by students from underrepresented groups.

(4) Establish procedures for prompt communication with student groups and admits, to enable recruitment of minority students as soon as they are admitted.

(5) Support proposals for alumni and other private sector law employers to recruit, mentor, and employ Boalt minority admits and students, and to provide scholarship funds for them.

With respect to admissions practices, the report included the following recommendations that could be acted on by the faculty:

(1) End the practice of adjusting UGPAs and provide guidance to Admissions Committee readers for uniformity in evaluating UGPAs.

(2) Convert to using LSAT score bands. Provide guidance to Admissions Committee readers in the use of the LSAT. Send to the Committee files of applicants whose college grades outperformed their SAT scores. Ex-

periment with reading a percentage of applicant files without the LSAT, which could be disclosed after the Admissions Committee had made a more tentative decision.

(3) Conduct workshops for the Admissions Committee on how to read files to look for a broad range of potential contributions and strengths; to understand the relevance of disadvantage and diversity if it appears in files; and to understand what is permitted under SP-1 and 209 as well as what is not.

(4) Request socioeconomic information in quantifiable and indexable form to be used at a minimum to study how it would affect admissions; at a maximum to use if the faculty adopted a socioeconomic index.

(5) Make clear in the Catalog that with respect to the personal statement on overcoming adversity, specific racial and ethnic prejudice can give rise to obstacles that applicants can mention when relevant and which can be taken into account. Indicate what other racial and ethnic experiences can be included. Change instructions to writers of recommendation letters, calling attention to the relevance of such matters. Make demonstrated commitment to practice in communities under-served by lawyers a relevant consideration in admissions.

(6) Change curriculum to make it more attractive by establishing a Center for Social Justice and including social justice courses among first-year electives.

Student activists were pleased with the Cole Report. In seeming to echo student recommendations, Associate Dean Cole legitimized student efforts, and in making additional suggestions, Cole indicated a number of areas where the law school could work toward eliminating embedded preferences. However, students felt that the most damaging embedded preference—the LSAT—was not adequately addressed. Certainly the recommendations that the law school use LSAT score bands and that it further study the use of the test were important, but they were not enough. Furthermore, the recommendation for an experiment in LSAT-blind reading was welcome, but it would not be acted on. Student activists were critical of the continued weight given to the LSAT in the admissions process. Cole was also personally concerned about the use of the test, but he had not pursued a possible reweighing of the LSAT in his report because, as a matter of practicality, he felt that the faculty would be unwilling to consider lessening the importance of standardized test scores.

Some members of the faculty still considered the LSAT an objective measure of "merit." Other professors were hesitant to lessen the weight of the test because it might affect the school's national ranking. The average LSAT score of a law school's entering class determined, in part, its national ranking in the *U.S. News and World Report* magazine. Boalt had long been a highly ranked law school, and many on the faculty wanted to assure its continued placement in the top ten. The faculty's concern with ranking bordered on obsessive, and it was often said that the faculty would not do anything that might jeopardize the school's ranking unless higher-ranked law schools acted similarly. Some professors at Boalt told lobbying students that the best way to get the faculty to change its policy was to get Harvard to change its policy first. Once a leader in the inclusion of minority students, Boalt appeared to be a leader no longer.

Student activists pressed on with their efforts to reach out to minority applicants. Students Supporting Students used the funds given by the Alumni Association to dispatch small and racially diverse groups to undergraduate institutions across California, including every campus of the California State University. Visits to CSU campuses were particularly important, since the director of admissions at Boalt included only a few of these campuses on his nationwide outreach tour. In addition, several students independently contacted undergraduates at historically black colleges, such as Howard University in Washington, D.C., which had not been visited by the director of admissions.

On their outreach visits, Boalt students spoke to pre-law and minority undergraduate students, many of whom were underclassmen not yet ready to apply. Students were given admissions packets prepared by SSS that contained an application to Boalt, guidance on how to fill out a law school application, sample essays, and phone numbers of student organizations, including student-of-color groups, that applicants could contact for additional guidance. Potential applicants were also given honest answers to direct questions about what it was like to be a minority at Boalt. Daniel Tellalian recalled,

We gave [undergraduate students] some hope. We educated them and answered their questions. We showed them where the scholarship money was. We found that many advisors at these campuses just told their students not to apply to Boalt because they would never get in. We saw that Kaplan didn't offer LSAT classes within 200 miles of some schools. We saw a real communication gap. We exposed a lot of underlying causes for under-representation from these schools—causes that are not fixed today and may never be.[64]

SSS was successful in contacting students from underrepresented and rural communities. Boalt had never conducted the level of outreach in California that was conducted that semester. The number of applicants from California State University went up. However, overall, the number of underrepresented minority applicants went down slightly. Anti–affirmative

action measures had a chilling effect on applications, despite an unprecedented amount of outreach.

At the end of October, Jesse Jackson marched on the state capitol in
Sacramento, again protesting the repeal of affirmative action. Eric Brooks
was at his side, introducing Jackson to the protesters gathered at the
march. Before taking the stage, Brooks gave an interview to a BBC reporter doing a series on race in America. The reporter asked him, "Would
you recommend that black students come to Boalt in future years?"
Brooks answered, "I would tell them that you can get a good legal education here and that it is a supportive environment. But," he added, "I
wouldn't wish this situation on anyone—it's a lot to ask of someone to
have all this attention and still try to go to school. But it's important that
people come to the school after me and try to do what I am doing. When
I walk down the halls, the administration [at Boalt] is always reminded
that I am here." "Were I not here," Brooks continued, "they just might
be able to forget about black students altogether."[65]

Despite these comments, Brooks considered transferring after the
march. As part of his work with the CDF/SB, he had researched the admissions policies at Boalt and talked to professors about changing those
policies. He thought change was unlikely and believed that few blacks, if
any, would be admitted to Boalt in subsequent years. Quite simply he
didn't know if he could continue to handle the attention. "It just kind of
hit me that this situation was never going to go away and that I would
have to deal with it my entire career here." But the debate over affirmative action had become very real to him, and he decided to stay.[66]

On November 4, the U.S. Supreme Court decided not to hear the legal challenge to Proposition 209, clearing the way for a full-scale dismantling of affirmative action in California. One month later, Dean Kay
adopted the Cole recommendations concerning outreach and recruitment, and the faculty adopted recommendations concerning the admissions policy. In addition, the faculty adopted an experimental pilot project
for admitting students from a pool of the most socioeconomically disadvantaged applicants. Though these changes were important and would
serve to mitigate to some extent the impact of anti–affirmative action
measures, they were not enough to offset the devastating impact of the
LSAT on minority applicants. Even in adopting their experimental
project, the faculty felt compelled to set a minimum LSAT score that
effectively kept underrepresented minority students—the students for
whom the project was conceived—out of the pilot pool. Student activists
perhaps undervalued the full set of changes the law school had made.

Nonetheless, they grew skeptical that either the dean or the faculty had the political will to make any changes to the admissions policy that would substantially increase diversity. The changes that were made were welcome, but they seemed to be only improvements at the margins.

Lingering after class one day, Adam Murray, a white third-year student who had participated in the student protests, and I asked ourselves what recourse remained to maintain diversity not only at the law school but also in higher education institutions across the state. Having been involved in a broad range of social justice issues, particularly those related to poverty, Murray was concerned with matters of equity in a land of uneven opportunity. He and I both viewed the elimination of affirmative action as a step backward in the struggle to balance the scales of privilege, and thought about what students could do to ameliorate a situation that was about to worsen. The impact of "race-blind" policies had yet to be felt at the undergraduate campuses, but administrators predicted that the number of underrepresented minorities would drop drastically at Berkeley and UCLA—the flagship campuses of the University of California—in the first year of post–affirmative action admissions.

Student activists had expended an extraordinary amount of energy to alter the admissions process at Boalt, and this effort had yielded what many felt were inadequate changes. If that energy was necessary at every school in California just to hold the line against declining diversity, students would become exhausted without effecting any real change. However, if student activists across the state could join their resources and direct their collective energy at a larger change, then they might be able to keep the doors of education open. Assessing the situation, Murray and I concluded that what was needed was an amendment to the state constitution that would, once again, make affirmative action programs permissible in higher education.

Murray had taken a class the previous year on the initiative process and had listened to a number of guest speakers—Ward Connerly among them—discuss the intricacies of the campaign process. From this class and his own reading, Murray understood that a statewide initiative campaign was a formidable task—we would need to write a viable ballot measure, gather more than seven hundred thousand signatures, and win a majority of the vote—but he felt that students were up to the challenge. He had learned how previous campaigns had succeeded or failed on the basis of their resources or lack thereof, and he knew that a student-run campaign would be at a disadvantage in this respect. But he believed that a student campaign was feasible, and I agreed.

In a legal research course, I had undertaken my own study of the initiative process and appreciated the challenges that an initiative campaign posed. But given the talent and energy of student activists at Boalt, I felt that those challenges could be met. Boalt students were computer savvy and well connected to students at other universities across the state, and I believed we could mobilize a grassroots campaign through the networks created by the outreach efforts and political actions of the previous semester. I also thought we could use the Internet to connect volunteers, bring visibility to the campaign, and even distribute petitions, thereby mitigating a lack of financial resources. A student-run campaign would not be easy, I thought, but it was possible.

Murray and I called a meeting of student activists and presented the idea of an initiative campaign. Many were hesitant. This was a much bigger step than we had taken before. Aman Thind, a third-year student and co-chair of the South Asian Students Association, was the first to speak. She recognized the necessity of doing something, and conceded that there were no other viable alternatives. Thind had arrived at Boalt just after the regents had voted to dismantle affirmative action, and she had spent the last two and a half years lobbying the administration and faculty to do all that it could to preserve diversity at Boalt. But she had seen the limited results of those efforts and thought an initiative was a good idea. At the meeting she stated, "We are the best situated to take up an initiative campaign. We are the ones who have suffered the repercussions of anti–affirmative action measures. We are the ones who can best articulate the need for race-conscious and race-inclusive policies." She added, "If we don't do this, who will?"[67]

Dawn Mann Valentine, a white second-year student who had been very active in student outreach efforts, agreed. Valentine had spent the semester counseling minority undergraduates on how to apply to law school. She spoke to students directly about how important the LSAT was and helped them find funding to pay for test preparation courses. But she knew that these efforts would not be enough. She recalled, "We had learned how a race-blind admissions process works to exclude underrepresented minority students, and we knew that absent a change in the law, Boalt would continue to be devoid of a meaningful number of these students."[68] The idea of an initiative campaign excited her; it was the chance to make substantive and systemic change.

Student activists concurred. There was no direction to move but forward. Murray and I set to work writing a ballot initiative. With the help of other students, we looked at opinion polls, reviewed case law, talked with political consultants, and brainstormed with those who had led the opposition campaign against Proposition 209. With draft language in hand, we sought support and initial funding from area attorneys, many of whom were alumni of Boalt. There was no time to lose. It was late fall 1997. The next scheduled statewide election was in November 1998, which meant that the initiative language would have to be submitted to the attorney general immediately and signatures collected by the end of April in order to qualify for the election. We would be starting late in the election calendar and would have two months less than normally given for gathering signatures.[69]

Of course, there was always the following election, but the next statewide election was not until the year 2000, and we feared that would be too late. With the dismantling of affirmative action coming into full effect, every passing year would mean the loss of thousands of already underrepresented minority students at public institutions of higher education. In addition, anti–affirmative action measures had been introduced in other states and were gaining ground. If students across California joined forces and launched a counterattack now, at ground zero of the affirmative action struggle, then perhaps anti–affirmative action measures in other states would falter, even if the student campaign failed.

Most important, we reasoned that if we waited, we would lose the people power necessary to sustain a high level of activism. Up to this point, the majority of students fighting for diversity had been students of color who would not be replaced in subsequent admissions cycles. Minorities were in danger of dropping below a critical mass: the time to act was now. The issue of declining diversity had held the attention of the public and the media for the last six months and would continue to hold their attention as the decline in the numbers of underrepresented minority students admitted to undergraduate schools was reported that spring. The gubernatorial race was under way and the front-runners had put education at center stage. Moreover, interstudent networks and student-alumni networks were stronger than ever as a result of the diversity crisis.

On the day before Thanksgiving, Adam Murray and Aman Thind drove to Sacramento and delivered the text of the initiative and a check for two hundred dollars to the attorney general, who would have until January to provide a title, summary, and fiscal analysis to be included with the text on the petition circulated for signatures. Called the Equal Educational Opportunity Initiative (EEOI), the student-written amendment would undo the educational portion of Proposition 209 and would once again allow affirmative action to be used in public education. It was only one sentence long and read, simply, "In order to provide equal opportunity, promote diversity, and combat discrimination in public education, the state may consider the economic background, race, sex, ethnicity, and national origin of qualified individuals."

Identifying ourselves as Students for Educational Opportunity (SEO), a group of more than fifty committed Boalt students spent the vacation following exams preparing for the daunting task that lay ahead—the collection of approximately seven hundred thousand signatures of registered California voters by mid-April. The strategy was to organize SEO chapters at more than thirty campuses across California. Boalt students contacted friends and colleagues at other campuses and garnered their support. In addition, they prepared informational materials on signature gathering and voter registration to distribute to campaign volunteers. "It was a lot of work," recalled Aman Thind, the Southern California coordinator for the campaign. "But we didn't think about it. There was so much to do and we just did what needed to be done, all day, every day, seven days a week."[70]

With pamphlets in hand explaining the EEOI and the mechanics of an initiative campaign, Boalt students spent the better part of January in their cars driving around California, organizing SEO chapters, and training students on how to gather signatures and register new voters. "It was kamikaze organizing," reflected Dawn Valentine, the Northern California coordinator. "We had no time to waste. We had to get SEO chapters up and running immediately." [71]By mid-January, SEO chapters had been established at more than thirty campuses across the state, and the EEOI campaign was quickly becoming the largest student-run grassroots effort in years. Student volunteers numbered well over a thousand, and the number of nonstudent volunteers was also growing.

Civil rights leaders, such as Eva Paterson, remained skeptical of the campaign. Disillusioned with the initiative process, which in recent years had worked against minority interests, she felt that an initiative campaign was a losing battle of resources, and that another loss in the struggle for racial inclusion would be another nail in the coffin. Nevertheless, she supported student activists who felt that running a proactive campaign, even if it was not successful, was of great value.[72] Students felt that a proactive campaign would help reinvigorate the civil rights community and put opponents of affirmative action on the defensive for a change. The EEOI campaign was the only effort under way in the state that could effect any real change. "The initiative was the only option. We had to try it," recalled Adam Murray, who co-chaired the EEOI campaign with me.[73]

At the end of January, Governor Wilson identified eleven state-funded education programs that he sought to eliminate or curtail, purportedly in order to comply with Proposition 209.[74] The threatened programs had all been designed to meet the needs of minority students who were un-derrepresented in higher education, though the programs did not exclude anyone based on race or ethnicity. These programs included K–12 educa-tion programs that provided underprivileged children with the readiness, motivation, and technical skills they would need to advance to higher ed-ucation. They also included community college programs that provided counseling, financial assistance, and support services for students affected by economic, social, and language disadvantages. Governor Wilson's at-tempted elimination of these programs was an appalling reminder of why the EEOI was so important.

At the end of January, having finally received the official title, sum-mary, and fiscal analysis from the attorney general, students designed a one-page petition following the specifications of the secretary of state and ordered ten thousand copies to be printed overnight. With space for eight signatures to a petition, this large order was just a fraction of the num-ber that would need to be printed before the campaign was over. In the morning, volunteers climbed into their cars and spent the next twenty-four hours delivering petitions to SEO chapters up and down the state of California. The race against the clock had begun.

The spring semester started, but student activists continued to focus their time on the initiative. "The campaign was our first and foremost priority," reflected Aman Thind.[75] For students involved in the campaign, learning that semester would come as much from the campaign as it would from their coursework. In early February, SEO formally launched its campaign, issuing a statement to the press that read, "We are outraged by the dismantling of programs designed to ensure equality of opportu-nity from kindergarten through college. If California is to prosper in the next century, our schools must educate all of the state's children, and our graduates must reflect the diversity of our many communities."[76] The *Stanford Daily*'s editorial board threw their support behind the EEOI, stating, "Although Stanford, as a private institution, is not bound by Prop 209 it suffers indirectly from the perception that California is not as wel-coming to minority students as are other states. We believe that the Boalt law students' cause is worthy and that concerned Stanford students who enjoy the diversity of the Stanford community should join the Boalt stu-dents and students across the state in fighting for this ballot measure."[77]

Volunteers set to work gathering signatures. Apart from students, SEO solicited the help of unions, churches, community groups, profes-sional associations, and civic leaders to gather signatures. In mid-Febru-ary, SEO received a big boost, winning the support of Reverend Jesse

Jackson, who stated in the press, "Their sense of idealism is encouraging. What would be really sad is if they did nothing."[78] Jackson added, "[They] remind me so much of the students from the '60s. They have so much hope and so much resilience, and they are not giving up. What excites me is students coming alive and seeking to fight for more diversity." SEO also received a letter from Coretta Scott King, encouraging student efforts. Endorsements came from U.S. Representative Barbara Lee,[79] several California state legislators, the California Democratic Council, the California Teachers Association, the California Faculty Association, the California chapters of the NAACP, ACLU, and NOW, the Hispanic National Bar, the Asian National Bar, and a number of other organizations.

Boalt alumni, who were now in prominent positions in many of these organizations, assisted the students in soliciting financial contributions. One alumnus who was on the board of the Hispanic National Bar Association urged members to contribute funds to the EEOI campaign. In a newsletter to HNBA members, he wrote, "To do nothing and accept the complete dismantling of affirmative action spearheaded by individuals like Pete Wilson and Ward Connerly, would be to imply that their interpretation of justice, fairness and opportunity is not only right, but shared by a majority of Californians and Americans. I am not willing to make such a concession."[80]

SEO was able to raise enough money to lease a small office above a restaurant in Berkeley, which served as headquarters for the campaign and the receiving office for completed petitions. The office also functioned as home base for the three Boalt students who coordinated signature gathering in Northern, Central, and Southern California. Together they kept the SEO chapters supplied with petitions and signature-gathering materials, such as homemade clipboards (made of cardboard) and pens, and helped to circulate petitions. Though volunteers did much of their signature gathering on school campuses, they also stood in front of retail stores, set up tables at concerts and sporting events, circulated petitions at conferences and meetings, and approached people waiting for buses and subways. "It was hard to approach strangers off campus," recalled Adam Murray. "People would ignore you, be suspicious of you, or would not want to be bothered.... But we were committed to doing what we needed to do." [81]

"It was hard to get people to listen, but once they did, they were generally supportive," remembered Aman Thind.[82] However, there were exceptions. Murray recalled a white woman who yelled at him in front of a K-Mart store: "You are a traitor to your race."[83] Dawn Valentine remembered another occasion in which a white man identifying himself as a veteran told her, "How dare you ask me to sign a petition like that," and shoved her. But she remembered many more rewarding experiences. "On one occasion, a couple who signed the petition thanked me, not only for gathering signatures, but also for involving myself in the democratic process the way it was supposed to work."[84]

Gathering signatures through the Internet was also important. Though volunteers numbered as many as three thousand at the height of the campaign, they were not enough to collect the number of signatures needed by mid-April, partly because the majority of volunteers were working or studying full-time, and could give only so many hours to the campaign. Another reason was that El Niño had inundated California with an unusual amount of rain, making the gathering of signatures outdoors difficult. As a result, signature gathering over the Internet became more critical. Internet-based signature gathering took place in one of two ways. The first was through a web site established by SEO, where an individual could download and print a petition, sign it, and mail it in. The second way was through a petition attached as a file to e-mails sent to potential signatories who could open the attachment, print the petition, sign it, and mail it in. The key to maximizing signature gathering over the Internet was in locating sympathetic registered California voters. Volunteers sent e-mails to friends, colleagues, and family members, requesting recipients to do the same. In addition, SEO distributed the petition to list-serves, reaching large numbers of people at once.

The Internet also served as a means of communication between volunteers, who shared logistical information, signature-gathering tips, and stories from the campaign trail. In addition, it provided a means by which students from around the country could stay informed about the campaign, express their support from afar, and ask questions about how to organize against the dismantling of affirmative action in their own states. The campaign had a tremendous politicizing effect. Though some volunteers were seasoned activists, many had limited experience and came alive during the campaign. Sandra Alvarez, an undergraduate student at the University of California at Davis, was one such student. Alvarez had some political experience but had never taken a leadership role to the extent that she did during the campaign. She recalled, "The campaign created a space for new leaders and a need for students to take on a large amount of responsibility. I stepped up as the point person for Davis and learned a lot about the initiative process and about politics in general in California."[85]

Over the course of the campaign, the number of signatures gathered grew exponentially. The more practice volunteers had, the more signatures they collected in person and through the Internet. As the campaign became more prominent, however, students also began to receive harassing phone calls, both at the SEO office and at their homes. Petitions signed with excrement were mailed into the office, and SEO received letters full of racial epithets. These hateful incidents were an unnerving reminder of the racial hostility that still existed in America. They made many students more cautious about their personal safety but otherwise did not slow them down. By the beginning of April, though petitions were coming into the office in greater numbers than ever before, the number of signatures gathered did not approach the number required to place the EEOI on the ballot. With a little over $20,000 and some 3,000 volunteers, SEO had managed to collect an estimated 200,000 signatures. But the campaign was still short 500,000 signatures.

Around this same time, the University of California announced a dramatic decline in the number of underrepresented students admitted to its most selective undergraduate campuses. Berkeley experienced the most stunning drop. Calling the admissions cycle the most competitive admissions process in campus history, Berkeley Chancellor Berdahl remarked, "Out of this pool of applicants we could have admitted two or three classes that would be the envy of other universities."[86] Berkeley admitted only 27 percent of the record number of students applying. Chancellor Berdahl expressed his dismay that only 10 percent of those admitted were underrepresented minorities—a drop of 57 percent from the 23 percent admitted in the previous year. The largest decline had occurred among African Americans—of the roughly 8,000 students admitted, only 191 were African Americans (see table 4).

Unwavering in his position, Ward Connerly stated again that he felt vindicated by the statistics. He said that to keep the high quality of education in the UC system, the university should only accept the top high school students, regardless of race. He suggested that the underrepresented minority students who were denied admission to Berkeley were not qualified. But the fact was that more than eight hundred of the underrepresented minorities denied admission had a grade point average of 4.0 or above[87] and an average SAT score of 1200 (out of 1600).[88] Commenting on this fact, Chancellor Berdahl stated, "There are a lot of underrepresented students who could have done exceedingly well here."[89]

One such student was Jamese LaGrone, a seventeen-year-old African American senior at Oakland's Holy Names High School, who had thought she had what it took to get into Berkeley.[90] LaGrone served as junior class president, was a scholar-athlete, worked on the yearbook, and took many advanced placement courses. She earned a 4.0 GPA and

TABLE 4. 1998 Freshman Admissions to UC Berkeley by Ethnicity

Race/Ethnicity	1997 Admissions	1998 Admissions	Percent Change 1997 to 1998
African American	562	191	–66
Latino/Chicano	1,266	600	–53
Native American	69	27	–61
Subtotal	*1,897*	*818*	*–57*
Asian American	2,925	2,998	+2
Caucasian/Other	3,407	4,012	+18
Total	*8,229*	*7,828*	*–5*

SOURCE: Fall admissions data released March 30, 1998, University of California, Berkeley, Office of Student Research and Office of Undergraduate Admissions.

scored 1390 on the SAT. But in early April she had received a rejection letter from Berkeley. LaGrone commented that even if she were to be accepted now, she would not go. Instead, she would study political science at San Francisco State University. Referring to Berkeley, she commented, "It's obvious they don't want me there."

Bob Laird, the director of admissions at Berkeley, said that administrators were disappointed by the drop in numbers, but he stated, "[W]e admitted those students that we felt were the strongest within the constraint of the law." The ACLU and other civil rights organizations countered that Berkeley could have done more to admit qualified underrepresented minorities and began to prepare a lawsuit, which they would file in less than a year, challenging the admissions process as "discriminatory."[91] Remarking on the drop in numbers, Berkeley sociology professor Troy Duster stated that the admissions results signified a huge loss in diversity for the university and emphasized the need for immediate steps to remedy the problem. "It has reached a crisis in terms of the university's serving the state's population and I think it should be framed as a crisis." June Jordan, a professor of African American studies at Berkeley, felt the statistics proved that the law was morally wrong. Jordan said, "In order for the university to maintain its diversity, California voters must approve the Equal Educational Opportunity Initiative, which calls for the reinstatement of affirmative action policies in higher education." She added, "We are trying to get signatures in to put it on the ballot in the fall of 1998 and I believe the administration should put forth whole-hearted support for the initiative."[92]

SEO volunteers were appalled by the devastating admissions results but were unable to qualify the EEOI for the November 1998 election.

Fueled by the desire to halt the resegregation of California's public schools, SEO decided to take an additional two months to try to qualify for the subsequent statewide election in the year 2000. In announcing the continuation of the campaign, Adam Murray stated in a press release, "If we allow our schools to become segregated and we restrict educational opportunities for whole segments of our population, we fail our children and we jeopardize our future. We need affirmative action to ensure equal opportunity in our state and diverse perspectives in our classroom."[93]

In a letter sent to supporters, SEO asked for further assistance: "It is imperative that we qualify the EEOI for the ballot. Proposition 209 has decimated minority populations at the most prestigious public universities in California. This loss not only threatens the moral integrity of this nation and calls into question its commitment to equality of opportunity, but also compromises the quality of education that our public institutions can provide to their students."[94] Dawn Valentine and Aman Thind, the Northern and Southern California coordinators of the signature-gathering effort, e-mailed all volunteers, calling for a redoubling of effort. They wrote, "Education's door is shutting to all but the most privileged and elite Californians. By next fall, the door will be shut. Diversity in our schools will have plummeted. Who then will lead the fight against the far right to ensure equal access to education for ALL?"

SEO volunteers marched forward in the late spring of 1998, circulating petitions far and wide. Students carried petitions to classes, parties, clubs, sporting events, family gatherings, the beach, the library, the gym, and on the subway and the bus. They registered new voters everywhere they went and educated people along the way about the impact of "race-blind" policies. In addition, SEO expanded its efforts on the Internet, finding a growing number of list-serves through which to distribute the initiative. Toward the end of the campaign, in May 1998, students became aware of a list-serve maintained for the state Democratic Party that reportedly contained the e-mails of 1 million registered California Democrats—the voters that SEO had learned through experience were most likely to sign and support their initiative. If students could secure signatures from even a fraction of the voters on the list-serve, they would have a realistic shot at qualifying the EEOI for the ballot. SEO approached the individuals who maintained the list-serve about distributing the EEOI—an initiative that the Democratic Council, the liberal wing of the Democratic Party, had endorsed—over its list-serve. This was something that the managers of the list-serve had never done and hesitated to do for the EEOI. Recalled Adam Murray, "The people we contacted were fascinated with the idea of distributing a petition through the list-serve; they had never thought of it before. But I think when they realized the financial value of the idea they were hesitant to let us do it for free. We were never quite sure why they hesitated; they stopped returning our phone calls."

During this time, the state Democratic Party was caught up in the gubernatorial race, as were a number of prominent civil rights organizations. The number-one concern among political activists that spring was making sure that the Democratic candidate, Gray Davis, was ahead in the polls. Many civil rights activists believed that as governor, Davis would ameliorate the diversity crisis at the University of California. Student activists were not so sure. They had approached the Davis campaign team to solicit the candidate's support for the initiative and had been told that, though Davis supported the student effort, he could not jeopardize his campaign with a public endorsement of EEOI. Davis sounded a lot like President Clinton, and students did not count on the gubernatorial candidate or the Democratic Party to help them qualify the initiative. But they were disappointed by civil rights organizations, which had been quick to endorse the EEOI but were not forthcoming with financial support or signature-gathering volunteers in the final months. Pinning their hopes on Davis, these organizations were directing their efforts toward the gubernatorial race.

Also occupying the minds of civil rights organizations that spring was Proposition 226, one of the latest assaults from the conservative right that was up for a vote in June. Proposition 226, the "Paycheck Protection Act," would have required unions to obtain annual written permission from each of their members for the use of dues for any political purpose. The effect of the measure would have been to reduce the political clout of unions, which were a financial mainstay of Democratic candidates such as Gray Davis and a powerful barrier to conservative successes in the legislature and in initiative campaigns. The unions, as well as the organizations and candidates that relied on them, considered the battle over 226 to be a life-or-death struggle and poured everything they had into defeating the proposition.[95] Consequently, in the last stages of the EEOI signature-gathering campaign, SEO had a hard time capturing the attention or support of political activists who had helped in the first stages of the campaign.

Before the deadline in June, SEO volunteers collected another hundred thousand signatures. Though they had fallen short of the signatures needed, students counted the EEOI campaign a success. Boalt students and students across California had stood up for what they believed in and had done the best they could with what little they had to halt the resegregation of higher education. We had raised and spent close to thirty thousand dollars on the campaign for the EEOI. The typical winning initiatives spend millions.[96] Many students who had come to the campaign without prior political experience emerged as student leaders, public speakers, community organizers, and political strategists—myself included. At the conclusion of the campaign, student volunteers parted ways, some to begin summer jobs, some to study for the bar exam, and some to join other grassroots political efforts. The experience had forever altered us: we had all learned something about ourselves and about the world around us. Perhaps it was about hope and confidence, strength and solidarity, equality and diversity, or policies and politics. Regardless, the students involved in the EEOI campaign would carry the lessons they learned proudly into their future endeavors.

In the fall of 1998, Boalt enrolled 34 underrepresented minority students in the first-year class, a marked increase from the 15 students (including 8 who had deferred admission) who had enrolled in 1997. This number, however, was still much lower than 52—the number of students who had enrolled in 1996, the year prior to the dismantling of affirmative action. The dean credited the increase to greater outreach and recruitment efforts and to a more whole-person review of law school applicants. It is also noteworthy that the Bar Association of San Francisco had given twelve race-based private scholarships to Boalt minority admits that defrayed part of the financial burden of attending law school. Unfortunately, the admissions results would prove to be only a temporary reprieve in declining minority enrollment.

Khari Tillery was one of the eight African Americans who enrolled that fall. As a senior at Berkeley the year before, he had been hesitant to apply to Boalt. "I had watched what Eric Brooks had gone through and didn't want to be in his position. I had also come to feel unwelcome at the University of California." But the reasons to apply outweighed the reasons not to. "I wanted to stay in California, Boalt was a good school, and I could afford it. I also felt that it was important for African-American students to follow Eric."[97] Law students heavily recruited minority students to come to Boalt. The dean and other faculty members called minority admits, but student recruiting seemed especially important. Sonya Enchill, the outreach and recruitment coordinator for Law Students of African Descent, and several other students had organized a recruitment weekend for students of color the previous spring. With the financial and moral support of a prominent black alumnus and former mayor of Berkeley, Warren Widener, students put on a whole weekend event complete with housing, dinners, and tours for more than fifty minority students. Enchill recalled, "All except one black student from the subsequent class attended our weekend and all those in attendance said the weekend event led them to choose Boalt."[98]

The extensive outreach conducted through Students Supporting Students and the recruitment organized by Enchill and others were made possible by the presence of a significant number of minority students who were committed to maintaining diversity at Boalt Hall. But the numbers of minority students, particularly African Americans, were dipping below a critical mass. Though the dean had hired an outreach director, an impressive African American experienced in admissions, it seemed unlikely that one person could replace the effort of so many committed students or that the administration would support targeted outreach and recruitment.

The entering class did not manifest the racial diversity of the class that had just graduated, and the school as a whole became less diverse. Underrepresented minorities, who had composed 17 percent of the student body the year before, and 24 percent the year before that, now constituted only 13 percent. The diminishing numbers, particularly of African Americans, were taking their toll. Khari Tillery reflected on his first semester at Boalt: "I was really uncomfortable the first two months of school and was very reserved. I felt isolated and had a hard time finding someone to connect with, even among the African American students who were so few in number and consequently far less diverse—there were only two other black men and they were older with families."[99] He considered transferring, but one of his professors encouraged him to stay.

The second- and third-year students who had poured their hearts and souls into activism the previous year were physically and emotionally exhausted. "I was burned out," recalled Dawn Valentine. "I was also going through a mourning process. It had been a tremendous accomplishment to get people to listen, but I was tired of confronting people with destructive and intolerant views. California had taken one giant step backwards and nobody seemed to be doing anything about it except students who had already given it their all." Expressing the sentiments of other third-year students, Valentine continued, "On top of the fatigue, I was focused on finishing my coursework so I could graduate."[100] Activism surrounding racial diversity, which had been a constant of school life the year before, became virtually nonexistent in the 1998–99 school year. The few instances of activism focused on securing minority student involvement in the outreach, admissions, and recruitment process. Student activists hoped that the presence of minority students in the admissions process would in some way mitigate the results of a race-insensitive policy.

The heavy reliance on the LSAT in admissions decisions continued to disproportionately affect minority students. The reliance on undergraduate grades also affected minorities but not to the same extent as the LSAT. In September 1998, Testing for the Public—a Berkeley-based, nonprofit education research group headed by test scholar David White—completed a study that exposed the extent of cultural bias in the LSAT.[101] The statistics for the study had been compiled by first-year Boalt student William Kidder, who worked for Testing for the Public prior to coming to law school, and continued to work there once at Boalt. Kidder was a white student who grew up in a predominantly white area of Los Angeles and was aware of the benefits that he had been afforded. Applying to college, he had not scored high enough on the SAT to get into the most competitive schools, but his parents had paid three hundred dollars for a private admissions counselor to help him get into Berkeley. In applying to law school, knowing that he had not done well enough on the SAT, Kidder paid for an LSAT preparation course to help him get into Boalt.[102] He recognized that his space at the prestigious campus was a scarce resource and that he was privileged to attend. He felt obliged to use his learning as a tool to help others, so after completing his undergraduate degree, Kidder taught test preparation courses for Testing for the Public, which catered to economically disadvantaged and racially underrepresented students. In the LSAT preparation courses that he taught, Kidder noticed that extremely bright minority students consistently did not score well on the practice tests. The racial screening process taking place prompted him to undertake a study with his mentor, David White, to examine the extent of bias in the LSAT.

The study they completed confirmed Kidder's suspicions—that minority students earning top grades in their undergraduate institutions were undermined in the admissions process by their LSAT scores. The study looked at all applicants from Boalt's top five feeder schools—Harvard, Yale, Stanford, UC Berkeley, and UCLA—in the years 1996 to 1998. Each student from a minority group was matched with all white students from the same college who also had an undergraduate grade point average that was nearly identical with the minority student's (within plus or minus .10 on a 4.0 scale). White and Kidder reasoned that, theoretically, students who had achieved the same success at the same college should earn comparable scores on the LSAT. But the study showed that this was far from the case. All minority groups consistently scored lower on the LSAT than their white peers. On a scaled score of 120 to 180, African Americans consistently scored 9.30 points below whites, Latinos scored 6.87 points below, Native Americans scored 3.77 points below, and Asian Americans scored 2.48 points below.[103] Officials from the Law School Admission Council acknowledged the racial gaps, but could offer no explanation.[104]

White and Kidder suggested that societal factors might contribute to the gap. Claude Steele, a Stanford psychology professor, had found that, in a standardized test situation, academically strong minority students suffered from additional anxiety, which he termed "stereotype threat." He demonstrated that "when strong black students sit down to take a difficult standardized test, the extra apprehension they feel in comparison with whites is less about their own ability than it is about having to perform on a test and in a situation that may be primed to treat them stereotypically." Steele stated that "African Americans have endured so much bad press about test scores for so long that ... they are instinctively wary about the test's fairness" and tend to score lower because of this anxiety.[105]

In addition, White and Kidder pointed to earlier studies undertaken by White and others suggesting that intimidating testing conditions—such as when a student is the only, or one of the few, minorities in the room—might also explain the gap in LSAT scores. They suggested that the gap might also be explained by cultural bias in the test questions themselves, commenting that "[t]he test is normed on a [testing] population that is 75 percent white ... contribut[ing] to a significant ethnic bias on the test that places minorities at a disadvantage."[106] Regardless of how the score gap might be explained, the Testing for the Public study made clear the LSAT's disparate impact on minority students. Kidder observed that the bias in the LSAT was not a reflection of the receding past, but rather was the expression of a present-day bias that recurred on a regular schedule—four times a year. "People walk in [to the LSAT] after four years of college with essentially the same credentials, and after a four-hour test, those people with the same credentials are either rewarded or destroyed."

He pointed out that a nine-point score difference between a black student and a white student might not otherwise be significant, but in a highly competitive law school market, this gap could determine whether an applicant was admitted into a top-twenty law school or not. At Boalt, for example, in the 1997 admissions cycle, nine points meant the difference between a 90 percent chance and a 30 percent chance of being accepted for students with UGPAs of 3.75 or above. For students with this same UGPA, six points or even three points meant the difference between a 90 percent chance and a 54 percent chance of getting into Boalt. Likewise, for students with a UGPA of 3.50 to 3.74, as little as three points meant the difference between a 55 percent chance and a 22 percent chance of acceptance (see table 5).

Responding to the Testing for the Public study, Dean Kay admitted that the school had long been aware of the differences in scores based on race.[107] She stated that Boalt used the LSAT to a lesser extent than did other law schools. Where other law schools used a 70 percent LSAT and 30 percent UGPA balance, Boalt balanced the LSAT and the UGPA equally. However, the disproportionate impact of even this balance on minority students called into question its appropriateness.

This subject was taken up by a New Definitions of Merit Committee, which had been recommended in the Cole Report and appointed by Dean Kay the previous spring. In November, the committee released a progress report stating, "Although the LSAT appears to have moderate success in predicting academic performance (or more precisely grades in the first year of law school), it is not so good that there is no need to search for ways to supplement it. Indeed we think that there are enough problems with the LSAT, and aptitude tests more generally, to warrant a serious and sustained search for supplemental predictive tools."[108] The committee recommended an expanded investigation and called for collaboration with other institutions that could provide statistical and technical expertise. The scope of the investigation would require a substantial budget and several years of study. In the interim, the faculty did not appear ready to adjust the weight of the LSAT, despite clear indications that the test, as used by Boalt, had a disparate impact on minority applicants.

The admissions process in the coming year—1999—would yield fewer minority students, leaving unanswered the question of what could or would be done to maintain racial diversity in the years to follow. Certainly the LSAT was an obvious target, but vestiges of past discrimination and instances of present discrimination, reflected in other areas of the admissions process, also inhibited the selection of a diverse student body. These problems would soon be exacerbated by a diminished number of minorities in the applicant pool as a result of decreased minority enrollment at Boalt's two top feeder schools—Berkeley and UCLA.[109] In the year 2002, the first class to be admitted to the undergraduate schools un-

TABLE 5. Percentage of Admissions to Boalt in 1997, Based on LSAT Scores

LSAT Score Bands	150–155	156–161	162–167	168–173	174–180
National Percentile	*47.3–67.8*	*71.3–85.7*	*88.4–95.6*	*96.4–99.1*	*99.3–99.5*
GPA					
3.75+	7 %	30 %	54 %	90 %	98 %
3.50–3.74	2 %	8 %	22 %	55 %	89 %
3.25–3.49	0 %	2 %	7 %	29 %	53 %
3.00–3.24	0 %	1 %	2 %	6 %	21 %

SOURCE: Boalt Hall, 1998 *Admissions Handbook* for the Committee on Admissions, Section 3.

der SP-1 would be applying to law schools. They would be composed of far fewer minority students than in years past and would signal another dramatic decline in the number of underrepresented minorities enrolling in law school.

In February 1999, a group of civil rights organizations that included the ACLU, MALDEF, the NAACP Legal Defense Fund, the Lawyers' Committee for Civil Rights, and the Asian Pacific American Law Center, filed a class action lawsuit against the University of California on behalf of the highly qualified minority students who were denied admission to the undergraduate school at Berkeley in 1998.[110] The civil rights groups claimed that the admissions process discriminated against minority students, stating, "In the past, affirmative action policies attempted to compensate for some of the unfair components of the admissions process. In the absence of affirmative action, we are simply left with a discriminatory system."[111]

The lawsuit stated that the Berkeley undergraduate admissions process was discriminatory; first because it placed weight on Advanced Placement test scores when approximately 50 percent of high schools in the state did not offer any AP classes. Students who had the opportunity to take AP courses were graded on a 5.0 scale and could earn a high school grade point average (HSGPA) above a 4.0, giving them a significant advantage over students who did not have the opportunity to take such courses. Prior to the elimination of affirmative action, Berkeley capped HSGPAs at 4.0 in the admission process, minimizing the disparity between schools with and schools without AP course offerings. But following the elimination of affirmative action, Berkeley uncapped high school grade point averages, allowing the disparity between schools to work to the full advantage of students from schools with greater offerings of AP courses. The lawsuit asserted that minority students were at a disadvantage in this respect in the admissions process because many schools with high minority populations did not provide the same number of AP courses, if any at all.[112]

Second, the lawsuit alleged that the admissions process was discriminatory because it relied heavily on the SAT, which had been shown to have a cultural bias and to correlate more with parental income than freshman-year grades. A UC task force charged by the regents with examining Latino eligibility for admission to the university had concluded as much in 1997, when it issued a report finding that the SAT was a poor predictor of college performance and was biased against Latinos and other minorities.[113] This finding had led the task force to recommend eliminating the test as an eligibility requirement. The regents, however, hesitated to eliminate the SAT without replacing it with another means to select among a highly talented applicant pool. The lawsuit argued that students who took SAT preparatory classes fared better on the test, but most minority students did not have the financial means to take such classes. Even for those minority students who did, however, it was not clear that such courses could adequately correct for bias in the test.

Michelle Alexander, an ACLU attorney, stated in a press conference, "This is not just unfortunate, it is absolutely illegal." She added, "UC Berkeley [has gone] back to a system where people of privilege get to attend these schools."[114] Ward Connerly responded, "I certainly don't think that the university is engaged in discrimination towards anyone or any group, because we apply the same standards to everybody."[115] Connerly suggested that minority students simply needed better grades to get into the prestigious schools. But he was ignoring the fact that minority students who did well in school and received top grades were still being denied admission to Berkeley.

In the course of the next several months, in an attempt to correct for the disparity between high schools and to increase minority enrollment under SP-1, the regents adopted the "4 percent plan." The plan, which was modeled on the "10 percent plan" in Texas, provided for the admission of the top 4 percent of seniors at every high school in the state to the University of California. The previous policy had provided for the admission of the top 12.5 percent of high school seniors statewide, rather than by high school. Though the 4 percent plan would more equitably allocate spots to the university among high schools, it was not expected to affect the racial composition of the group of students who were UC-eligible.

TABLE 6. Simulated Racial Composition of UC-Eligible Class for 1996

Race	Previous Plan: 12.5% Statewide	Adopted Plan: 4% by High School	Rejected Plan: 12.5% by High School
White	54 %	53 %	45 %
Asian	30	30	28
Latino	9	10	17
Black	2	2	4
Other	5	5	6

SOURCE: Pamela Burdman, "Two Challenges Set for UC's Race Blind Admissions," *San Francisco Chronicle,* February 8, 1999.

The 4 percent plan had originally been designed by California Senator Teresa Hughes as a 12.5 percent plan, whereby the top 12.5 percent of seniors at *every* high school would be admitted to the University of California. In contrast to the 4 percent plan, this plan would affect the racial composition of the students who were UC-eligible.[116] Simulations showed that for the high school class that had graduated in 1996, under the previous statewide policy, 9 percent of the UC-eligible seniors were Latino, and 2 percent were African American. Under the new 4 percent plan, 10 percent would be Latino, and 2 percent would be African American. But under the alternative 12.5 percent plan, 17 percent of UC-eligible seniors would be Latino, and 4 percent would be African American (see table 6). However, concerns about lower academic standards and space constraints prompted the regents to reject this alternative.

In addition to not altering the composition of the UC-eligible class, the 4 percent plan adopted by the regents would not alleviate the problem of "cascading," whereby minority students admitted to the University of California would be admitted to less prestigious campuses. These campuses, such as Santa Cruz and Riverside, accepted all UC-eligible students. But the more prestigious campuses at Berkeley and UCLA only accepted the most competitive of the UC-eligible students. In this respect, the 4 percent plan was markedly different from the 10 percent plan in Texas, where eligible students were admitted to *all* campuses, and individual campuses competed for these students.

Newly elected Governor Gray Davis applauded the 4 percent plan, ignoring the fact that it would have little effect on the diversity of undergraduate schools and would not even apply to graduate school admissions. Recognizing the inadequacy of the 4 percent plan and other measures to achieve diversity in highly competitive public programs, the state legislature passed a bill (S.B. 44) that would have allowed governmental bodies to use outreach programs to increase the number of minorities in public education and employment.[117] Believing it violated Proposition 209, Governor Davis vetoed the bill. Davis contended that effective outreach programs could be fashioned like the 4 percent plan, and could be based on socioeconomic factors, geographic area, and other non-race-based characteristics. His position was surprising, given that his gubernatorial opponent, former Attorney General Dan Lungren—a staunch opponent of affirmative action and proponent of 209—had supported the measure, recognizing outreach as necessary to prevent reliance on "old boy networks." Notably, while rejecting outreach for minorities, Davis signed a bill that would require local governments to implement an employment preference program for veterans. Far from being the liberal hope that civil rights organizations had campaigned for, Davis appeared to be another shade of his Republican predecessor.[118]

The consequences of SP-1 and Proposition 209 demonstrated that highly competitive schools that were able to select from a large pool of qualified applicants but unable to take into account the race of those applicants were not then able to select for a racially diverse class. Studies had repeatedly shown that there was no proxy for race. Socioeconomic factors were often suggested as a means of achieving diversity and were important for consideration in their own right, but they could not substitute for race. Economist Thomas Kane and others had looked at the possibility of using socioeconomic factors to admit a racially diverse class and concluded that they were an inadequate replacement for race-sensitive affirmative action. "The problem is one of numbers," Kane stated. While blacks and racial minorities are much more likely than whites to come from poor families, they still make up a numerical minority of all applicants with low incomes. Furthermore, poor, underrepresented minority applicants are less likely than poor white applicants to have high test scores and are still at a disadvantage in the consideration of numerical indicators.[119]

As had been predicted, the experiment with socioeconomic admissions at Boalt did not contribute significantly to the increase in enrollment of underrepresented minorities in 1998. At UCLA's law school, which had moved to a system of computerized socioeconomic admissions, the results in 1998 were much worse than Boalt's discretionary process of reading individual files (though in 1997, when Boalt had done nothing to mitigate "race-blind" policies, UCLA had fared better using socioeconomic criteria).[120] At Boalt, this meant that, regardless of so-

TABLE 7. Racial Diversity at Boalt Hall, 1994–1999

	Entering Class		School Total	
Year	Underrepresented Minorities	Total Minorities	Underrepresented Minorities	Total Minorities
1994	26 %	40 %	25 %	40 %
1995	24	36	25	39
1996	21	35	24	37
1997	5	19	17	30
1998	13	31	13	28
1999	10	23	9	24

SOURCE: Admissions statistics printed in *One Community, Many Perspectives,* Boalt Hall, 1999.

cioeconomic considerations, as long as the law school employed traditional admissions criteria without regard to race, the school would admit significantly fewer underrepresented minorities than it had in the past under affirmative action.

In May 1999, the last class to be admitted to Boalt under affirmative action—my class—graduated. At the commencement, Dean Kay asked the audience to celebrate the diversity of the graduating class. These graduates, she said, "are uniquely qualified to deal with the problems we face in society." She stated, "Perhaps more than at any time during the past thirty years, the unifying concepts of equality before the law and justice for all people regardless of their condition are being challenged. Beyond all other segments of our society, we, the members of the legal profession, have a special obligation to respond to those challenges." Addressing the graduating class, she said, "[A]s you enter upon your chosen work, you will have a great responsibility and a great opportunity, for the divisions that confront us are profound. I know that you are well equipped to deal with these challenges, and I am confident that each of you will live up to your high calling."[121]

The year that the class of 1999 entered Boalt Hall, students had thrived in the school's racial diversity. In 1996, Boalt boasted of being one of the most diverse law schools in the country, with a student body made up of 24 percent underrepresented minority students and 37 percent total minority students. But in the following years, as the two classes above them graduated, the diversity at Boalt Hall declined precipitously (see table 7).

Like the more than two thousand minority graduates who had come before them, this year's graduates were headed for corporate law firms, public interest law firms, public defenders' offices, and district attorneys' offices.[122] Others were on their way to the courts, to clerk for state supreme courts, federal district courts, federal appellate courts, and one was headed to the U.S. Supreme Court. Many among them had spent the better part of their law school careers fighting side by side with progressive white students to keep the doors of Boalt Hall open for students of all racial and ethnic backgrounds. Now they were leaving and, as in the two previous years, far fewer would take their place.

As they prepared to leave, minority and white students who had fought to halt the resegregation of Boalt Hall issued one last statement. In a brochure distributed at graduation, the students expressed these closing thoughts.

We are honored to graduate today, and to celebrate this occasion with you, the friends and families of the Class of 1999. Yet, we are also deeply saddened because this day marks not only a passage for us, but a devastating blow to the struggle for equal opportunity as well. Our class is the last class to be admitted to Boalt Hall in the near future, whose diversity comes close to approximating the diversity of California, the state in which the majority of us will serve as legal professionals.

For many of us, this graduation marks not just our completion of law school, but the sorrowful moment at which this state's doors to higher education and opportunity finally whisper shut. Months before we began law school in the fall of 1996, the Regents of the University of California passed Resolution SP-1, and only months later we witnessed the passage of California's Proposition 209. Instead of taking an independent stance for the continuing legality and necessity of race-based affirmative action as a remedy for systemic racial inequality in our educational systems, the majority of the faculty of Boalt Hall assumed defeat at the hands of this legal interpretation without a fight. Students were forced to assume their responsibilities to maintain diversity in legal education, and investigated alternatives to our current admissions process to offset the devastating effects of an admissions policy based on racially exclusionary definitions of merit on the next classes at Boalt Hall. The administration and faculty claimed defeat to an overly conservative interpretation of the law, and many of them did nothing to change the admissions policy until compelled by the efforts of the (still diverse) student body.

The struggle for affirmative action has taught us that many people who teach the law are afraid to use the law, to mobilize it to achieve racial and social justice. From the poor example of our faculty and their inaction, we learned that respect for the law does not compel fear of using the law. In organizing meetings, in protests in the halls of Boalt, in lobbying sessions before the California legislature, in organizing rallies for a statewide campaign to reinstate affirmative action, in our own press conferences, we found an education for justice. We taught ourselves and each other to be the lawyers people need, the lawyers that justice requires, and *not* the lawyers that Boalt Hall taught us to be, the lawyers of inaction who protect only injustice. We learned not to be afraid of the adversarial system, and we learned that, win or lose, we are willing to use the law to fight for our rights in an equitable society.

While we recognize the privilege that a degree from this institution confers upon us, we reject the administration's and faculty's common refrain that Boalt Hall is an "elite" school. While they use the word "elite" to mean academically superior, we recognize that the term "elite" also means that Boalt Hall is exclusive, discriminatory and classist. We believe that excellence in education should not only be available to a diverse group of people, but that excellence in education can only be achieved with a diverse student body. A school that excludes people of color, whether "incidentally," or "intentionally," can never achieve this excellence.

Our experience as the last racially diverse class at Boalt Hall has recommitted many of us to the struggle to ensure that others have the opportunities we have. Sadly, we leave today, unsure that Boalt Hall feels the same commitment. We leave knowing that we have succeeded at Boalt Hall, and will continue to succeed, not because of Boalt Hall, but because of each other and in spite of Boalt Hall. And we leave hoping that Boalt Hall will recommit itself to educating diverse lawyers for a diverse society, and to recognizing that Boalt Hall never succeeded in spite of racial diversity, but succeeded, and will succeed, only because of racial diversity.[123]

CHAPTER 5

Listening to the Silence

The month is August 1999—the beginning of the school year at Boalt Hall. Rafael Mandelman, a white student who entered Boalt in 1996 as part of the last class to be admitted under affirmative action, and who spent the last two years at Harvard completing a joint degree in public policy, sits in his constitutional law class.[1] Looking around the room, he thinks about how the law school has changed. Boalt is different than it was when he was a first-year student. The most obvious difference is the makeup of the student body. When Mandelman started law school, underrepresented minorities composed 24 percent of the student body. Now they compose only 9 percent.

When he was a first-year student, the issue of affirmative action politicized Mandelman. Though he grew up in a mostly white environment, largely oblivious to issues of race, his undergraduate experience at Yale afforded him the opportunity to interact and converse with minority students. Through an accumulation of interactions and conversations, Mandelman developed an understanding of how different the world was for those who were not white. At Boalt, this understanding took on added meaning when he became aware of the ways in which the law school was going to change as a result of the elimination of affirmative action. He involved himself in the discussions then taking place, and remembered in his first year talking about what would happen to the law school once affirmative action was stripped away. Having been away for the last two years, he did not witness the actual transformation. But now, sitting in a classroom of more than seventy-five mostly white students, he is living the result.[2]

In his first year, student activists pushed the administration and faculty to do all that they could to prevent the worst from happening. They painted horrible scenarios of what classes would be like with a diminished number of minorities: "Imagine, we're going to get to *Brown v. Board of Education* in our constitutional law class and there's not going to be a single black person in the room." Now, Mandelman's constitutional law professor turns the attention of the class to *Brown v. Board of Education,* the landmark school desegregation case. Mandelman looks around the room. There are no black students.[3]

Oscar Cisneros, a second-year law student, sits in his criminal law class amazed at what he hears.[4] The class is discussing the case of two Native American parents who were charged with manslaughter for failing to bring their child to the governmental agency on the reservation for medical treatment. In the past, the federal agency had taken Indian children away from their parents and put them in boarding schools. The parents, unaware of the seriousness of their child's infection and fearful of the federal agency, delayed taking their child for treatment. The question for the class is whether it was reasonable for the parents to have known about the seriousness of the infection. If it was, then they are guilty of manslaughter. A white student in the room opens the discussion: "These people could have gone to the library and done research. They should have been fully aware of the child's medical condition." Other students in the room echo her statement.

Cisneros is not Native American—no one in the room is—but he imagines that the reservation did not, and perhaps still does not, have a "library" or a place to do "research," and finds the comment disturbing. Cisneros is Mexican American—one of the few admitted following the elimination of affirmative action—and grew up in the Lower Rio Grande Valley, in the impoverished borderlands of Texas and northern Mexico without access to the information resources that are common to many big cities. He can imagine a world without information resources and is not so sure that the white students who spoke up in class can. Cisneros contributes his own experience to the discussion, bringing in an "other" perspective. But his is the only one.

One month into the school year, Eric Brooks prepares for the first meeting of the staff of the *African American Law and Policy Report (AALPR)*. Brooks was the only African American to enter Boalt Hall in 1997; now in his third year, he is the editor of *AALPR* as well as the chair of the student group Law Students of African Descent. The meeting is being held to determine the future of the law journal—the only one of its kind in the nation.[5] He is concerned. "It's difficult to see the survival of this law journal," Brooks remarks. "Its survival requires a core group of students dedicated to publishing the journal. African Americans here are stretched thin." He points out that there are fewer than twenty African Americans at the law school. In the first-year class, from which journals draw much of their people power, African Americans number only seven, one less than the previous year. Of these few first-year students, several have spoken to him about transferring to a more diverse school where they think they might be more comfortable.[6]

Brooks admits, "The journal might be the first casualty." The meeting draws four black students and four white students, of whom Rafael Mandelman is one. Mandelman was one of two white students on the journal staff in 1996, when it included twenty African American members. "Coming back to Boalt, I wanted to make a contribution," he says.[7] Mandelman, along with one other white student and two black students, volunteers for the editorial board. The journal is saved, at least for this year. Khari Tillery, now a second-year student, is one of the black students who volunteers for the editorial board of *AALPR*. He comments on the predicament of minority-based student organizations. "As a result of SP-1 and 209, there are so few students of color. Our organizations are struggling, and we are trying to figure out how to survive with fewer numbers and learn where our limits are." He adds, "We need more people at Boalt who are willing to step up and take leadership positions. We don't have the numbers to afford minimal involvement."[8]

Mandelman laments the lack of underrepresented minorities at the law school, particularly African Americans. "It feels very wrong," he remarks. He feels angry with the people who do not know how wrong it is. But he observes, "There is no way for them to know what Boalt should be like, what Boalt used to be like." Mandelman comments that in most of his classes there are no black students. He states, "When students here see that there are no black people, they think that this is the way it is, that this is normal, that black people don't go to law school." He adds, "This is not something they even think about." He reflects on the value of diversity in his own life: "To the extent I have realized that a black man my age sees the police very differently than the way I see the police, that understanding has come from personal interactions with black students at school. It is not something I learned from reading a book. I imagine that people are having a lot fewer of those interactions and conversations."[9]

The few underrepresented minorities at the law school continue to share their views with their colleagues and to bring up the "other" perspective in class, but they are less comfortable doing so. They are so few that their every move is noticed. If they speak, their voices are scrutinized and their contributions sometimes ignored. If they choose not to speak, their silence is scrutinized and sometimes used by conservative students and faculty to assert that minority students add nothing to the classroom and that diversity is a "hoax."[10] So, minority students speak when they can and are sometimes rebuked. After a professional responsibility class one day, a white second-year student says of a black student in the class, "I get tired of the way he always feels like he needs to raise the black perspective."[11] Khari Tillery, the black student to whom the student refers, later responds to this statement. "I bring up another perspective because I feel that the students in my classes are working on false assumptions that our system works and that the distribution of power and resources in this country is fair. This is not reality, and I feel compelled to bring that to light." He adds, "I question whether students who are 'tired of hearing the black perspective' want to hear that perspective at all, regardless of who it comes from."[12]

In a class on the topic of "difference," conducted in a required course for those enrolled in the East Bay Community Law Clinic (EBCLC), where Eric Brooks assists mostly low-income and minority clients, Brooks raises the issue of race. As part of the class, students are encouraged to explore questions of race, class, and privilege in connection with the judgments and assumptions made about their clients and the impact those assumptions have on their ability to provide competent advocacy. Brooks raises the issue he faces whenever administrative law judges presume that blacks are lazy and dishonest when they assert their inability to work. No one responds to the observation, and the conversation quickly turns to a separate discussion about economic disadvantage.[13] The topic of race, alone or in the context of other issues, is never addressed in the class.

In a reflection piece he later writes about the class on "difference," Brooks states,

What happened in our class is a symptom of the unconscious racism that infests our society. Our class discussion reflects how society turns away from frank discussions about racial differences to more socially acceptable discussions about socioeconomic differences. The current affirmative action debate is a perfect example. Those who support an end to affirmative action no longer want to look at people being disadvantaged by their race or gender, instead they want to look at those who are economically disadvantaged.

In his reflection piece, Brooks cites race scholar Charles Lawrence: "When an individual experiences conflict between racist ideas and the societal ethic that condemns those ideas, the mind excludes his racism from consciousness." Brooks notes that the class, filled with progressive, racially conscious people, still fell into the same problem that Lawrence describes. He reflects,

We, as a class, gravitated to the differences that we had encountered that caused us tension yet were socially acceptable. It would have been too troublesome for most people to say that the difference of skin color had caused them difficulty. How can a white person say that they are having a hard time relating to black people when society has told them that they should not have such feelings? What is truly troubling is that while this person is being told by society that all people are equal, they are also being told, in much more subtle ways, that people of color are different. Because of this conflict of societal norms, people have developed a tendency to shy away from the issue of race altogether. And our class discussion...was a perfect example.[14]

Bernida Reagan, the executive director of EBCLC, is also troubled by the class on difference, and by the larger impact of "race-blind" policies.[15] This is not the first time that a minority student has raised the issue of race in one of her classes and other students have been too uncomfortable to continue the discussion. She is concerned about what this means for the clinic and for society at large. In a law journal article discussing her concerns, Reagan notes that following the class on difference, many of the reflection pieces written by students were either silent on race as a difference or minimized its impact on clients or on the advocacy relationship. She states that this is symptomatic of what is happening in a "race-blind" society. Individuals, feeling it is inappropriate to see race, turn a blind eye to race, and consequently do not see the differences they need to understand in order to work across those differences. Reagan remarks,

The issues of race profiling, police abuse, and discrimination are issues that large numbers of white Americans never have to think about. White people do not have to think about racism, whereas people of color experience frequent acts of brutality, injustice, and unfairness on a daily basis because of their race. But differences in perception and experience are exactly the reasons why we must discuss race in "mixed company." If we are ever to move forward to true social equality, we must be able to honestly explore the power systems which govern our world and gain a greater understanding about how each person's experiences may limit opportunities or allow privilege.[16]

She adds, "Without the participation of diverse students and their forthright reflection and discussion, important issues will go unnoticed." Diversity in the student body and at the clinic, she asserts, is essential to broadening the perspectives of students who will be exposed to many different clients with many different perspectives. In learning to see difference and respond to it, students will become better lawyers, the kind that are needed in a racially diverse society. Reagan notes that at EBCLC, having a diverse staff of attorneys and law students is important to the clinic's diverse clients. She states, "[H]aving students of color and those reflective of the community serving as advocates can help reduce some of the inevitable barriers inherent in the advocate-client relationship. Similarly, having an advocate who is likely to have shared similar experiences, or who can communicate in the same language as the client, often increases the client's sense of trust and faith."[17]

Reagan, herself African American, observes, "It is also important that our clients see us—women, people of color and other subordinated groups—as capable, intelligent beings. Our clients and their children share a sense of pride and comfort when they see us in roles as lawyers, law students and people in charge. It gives them hope and optimism that is rare in this day and age. It challenges stereotypes to which we have all become accustomed." In her article, she laments the loss of affirmative action—a policy from which she has benefited—and worries about the consequences of this loss on communities of color. Reagan concludes, "The demolition of affirmative action is not just the loss of a remedy. It is a signal to my community that we can no longer take for granted a commitment in this society to equality and justice."[18]

What is happening in California and at Boalt in particular is distressing. The law school that once actively pursued diversity and flourished as a result, now sits by as anti–affirmative action measures take hold, and the ethos of diversity and excellence is replaced by an ethos of excellence and individualism. Reflecting on this change, Boalt alumnus Daniel Tellalian remarks, "The faculty and administration have sacrificed an incredibly proud legacy of commitment to diversity and excellence in order to avoid a confrontation that might affect their cozy careers."[19]

The situation on the larger campus at Berkeley is no better. In an editorial in the *Daily Californian,* Pedro Noguera, a Latino professor in the Ethnic Studies Department, speaks of the changes that anti–affirmative action measures have wrought on the Berkeley campus and expresses his intention of leaving the university:

[B]ecause of the law and the politics of California, I fear that this place has been changed forever, and that people like me will increasingly not be present. If I do leave Berkeley, it will not be with bitterness, but with sadness, because this was once a university that genuinely embraced the ideal that diversity and excellence were attainable, and that noble ideals such as free speech and human rights were important.

I sense this is no longer the case, and that we are becoming like so many other large universities more concerned with money than the values that previously distinguished us among the great universities of the world.[20]

Despite the alarming changes that have taken place at Berkeley and at Boalt, few people are discussing the issue. Sunil Gupta, a South Asian student who was away from Boalt for two years completing a joint degree, notes that the diversity issue is not foremost in the minds of most students. During his first year at Boalt, Gupta was very involved in the diversity issue. He had attended Berkeley as an undergraduate and had watched in amazement as the regents voted to end affirmative action. Once at the law school, he joined his voice with others in pleading with the administration and faculty to mitigate the impact of "race-blind" policies. Two years later, he returned to Boalt and asked several students, "What are the numbers like?" and no one seemed to know. In fact, it appeared that not many cared.[21]

Assistant Dean Lujuana Treadwell echoes this observation, stating that after several turbulent years, the most troubling time is now. People are no longer upset about diversity. "The numbers have gone down," she exclaims, "and the fact that no one seems to be talking about this, not the faculty, not the students, and not the administrators, is very troubling." She notes that in focus groups conducted over the previous summer to determine what students are concerned about, the issue of diversity did not come up. She is angry that the faculty has not engaged in the issue. "They could do something," she states, adding, "Diversity has always been important to me. The loss of diversity here makes me question whether this is where I want to be."[22]

Commenting on the attitude of resignation at Boalt, Sunil Gupta remarks, "There is a sense among students that there is no way to alter the situation." He notes, "Students are not thinking about pressuring the administration to change things for the better. Protest is not something people think about."[23] Khari Tillery admits, "I'm not sure what more we could do that hasn't been done already to pressure the administration."[24] He adds regretfully, "It's hard to mobilize students to take part in political action right now. Minority students are stretched thin, trying to hold student organizations together and survive the law school experience."

Norma Aguilar, now a third-year student, is herself disheartened. She has participated in the protests and advocacy efforts of the last several years and has worked closely with the outreach director to ensure that underrepresented minority students are contacted and encouraged to come to

Boalt. Referring to the decline in minority student enrollment that year, she notes that the admissions policy is still a major problem and that the real need is for the faculty to consider substantive changes to the policy. She notes, however, "We have tried for several years to get the faculty to look at substantive changes, but they are unwilling to do so. I'm not sure what more pressure from us would yield. They seem immovable."[25]

Aguilar regrets that no matter how much outreach or recruitment students undertake, whether the law school enrolls a significant number of underrepresented minority students still comes down to admissions. She reflects on the previous admissions cycle, "We didn't admit enough people, and those that got in were really worried about coming here because it doesn't seem like the school is trying too hard to increase the numbers of minority students." Expressing despair, she states, "Now it is a much larger problem than students can deal with because the reputation of Boalt among minority students is that it is an unfriendly place for students of color. You can't get over that within a thirty-minute conversation you have with someone over the phone."[26]

Khari Tillery remarks, "Sometimes I feel like there is no point in recruiting, since all we are doing is helping the school stay comfortable, when they are not supporting us in any way. I have often thought that if we did nothing and let the numbers fall even further, that Boalt would feel pressure to do something. But then there would be no students here to fight, and on balance, it is still a good idea to recruit students to Boalt." He expresses his disappointment with the law school. "I don't think the school really cares about the lack of diversity. If they did care, they would act, even if that meant challenging discriminatory laws. Instead, they have stayed well within the boundaries of the law. This is my biggest criticism of the administration."[27]

Tillery and Aguilar both agree that recruitment is not enough to bring about a diverse student body. According to Tillery, "It all comes down to how many people are admitted." He sighs, "I don't think the numbers are going to change much. I think three years of results of race-blind admissions show a pattern."[28] Dean Kay admits, "I don't think the situation is going to get better. It's a constant struggle."[29] Professor Robert Berring, who has chaired the Admissions Committee for the last several years, agrees: "We have to move away from strict numerical indicators. As long as we are wedded to these indicators as measures of merit, we will not be able to admit a substantial number of underrepresented minority students."[30] Nevertheless, former Associate Dean Cole, who stepped down when the 1998 enrollment was complete, believes that incrementalism could still make an important difference in a situation where each additional underrepresented minority student matters. Boalt lost momentum, he believes, when it should have built on the momentum from the 1998 turnaround, especially by finding ways to promote more private, race-based scholarships from Boalt alumni and Bay Area law firms and by appointing a faculty member to replace him to keep pushing new policies and experiments, implementing unfinished ones, and troubleshooting each stage of the admissions process.[31]

The LSAT—which the faculty has chosen to give "substantial" weight—continues to heavily influence admissions decisions that exclude many talented minorities. In a recent study, test scholar Linda Wightman demonstrates that as long as law schools rely heavily on the LSAT and on undergraduate grades to determine admissions, they will not be able to attain the level of diversity achieved under affirmative action. Such an admissions model, she asserts, will result in a law school student body that mirrors the ethnic makeup of law schools thirty years ago.[32] Subsequent studies conducted by William Kidder, using data compiled by Wightman, show that if admissions decisions are made exclusively on the basis of numerical indicators, the number of minority students will fall by more than half, as they have already done at Boalt. Illustrating the effect that the LSAT has on admissions, Kidder observes that minority students fare better when grades alone are considered (see table 8).

In their studies, Kidder and Wightman illustrate how the use of a "numbers-only" policy works to the disadvantage of *all* minority students, including Asian American students, and how, if adopted by law schools across the country, such a policy would eliminate a substantial number of minority lawyers in America. Wightman found in her study that, of the minority students who would have been rejected under a numbers-only policy, the vast majority graduated from law school and passed the bar. She concludes that a numbers-only policy is unjustifiable, given the fact that most of the minority students who would be excluded by such a policy are "fully capable of the rigors of legal education and of entering the legal profession."[33]

As the University of California demonstrates, heavy reliance on numerical indicators drastically diminishes the diversity of the student body. In the aftermath of SP-1 and Proposition 209, the three UC law schools—Boalt, Davis, and UCLA—have witnessed a dramatic decline in the enrollment of underrepresented minorities and have seen only a marginal increase in the enrollment of Asian Americans. Neoconservatives, however, use the small gains made by Asian Americans to assert that the end

TABLE 8. Actual Admissions versus Projected "UGPA Only" and LSAT/UGPA "Numbers Only" Admissions for 1991 Applicants to Accredited Law Schools

Race/Ethnicity	Actual Admitted	UGPA Only	LSAT/UGPA Numbers Only	Percentage Excluded under Numbers Only
African American	3,435	1,769	822	76%
Latino/Chicano	2,304	1,670	1,228	47%
Native American	302	199	177	41%
Asian American	2,312	1,954	1,727	25%
Minorities Total	8,353	5,592	3,954	53%
White	42,287	45,048	46,684	(Increase: 10%)

SOURCE: William C. Kidder, "Portia Denied: Unmasking Gender Bias on the LSAT and Its Relationship to Racial Diversity in Legal Education," 12 *Yale J. L. & Feminism* 1, table 2 (2000); William C. Kidder, "Situating Asian Pacific Americans in the Law School Affirmative Action Debate: Empirical Facts about Thernstrom's Rhetorical Acts," 7 *Asian L.J.* 29 (2000): 47, table 5. Hispanic, Mexican American and Puerto Rican figures are included in Latino/Chicano figures.

of affirmative action has had no disparate impact on people of color overall. Describing a numbers-based admissions policy that is devoid of any consideration of race as a "fair, open, and color-blind process," Harvard historian and neoconservative pundit Stephan Thernstrom states that such a process "does not greatly disadvantage racial minorities in general." "Indeed," he asserts, "Asians are distinctly better off when judged strictly as individuals, on the basis of their academic qualifications."[34] But the ban on affirmative action has resulted in negligible gains for Asian students at the three law schools, as compared to the substantial gains made by white students (see table 9).[35]

The neoconservative rhetoric that allies whites with Asians in the celebration of "race-blind" policies falls flat in the face of reality. Asian American students do not fill the seats that underrepresented minorities once held. Though as a whole the number of Asian Americans has not diminished, the numbers of some Asian groups have declined precipitously. Particularly hard hit are Filipinos, who constitute one of the largest Asian subgroups in the United States but who are notably underrepresented in higher education, especially at the law schools. At Boalt, in the three years prior to the ban on affirmative action, the law school enrolled thirteen Filipinos. But in the three years following the ban, Boalt enrolled only three, all of them in 1998. Filipinos and other Southeast Asians are being "zeroed out." This phenomenon, coupled with the negligible gains made by Asians overall, leaves white applicants as the primary beneficiaries of "race-blind" policies.[36]

TABLE 9. Percentage of White and Asian Enrollment at UC Law Schools before and after SP-1 and Proposition 209

Years	Boalt		Davis		UCLA		Total	
	White	Asian	White	Asian	White	Asian	White	Asian
1994–1996	62%	15%	66%	16%	55%	20%	60%	17%
1997–1999	75%	16%	75%	15%	67%	22%	72%	18%

SOURCE: William C. Kidder, "Situating Asian Pacific Americans in the Law School Affirmative Action Debate: Empirical Facts about Thernstrom's Rhetorical Acts," 7 *Asian L. J.* 29 (2000): 39, 44, tables 1 and 3.

The disparate results of "race-blind" policies are due largely to the LSAT, which William Kidder and test scholar David White have shown to have an identifiable and negative impact on minority students. In an article published in the *Yale Journal of Law and Feminism*, Kidder reviews the possible sources of bias in the LSAT: stereotype threat, speededness, differential guessing, subject matter selection, and item bias.[37] Stereotype threat refers to a form of bias not on the test itself, but in the psychosocial environment in which standardized testing occurs. Speededness refers to the ability of test takers to complete the test within given time constraints. Differential guessing refers to possible differences between subgroups in their proclivity to guess when they do not know the answer. Subject matter selection addresses how choices about content can influence score differences between subgroups. Finally, item bias refers to individual questions that pose extra burdens for certain test takers based on differences in background.

With respect to item bias—an area of long-standing concern—Kidder notes that despite the Law School Admission Council's claims otherwise, biased and offensive questions continue to appear.[38] In the early 1980s, the LSAC removed the most egregious test questions, such as those that dealt with stereotypes of ethnic groups, and incorporated sensitivity review panels. But questions yielding different answers along racial lines persist on the LSAT. One such question, which appeared on the test in 1988, addresses opportunities in higher education for women and minorities. The passage, question, and answer choices read as follows:

The universities should not yield to the illiberal directives of the Office [for] Civil Rights that mandate affirmative action in hiring faculties. The effect of the directives to hire minorities and women under threat of losing crucial financial support is to compel universities to hire unqualified minorities and women and to discriminate against qualified non-minorities and men. This is just as much a manifestation of racism, even if originally unintended, as the racism the original presidential directive was designed to correct. The consequences of imposing any criterion other than that of qualified talent on our educational establishments are sure to be disastrous in the quest for new knowledge and truth, as well as subversive of our democratic values.

Which of the fol[l]owing, if true, would considerably weaken the argument above?

I.   The directive requires universities to hire minorities and women when no other applicant is better qualified.

II. The directive requires universities to hire minorities and women only up to the point that these groups are represented on faculties in proportion to their representation in the population at large.

III. Most university employees are strongly in favor of the directive.[39]

The test taker is asked to choose one or more of the statements above. Credit is given for choosing the first statement. But the second statement, for which no credit is given, is also a reasonable answer if a certain assumption—an assumption that many minorities are likely to make—is made about affirmative action. A test taker who assumes that women and minorities possess equal talent might reasonably conclude that the second statement—indicating that affirmative action hiring practices are capped by the proportion of women and minorities in the population—*weakens* the argument that affirmative action forces "universities to hire unqualified minorities and women." However, a test taker who assumes that hiring in proportion to population statistics ushers in hordes of unqualified women and minorities will likely conclude that the second statement *strengthens* the argument that affirmative action forces "universities to hire unqualified minorities and women." A test taker making this assumption will reject the second statement, choose the first, and be rewarded for having "legal aptitude."[40]

Kidder explains that in the sensitivity review process used by LSAC to determine whether a question is biased, a question is removed from the LSAT only if it creates racial disparities that deviate from disparities in overall test scores. In other words, bias is treated as a discrete, accidental deviation from the overall absence of bias on the test. However, Kidder and White have demonstrated that the test is not free of bias and that minorities from the same undergraduate schools with the same undergraduate grades consistently score lower than their white peers. In assuming that the test overall is free of bias, the sensitivity review process fails to identify anything but the most problematic questions, allowing questions with more subtle racial disparities to remain on the test.[41]

To the extent that law schools rely on the LSAT to determine who should and should not be admitted, the test serves as a gatekeeper, operating to keep out many minority students, most of whom would succeed if given the chance. But overreliance on the LSAT damages the statistical validity of the test.[42] The LSAT was designed for a narrow purpose—to predict grades in the first year of law school. When it is used for a broader purpose—such as predicting overall law school performance or performance in the profession—the test falters. While little research exists on the correlation between the LSAT and long-term success in the legal profession, evidence indicates that the correlation between the two is meager at best. A recent study of University of Michigan Law School alumni from the 1970s to the 1990s found that LSAT scores and UGPAs bore no relationship to measures of success in the legal profession—such as income or career satisfaction—for those alumni.[43] The rationale that heavy reliance on the LSAT is defensible because the test predicts first-year grades, which in turn predict second- and third-year grades, which in turn predict success as a lawyer, is flawed. Inferences about the LSAT become successively more tenuous the further one moves from the variable the test was intended to predict.[44]

Overreliance on the LSAT places law schools in a precarious legal position. In 1992, the U.S. Supreme Court held in *United States v. Fordice* that a university, guilty of past official racial segregation, cannot rely exclusively on a standardized test where the use of the test has an adverse impact on minorities—thus perpetuating the past illegal segregation—and where the producers of a test have recommended that it not be used as the sole factor in admissions decisions.[45] The situation of law schools is somewhat analogous in that LSAC consistently warns law schools not to give excessive weight to small differences in LSAT scores, urging them to use factors other than numerical indicators to make admissions decisions. The cautionary policies issued by LSAC forewarn,

Do not use the LSAT score as a sole criterion for admission. The LSAT should be used as only one of several criteria for evaluation and should not be given undue weight solely because its use is convenient. Those who set admission policies and criteria should always keep in mind the fact that the LSAT does not measure every discipline-related skill necessary for academic work, nor does it measure other factors important to academic success....

Do not place excessive significance on score differences. Scores should be viewed as approximate indicators rather than exact measures of an applicant's abilities. Distinctions on the basis of LSAT scores should be made among applicants only when those score differences are reliable.[46]

Law schools, however, rely heavily if not predominantly on LSAT scores, ignoring LSAC recommendations against such practices.[47] Such use of the LSAT by law schools that have engaged in prior state-sponsored segregation may subject them to lawsuits.

At Boalt, Professor Marjorie Shultz surmises that the emphasis on the LSAT as well as undergraduate grades is due in part to the absence of other validated predictors. This emphasis is unfortunate, she believes, because traditional numerical indicators are a narrow measure of the skills needed to be a successful law student and especially a practicing lawyer.[48] The LSAT, for example, only measures the ability to read and understand complex materials, to analyze facts and relationships that present legal problems, and to reason logically to draw legal conclusions. However, other skills are needed. The second and third years of law school focus more on substance, policy, and problem solving, and students are required to conduct research and write papers. As students enter the legal profession, they need all of the skills acquired in three years of law school courses as well as those acquired through clinical, work, moot court, and law journal experience. Lawyers must be able to identify legal and ethical problems, investigate and synthesize facts, research and analyze law, organize and manage information, counsel and serve as advocates for clients, and negotiate and solve problems. In addition, they must be motivated, self-disciplined, and ethical.

As head of the Merit Committee at Boalt, Shultz proposes identifying, developing, and measuring other factors that relate to success in law school and in the legal profession. She is seeking to translate these factors into predictable criteria for use in conjunction with traditional numerical indicators in the law school admissions process.[49] Shultz envisions this project taking several years and several hundred thousand dollars to complete, and has submitted grant proposals to undertake the project. Harvard Law School professor Lani Guinier suggests a less ambitious approach. She proposes broadening the criteria used to select for beneficiaries of affirmative action — criteria such as the ability to lead, overcome obstacles, and follow through on goals, as well as a record of community service — to select for all incoming students. Guinier asserts that because affirmative action has been so successful in identifying promising candidates, it should not be understood simply as a race-based exception to the general admission rule of rank-ordering test scores and grades; instead, it should be used to rethink how law schools admit everyone.[50] This approach, however, would require law schools such as Boalt to lessen the weight of traditional numerical criteria, particularly the LSAT.

Unfortunately, Boalt remains wedded to the LSAT as a measure of excellence, and a recent change in leadership has only increased its allegiance to the test. In the fall of 1999, Dean Kay announced her resignation, opening the door for new leadership to affect, for better or worse, the state of diversity at the law school. In the winter of 2000, over the objection of every woman and virtually every minority professor, the faculty recommended and Chancellor Berdahl selected Professor John Dwyer to become the new dean of Boalt Hall. Dwyer is a prominent environmental law scholar who joined the faculty in 1984. He is a graduate of Boalt who, prior to joining the faculty, clerked for U.S. Supreme Court Justice Sandra Day O'Connor. Among his many accomplishments, he was the 1997 recipient of Boalt Hall's Rutter Award for Excellence in Teaching. But Professor Dwyer's record on the diversity issue is cause for great concern, and for that reason women and minority faculty members opposed his candidacy.

While at Boalt, Dwyer has consistently opposed measures to mitigate the impact of "race-blind" admissions and has actively supported the use of the LSAT as an "objective" measure of merit.[51] For example, he voted against the Cole Report, which helped soften the blow of the affirmative action ban, and he resisted the elimination of a grade adjustment policy, which ended the practice of raising or lowering an applicant's UGPA based on the average LSAT score of his or her university. In addition, he opposed the "banding" of LSAT scores, which alleviated the reliance on statistically insignificant differences between scores. Dwyer has not shown a commitment to the issue of diversity in the past, nor has he shown a vision of how to increase diversity at Boalt in the future. This has served as a wake-up call to those concerned with diversity.

In February 2000, prior to Dwyer's appointment, a group of concerned students, representing eleven student organizations, including all of the student-of-color organizations, who had previously felt defeated and had not met to discuss the state of diversity at the law school that year, convened to respond to Dwyer's selection. Afraid that the situation might go from bad to worse, they wrote a letter to Chancellor Berdahl asking him to reopen the dean search:

Although Professor Dwyer is a well respected academic in his field... we believe he lacks several qualities essential for leading Boalt Hall at this critical juncture....
[With respect to diversity] Professor Dwyer has shown neither a history of commitment to this issue nor a current vision that Boalt so badly needs....

We need a Dean whose creativity and leadership in addressing these challenges will restore Berkeley's fundamental commitment to the diversity of its student body and to serving the public interest. We need a Dean with an innovative and inspired vision as Boalt takes the lead in this essential public debate. We do not believe that John Dwyer is that person.[52]

In an article in the *San Francisco Chronicle* covering the contentious appointment of Professor Dwyer, third-year law student Michael Murphy stated that the law school is at a critical juncture. "We are a public institution that this year will graduate two African Americans out of 300 graduates. If somebody is coming into the deanship and does not see [this] as a crisis, that is a disaster."[53] Former dean Jesse Choper, who served on the faculty committee that interviewed candidates for the position of dean, dismissed student complaints as "politics" and said Dwyer would make a "truly great" dean. Since the appointment, Dwyer has made clear his priorities for the law school.[54] Changing the admissions policy to increase minority representation at Boalt is not among them. High on the list of priorities, however, is improving the law school's ranking in *U.S. News and World Report,* a goal achieved in part by admitting students with higher LSAT scores. Dwyer is success-oriented, and the ranking of the school means a lot to him and to other members of the faculty. It appears to mean more than the inclusion of underrepresented minority students at the law school. This is disconcerting to Angela Harris, the only tenured African American professor at Boalt.[55]

Harris arrived at Boalt in 1988 after graduating from the University of Chicago Law School, where she was one of only four black students in her class. She was unhappy and felt alienated as a law student, and had reservations about joining the Boalt faculty, which was and continues to be predominantly white and male. As a leading critical race scholar, she won tenure in 1992, but thought about leaving when the regents eliminated affirmative action and the law school faculty failed to respond in a meaningful way. Following the vote to end affirmative action, Harris spent two years teaching at other universities, where she was offered tenured positions, but decided to stay in Berkeley because she found the then still diverse students at Boalt more interesting and more dynamic than students she had taught elsewhere. But remaining at Boalt has been difficult. She believes the faculty suffers from low morale and appears incapable of discussing difficult issues, not the least of which is the issue of minority representation. With respect to the LSAT, she feels that the faculty is in a state of denial. For the most part, faculty members do not perceive the test to be biased, or, if they do, they view the bias as insignificant and are unwilling to lessen the weight of the LSAT because doing so might threaten the law school's standing.

Harris sees this denial as a dangerous position to take, especially with no viable alternative to increase minority admissions. The law school is at a crossroads. The decline in minority enrollment affects not only diversity in the student body, but also interest in intellectual and policy issues that affect people of color. Issues of race are rarely raised in class discussions. When they are raised, they are often discussed in a superficial manner. A white first-year law student interested in having deeper discussions about race notes, "We never get past the things that everyone knows, and we never get to a more sophisticated discussion of race. The next level of critical thinking is totally missing."[56] Referring to a question asked in class, "When can we as middle-class white people stop feeling guilty for things that happened a hundred years ago," another white student observes regretfully, "A lot of people here think racism is something that happened a long time ago." He adds, "Nobody wants to talk about race anymore."[57]

The narrowing of perspectives within the law school community has made Boalt a less attractive place to be, not only for minority students but for minority faculty members as well. Professor Harris states, "We must attract a new generation of diverse students to help the faculty move towards interesting intellectual and policy issues, or else declining student interest in these issues will lead to an exodus of faculty of color."[58] Professor Robert Berring echoes these concerns: "Given the demographics of California," he states, "it is bizarre to maintain policies that perpetuate racially elite institutions." He adds, "If the law school does not actively include underrepresented minorities, the institution will falter for lack of legitimacy in a diverse state."[59]

Previous admissions cycles have made clear that business as usual will not yield an increase in the number of underrepresented minorities. If the law school is going to become more diverse, the dean and the faculty will have to do more than they have done already to remove embedded preferences and balance the scales of privilege. They will have to act creatively and affirmatively to mitigate the impact of "race-blind" admissions—something they have been unwilling or unable to do in the last several years. In a powerful editorial criticizing the inaction of the law school dean and faculty, Boalt alumnus Dirk Tillotson, an African American, writes in the *San Francisco Daily Journal*,

The relationship of silence to complicity is a well-worn path. However overused the metaphor, it remains apt in today's complicit approval of the ending of affirmative action and its devastating effects on the University of California's most elite campuses and programs, particularly in the law schools....

As the elite opportunities that were once available shrink, I shudder to think where we will be in a few years. We are a diverse state with a diverse populace, holding diverse understandings of our world. Law is supposed to be the universal glue that binds us. Law school is supposed to provide the discourse whereby our narrow understandings are enriched, to train lawyers who are able to move beyond their own frame of reference in assessing and shaping legal arguments.

In Boalt Hall's current incarnation that goal cannot be met. Instead of being a vehicle for improvement of the public by educating the excluded and broadening understandings, Boalt has emerged as an insulated institution that most likely will further undercut the link between justice, law and minority communities. We are sliding backward from the dreams of "one nation indivisible" toward division, separation and disparity of opportunity.

Increasing inequality will reach a breaking point sometime, and we will all pay the costs. The complicit whimper that saluted the passing of affirmative action will be augmented by a bang, whether it is the public support that leads to democratic action, or the crackling of timber under the heat of flames. Ultimately there is only one way to go. The question is how far back we will move before righting ourselves.[60]

In an extensive study of the long-term consequences of affirmative action, focusing mostly on African Americans, William G. Bowen, former president of Princeton, and Derek Bok, former president of Harvard, credit race-conscious admissions policies with creating a black professional middle class. Bowen and Bok estimate that had affirmative action not been used at the most competitive universities in the country over the previous thirty years, more than half of the black students who attended these universities would have been rejected. Of the black students who would have been rejected based on numbers alone, a sample survey shows that more than 30 percent attained professional degrees or doctorates, and more than 40 percent have become leaders in their communities. In their study, Bowen and Bok found that African American graduates from elite colleges, most of whom received affirmative action consideration, were significantly more likely than their white classmates to lead community service organizations. This held true for graduates who went on to get law, medical, business, master's, and doctoral degrees.[61] A recent study of law school alumni seconds these findings by showing that black and other minority alumni provide considerably more service to minority clients, tend to do more pro bono work, do more mentoring of younger attorneys, and sit on the boards of more community organizations than do white alumni.[62]

Since the 1960s, as a result of affirmative action in higher education, the number of black physicians in the nation has almost doubled, and their share of attorneys and engineers has almost tripled. Black representation in Congress has increased from four to forty-one members, and the total number of black elected officials has risen from less than three hundred to more than eight thousand.[63] African Americans and other minorities have made great strides, but they still have far to go. The playing field is not yet level, and affirmative action is still necessary to close the opportunity gap between minorities and whites. Despite the progress that has occurred, the black middle class is still much smaller, proportionately, than the white middle class. Furthermore, the lack of accumulated wealth (passed down from one generation to the next) puts blacks in a more precarious economic situation—even the highest-earning blacks have less than a quarter of the net financial assets of whites earning comparable incomes—making it much more difficult for blacks to pass on middle-class status to their children.[64] On average, racial minorities still earn less than similarly educated white men and are still subject to conscious and unconscious prejudice.

As of 1997, African Americans made up 11 percent of the workforce but less than 7 percent of all executive, administrative, and managerial employees, less than 5 percent of all editors and reporters, approximately 4 percent of all physicians and engineers, and less than 3 percent of all lawyers and dentists.[65] In contrast, white men constituted only 33 percent of the population but were 48 percent of the college graduates, 85 percent of tenured professors, 85 percent of partners in major law firms, 90 percent of the U.S. Senate, 95 percent of officers in major corporations, 97 percent of school superintendents, 99 percent of professional sports team owners, and 100 percent of U.S. presidents.[66]

Affirmative action at the universities has played an important role in furthering racial progress. Race-inclusive policies have not only created new generations of minority professionals and community leaders, but have also affected the learning environment on campus, making interactions between students of different races possible. In their study of long-term consequences of affirmative action, Bowen and Bok demonstrate that, contrary to claims that racial diversity has led to rigid self-segregation, a majority of students have known "well" at least two students of other racial backgrounds. They contend that racial diversity on campus has heavily influenced increased student acceptance of other cultures, participation in community service programs, and growth in other aspects of civic responsibility. They assert, "As educators have long surmised, racial diversity does appear to bring about positive results in increasing mutual understanding of whites and minority students, enhancing their ability to live and work together."[67] In a nation becoming more diverse every day, increasing cross-cultural understanding and communication is critical.

Recent studies have shown that people of different races still live separately from one another, residing in different communities, attending separate elementary and secondary schools, and rarely sustaining meaningful contact with one another.[68] This lack of contact fosters misconceptions and mistrust on all sides and affords little or no opportunity either to disrupt the perpetuation of racial stereotypes or to experience the richness of different racial and ethnic communities. Social psychologist Patricia Gurin contends, however, that the university provides an opportunity for students of different racial backgrounds to interact and plays a critical role in increasing sensitivity to, understanding of, and comfort with individuals of different racial backgrounds. In an in-depth empirical analysis measuring the educational benefits of diversity, Gurin shows that students who attend racially diverse universities "are better prepared to participate more fully in our pluralistic democracy when they are educated in such a setting." She finds that "[students] are better able to appreciate the ideas of others when they interact with diverse peers on an equal footing. They are more equipped to understand and consider multiple perspectives, deal with the conflicts that different perspectives sometimes create, and appreciate the common values and integrative forces that harness differences in pursuit of the common good."[69]

Gurin contends that patterns of racial segregation and separation historically rooted in our national life can be broken by cross-cultural interactions in higher education. Diversity experiences, she notes, have impressive effects on the extent to which graduates live racially and ethnically integrated lives in the postcollege world. She found that students with the most diversity experiences during college had the most cross-racial interaction five years after leaving college.[70] Other studies suggest that diversity experiences are most critical for white students, who disproportionately come from highly segregated neighborhoods and elementary and secondary schools. A national study of school segregation patterns in 1996–97 found that whites are by far the most segregated ethnic group in American schools and remain highly isolated even though the nation's school enrollment is approximately 36 percent nonwhite.[71] This isolation continues into college, where white students have the most segregated friendship patterns on campus of all ethnic groups.[72] But as Gurin and other researchers have shown, this segregation begins to break down as white students increase their interaction with students of different racial backgrounds.

A recent study of law students at Harvard University and the University of Michigan found that white students, because they lacked contact with persons of different racial backgrounds as they grew up, were most in need of diversity experiences in law school. Both white and nonwhite students overwhelmingly (90 percent) described diversity in their respective law schools as a positive experience.[73] When asked whether diversity had affected their "ability to work more effectively and/or get along better with members of other races," a clear majority (70 percent) of students said yes.[74] A large majority also stated that their views on a number of issues had changed as a result of cross-cultural interactions: on the issue of "equity in the criminal justice system" (81 percent); "conditions in various social and economic institutions" (82 percent); "civil rights" (77 percent); and "the kind of legal or community issues that you will encounter as a professional" (75 percent).[75]

The type of learning taking place at the Harvard and Michigan law schools is only possible in a racially diverse setting. To create such a learning environment, universities have to admit a racially diverse student body. At competitive institutions, this means looking at more than grades and test scores. It means deciding which set of applicants, considered individually and collectively, will contribute to a diverse and dynamic learning environment that will, in the words of the Association of American Colleges and Universities, "nourish the habits of the heart and mind... need[ed] to make diversity work in daily life." It means employing affirmative action to enroll a diverse student body that can "experience engagement across differences as a value and a public good," thereby fostering cross-cultural communication and understanding.[76] In California, at the most prestigious campuses, the ability to create such an environment is diminishing.

In a state that has become a racial plurality, where a racial majority no longer exists, it is tragic that the most competitive schools can no longer create a learning environment that is representative of and responsive to a diverse population. In 2002, California will be 49 percent white, 32 percent Latino, 12 percent Asian American, 7 percent African American, and approximately 1 percent Native American.[77] Yet in that year, Boalt will graduate a class that is 77 percent white, 6 percent Latino, 13 percent Asian American, 3 percent African American, and 1 percent Native American. Those students will enter the California Bar, which is 83 percent white, 4 percent Latino, 6 percent Asian American, 2 percent African American, less than 1 percent Native American, and 4 percent identified as "mixed race" or "other."[78] As Boalt alumnus Dirk Tillotson observes, "[T]hese imbalances are not random results generated by equal opportunity. They are the results of a historically exclusionary legal system and a present social and educational system that is formally tilted towards those advantaged in the past."[79]

In California, prior to the elimination of race-conscious policies, affirmative action had been a way to recognize these imbalances and correct for them. In other parts of the country, and in private universities in California, affirmative action continues to open doors of opportunity that would otherwise be closed, and proves to be an effective means of including historically excluded racial minorities in higher education. But race-conscious policies are under attack and in some states, like California, have already given way to the "race-blind" rhetoric of neoconservatives. In at least four other states—Texas, Washington, Florida, and Georgia—affirmative action has been eliminated at public universities, further limiting the opportunities of minority students.

At the University of Texas, affirmative action was eliminated by court order in 1996, one year after the regents at the University of California voted to adopt a "race-blind" admissions policy. In 1992, four white applicants who had been rejected from the law school in Austin brought suit against the university, charging that the law school's admissions policy—which used different cutoffs on standardized test scores for white students and minority students—violated their rights to equal protection under the Fourteenth Amendment. They lost their case in federal district court but appealed to the Fifth Circuit. In *Hopwood v. Texas,* a three-judge panel of the Fifth Circuit Court of Appeals ruled that the law school unconstitutionally used race in denying admission to the four students.[80] The three-judge panel also declared that colleges in the circuit—which covers Texas, Louisiana, and Mississippi—could no longer abide by the 1978 Supreme Court decision known as *Bakke,* which had permitted universities to use race as one factor among many in making admissions decisions.[81]

In July 1996, the Supreme Court declined to hear the *Hopwood* case on mootness grounds (in part because the law school had already abandoned the policy in question), and the Fifth Circuit decision stood. Supreme Court Justice Ruth Bader Ginsburg noted that the constitutionality of using race or national origin in higher education admissions is "an issue of great national importance," but stated that the Court would wait to hear a case in which a lower court had issued a judgment "on a program genuinely in controversy."[82] In 1997, in the first law school admissions cycle following the ruling, minority enrollment at the University of Texas plummeted—African American enrollment dropped 90 percent, and Latino enrollment dropped 50 percent.[83] Two years later, in 1999, the percentage of African Americans at the law school (1.4 percent) was lower than the percentage in the fall of 1950 (2.1 percent), when the U.S. Supreme Court voted to end de jure segregation in *Sweatt v. Painter.*[84]

The next state to end affirmative action in higher education was Washington. In 1998, voters approved a ballot initiative known as I-200, which mirrored Proposition 209 in California, prohibiting the consideration of race in public education, contracting, and hiring. The initiative was introduced by State Representative Scott Smith, who had once applied to the Seattle police force and been rejected because, he claimed, of reverse discrimination. Smith had difficulty getting the two hundred thousand signatures needed to place the measure on the ballot in Washington, but was rescued by Ward Connerly who, riding on the success of 209, supplied the campaign with close to $200,000 to obtain the necessary signatures to put I-200 on the ballot.[85] Connerly raised additional money through his American Civil Rights Institute and, in conjunction with publishing mogul Steve Forbes, funded the bulk of the I-200 media campaign that preceded the election.

Opponents of the initiative mounted a formidable opposition campaign, but in contrast to California, they enjoyed the support of the governor, Gary Locke—the first Chinese American to be elected governor in the continental United States. Locke was a Democrat, and with him came the support of the Democratic Party and some of the largest corporations in the state—Microsoft, Boeing, Starbucks, Eddie Bauer, and Weyerhauser. General Colin Powell also weighed in on the side of the opposition, telling voters, "The language [of the initiative] is simple and elegant, but the results are diabolical. Affirmative action has a goal of helping to remove a contamination from this country. Three hundred years of white male preference are slowly being eroded away. My fear is that Initiative 200 would stop that progress." Despite these words, in November 1998, in a state where 86 percent of the population is white, 58 percent of the electorate voted to end "preferences" in public education, employment, and contracting.[86] Relishing the victory, Ward Connerly told the press, "[T]wo down and forty-eight to go."[87]

In 1999, with momentum on his side, Connerly turned his attention to Florida, where he introduced a 209 copycat initiative called the Florida Civil Rights Initiative. But in Florida, Connerly ran into more difficulty than he had in Washington or California. From the start, Republican Governor Jeb Bush let Connerly know that he was not welcome in Florida. In a letter to Connerly, Bush wrote, "[A] bitter political cam-

paign that divides Florida by race and ethnicity would keep us from focusing on more pressing issues."[88] Florida was a diverse state and neither
the governor nor his brother in Texas, Governor George Bush, who was
running for president of the United States, could afford to lose the minority vote. In an effort to preempt Connerly, Governor Jeb Bush introduced the One Florida plan, which eliminated affirmative action in,
among other areas, university admissions but sought to maintain diversity by guaranteeing admission to a state university for the top 20 percent of each high school class.

The "20 percent plan" resembled the "4 percent plan" in California
and the "10 percent plan" in Texas and carried with it some of the same
problems.[89] Like the other percent plans, the 20 percent plan was not expected to substantially increase diversity by distributing admissions geo-
graphically. Though minority schools benefit from percentage plans that
draw students from each high school, many of these schools do not send
students to the university. In Texas, for example, though the University
of Texas admits the top 10 percent of each high school, only half of the
state's high schools send students to the university. Many of the schools
that do not send students are predominantly minority, and university officials suspect that the students coming from these schools lack the financial resources to enroll, are unaware of the academic programs offered by
the university, or are hesitant to move far from home.[90]

Schools that do send students to the university do not necessarily send
those—minority or white—who are best prepared to succeed in college.
The class-rank system, on which the percentage plan is based, is a narrow
assessment of student potential. It ignores "special talents, interests, or
experiences beyond the academic criteria that demonstrate unusual promise for leadership, achievement, and service."[91] Concerned only with
numbers, the percentage plan also discourages students from taking more
challenging classes, rewarding class rank over rigorous coursework. With
so much at stake, it is not clear that percentage plans will better serve universities to admit a capable and diverse student body that will contribute
to a dynamic and stimulating learning environment.

In February 2000, despite concerns surrounding percentage plans and
protests against the elimination of affirmative action (two black legislators
had staged a sit-in inside the governor's office, and more than eleven
thousand people had marched on the capitol, leading Governor Bush to
drop the provisions of the One Florida plan that dealt with state contracting), the Florida Board of Regents voted unanimously to endorse
the One Florida plan. In May, the legislature approved the plan and

ended affirmative action at the public universities in Florida.[92] In that same month, Ward Connerly, unable to focus public attention on his Civil Rights Initiative and unable to collect the five hundred thousand signatures necessary to put the measure on the ballot in Florida, called off his campaign. He vowed to return in 2002, and criticized Governor Bush for not going far enough in ending traditional affirmative action programs. He told reporters that he was considering campaigns in Colorado, Oregon, and Michigan, but still wanted a showdown in Florida "because Florida is sort of in transition between the old South and new America. It's a microcosm of the nation."[93]

Later that summer, Georgia added its name to the growing list of states ending affirmative action in university admissions. In July 2000, a federal district court judge ruled in a reverse discrimination case that the admissions policy at the University of Georgia—which gave an edge to a small fraction of borderline applicants who were black—was unconstitutional. In a strongly worded opinion that made *Hopwood* look subdued, the district court judge found that Justice Powell's opinion in *Bakke* is not binding precedent, though it does carry some persuasive weight. Citing *Hopwood* and applying concepts from remedial affirmative action cases—in which race-conscious policies were implemented to correct for discrimination and not to achieve diversity—the judge determined that diversity is not a compelling interest, stating, "To base racial preferences upon an amorphous, unquantifiable, and temporally unlimited goal is to engage in naked racial balancing." The judge found that the University of Georgia did not "meaningfully show how racial diversity actually fosters educational benefits," characterizing the evidence on the value of diversity (based on the testimony of a former university president) as mere speculation and anecdote.[94] One month after the ruling, the university decided to appeal the case to the U.S. Court of Appeals for the Eleventh Circuit but announced that it would discontinue its controversial admissions practices while the lawsuit was pending.[95] Georgia thus became the fourth state to eliminate affirmative action at its public university.

In December 2000, however, three federal courts issued decisions *affirming* the use of race-conscious admissions to admit a diverse student body, demonstrating that the debate over affirmative action is far from over. These decisions—issued in Washington, Texas, and Michigan—contradict previous federal court decisions in *Hopwood* (Texas) and *Johnson* (Georgia), holding that an interest in diversity does not justify affirmative action. The conflicting rulings may compel the Supreme Court to review—for the first time since *Bakke* in 1978—the constitutionality of race-conscious admissions programs. In *Bakke,* Justice Powell issued the guiding opinion for a divided court, holding that educational institutions can use race as one factor among many in the admission of a diverse student body as long as quotas (a specific number of places set aside for members of minority groups) are not employed. Since *Bakke,* the Supreme Court has taken a restrictive view of affirmative action and has stated that race can only be used in very narrowly tailored circumstances.[96] Some courts, such as the Fifth Circuit Court of Appeals in *Hopwood* and the federal district court in *Johnson,* interpret this to mean that the principles of *Bakke* no longer apply. But at least three other courts disagree.

In the first of three rulings in December, the Ninth Circuit Court of Appeals held that *Bakke* remains good law and that diversity remains a compelling interest justifying race-conscious admissions.[97] In *Smith v. University of Washington Law School,* four white applicants sued the law school in a class action lawsuit brought by the Center for Individual Rights (which also represented white plaintiffs in the *Hopwood* case). The CIR filed the suit in 1997, when students were denied admission to the law school, and charged the school with reverse discrimination. In 1999, a federal district court judge dismissed the case as moot, following the passage of I-200 in November 1998. The judge also ruled that Powell's opinion in *Bakke*—supporting the use of race as a plus factor to achieve educational diversity—is still good law.[98]

The CIR appealed, and in December 2000, the Ninth Circuit affirmed the district court ruling, finding that the case was indeed moot, in light of the voter-passed initiative, and that *Bakke* remains the law of the land.[99] In its ruling, the Ninth Circuit acknowledged more recent Supreme Court cases disapproving of race-conscious decisions in non-educational settings (such as in contracting and hiring), yet it concluded that only the Supreme Court can overrule *Bakke,* even if the rationale behind *Bakke* has been undermined by subsequent Supreme Court decisions. The CIR subsequently appealed the case to the Supreme Court, but the justices declined to review it, letting stand the Ninth Circuit ruling.[100] The ruling means that, for now, race-based admissions policies that meet the principles laid out in *Bakke* are legally permissible in the states—other than California and Washington, which have passed referendums prohibiting the consideration of race—within the Ninth Circuit. Apart from California and Washington, the Ninth Circuit includes Alaska, Arizona, Hawaii, Idaho, Montana, Nevada, and Oregon.

Two weeks after the Ninth Circuit affirmed the applicability of *Bakke* and the constitutionality of race-conscious admissions, the Fifth Circuit

Court of Appeals, in a strange turn of events in the *Hopwood* case, ruled the same. Following the 1996 ruling in *Hopwood*, in which a three-judge panel of the Fifth Circuit held that diversity-based, race-conscious admissions programs were unconstitutional because *Bakke* was no longer good law, the case was remanded to the same federal district court judge who issued the original ruling to determine remedies. Though the four white plaintiffs requested $5.4 million in damages and $1.5 million in attorney fees, the federal judge found that none of the plaintiffs would have been admitted to the law school under a "race-blind" admissions system and awarded the prospective students one dollar in damages and cut their requested attorney fees in half. But the judge also issued a permanent injunction prohibiting the University of Texas and all other public universities in Texas from using race as a consideration in admissions and financial aid. The injunction, issued in 1998, gave the university a legal basis to appeal the entire question of whether affirmative action is permissible and whether *Bakke* can still be applied.[101]

Having suffered the consequences of "race-blind" policies and having learned that, as in California, there is no substitute for the consideration of race in the admission of a diverse student body, the Board of Regents of the University of Texas voted to appeal the injunction. In asking the Fifth Circuit to hear the case again, a lawyer for the university told a different three-judge panel than had originally ruled in the case, "Four years ago, this court put the University of Texas in a crucible when it became the only circuit court to reject *Bakke*. This court must now confront the earlier panel decision."[102] In December 2000, the new Fifth Circuit panel lifted the district court injunction for failure to support the injunction with written findings of fact and conclusions of law, as required by federal rules of procedure.[103] Without findings of fact or conclusions of law, the panel could not rule on the validity of the district court injunction or the previous Fifth Circuit bar on affirmative action. The panel ordered the district court to conduct an evidentiary hearing to determine whether the injunction should be reinstated. But it also held that an absolute prohibition on affirmative action impermissibly conflicts with the holding in *Bakke*—that the consideration of race is permissible in some circumstances. In finding that *Bakke* is still good law and that affirmative action is still permissible (although not yet in Texas), the panel adds its weight—the weight of the Fifth Circuit—to that of the Ninth Circuit in affirming race-conscious admissions programs.

In the third ruling issued in December, a federal district court judge in Michigan upheld the use of race in one of two related cases that are expected to be appealed all the way to the Supreme Court. The two cases,

Gratz v. Bollinger and *Grutter v. Bollinger,* originated in 1997, when the Center for Individual Rights again brought a reverse discrimination case, this time on behalf of unsuccessful white applicants to the undergraduate college and to the law school at the University of Michigan. In both cases the CIR contests the use of race to admit "less qualified" or "equally qualified" black and Latino applicants and directly challenges the diversity rationale underlying affirmative action programs at universities across the country.

The University of Michigan maintains, however, that the Constitution and federal civil rights statutes, as interpreted by *Bakke,* permit it to take race and ethnicity into account in order to create a diverse student body. A racially diverse student body, contends the university, produces significant educational benefits because of the current state of segregation and separation along racial lines in America. These benefits, the university argues, constitute a "compelling government interest" which justifies the consideration of race and ethnicity in university admissions. In an opinion piece published in the *Washington Post,* Lee Bollinger, the president of the university, and Nancy Cantor, the provost, assert that the country cannot "afford to deprive institutions of higher education of the ability to educate generations of young Americans—minority and non-minority—in an environment that enables all to flourish, and understand each other, in a truly integrated society." They write,

> Until fairly recently, our society enforced the separation of the races in virtually all important areas—social, economic, political and educational. As a result of racial isolation, African Americans and white Americans often learned about each other by relying on unfounded images and stereotypes. Demeaning and hurtful images proliferated in the media, in textbooks, in movies and on radio and television. There were no countervailing institutions to perform the function of education and understanding. By design, we did not know each other.
>
> In the decades since,... institutions of higher education have strongly influenced a change in this design. They have opened the doors and aggressively recruited [and admitted] minority students... to create remarkably diverse student bodies.... [With a new] design in place, we have begun to know each other.

But this process of understanding is under threat from the suits brought by the Center for Individual Rights. Bollinger and Cantor explain, "[The] CIR seeks to eliminate all consideration of race in college admissions. If it is successful, as it was in an earlier lawsuit against the University of Texas, we will in all probability soon return to a largely segregated system—de facto rather than de jure, to be sure, but segregated nonetheless."[104] The lawsuits brought by the CIR are cause for concern. If they reach the Supreme Court and are successful, they will mean the end of race-conscious policies for public universities not only in Michigan, but also in the rest of the country. They will mean the loss of numerous underrepresented minorities in the most competitive and prestigious public universities in the nation. They will mean the resegregation of higher education in America, and this has many minority students concerned.

Adding to the interest in the Michigan cases, a group of minority students, represented by a number of public interest law firms, has sought and won intervention. As intervenors in both the undergraduate and law school case, minority students seek to justify affirmative action not as a means to achieve diversity, but as a remedy for discrimination.[105] In a historic ruling, the Sixth Circuit Court of Appeals granted students intervention, finding "persuasive their argument that the University is unlikely to present evidence of past discrimination by the University itself or of the disparate impact of some current admissions criteria, and that these may be important and relevant factors in determining the legality of a race-conscious admissions policy."[106] In *Bakke,* minority students had criticized the University of California for failing to raise discrimination as an issue and had sought intervention in order to raise the issue themselves. They were denied, as were students in subsequent cases at the University of Texas and the University of Washington. Now, as intervenors in the Michigan cases, minority students are able to do for the first time what universities have thus far been unwilling to do—raise discrimination as an issue and build a record of test bias and institutional racism for the courts to consider.

In December 2000, the federal district court in the undergraduate case (*Gratz*) issued a summary judgment on the diversity rationale offered by the University of Michigan in defense of its race-conscious admissions policy.[107] Citing the Ninth Circuit's decision from one week earlier, the district court held "that under *Bakke,* diversity constitutes a compelling governmental interest in the context of higher education justifying the use of race as one factor in the admissions process." The court rejected the Fifth Circuit opinion from four years prior, finding diversity to be no longer a compelling interest, and criticized the original three-judge panel in *Hopwood* for reading too much into the silences of the Supreme Court justices. In upholding race-conscious admissions, the district court found that the University of Michigan "presented this Court with solid evidence regarding the educational benefits that flow from a racially and ethnically diverse student body."[108]

In an unprecedented expenditure of resources to defend its admissions policy, the University of Michigan had spent several million dollars gathering research and providing testimony on the value of diversity in higher education. The defense was supported by *amicus* briefs from the American Council on Higher Education and other national higher-education groups asserting that college students benefit from working in a racially diverse environment. In addition, several major corporations submitted *amicus* briefs arguing that racially diverse public university campuses are a key source of the employees they need to remain competitive in a global economy. The Center for Individual Rights made little effort to rebut such claims, and instead argued that "diversity" was too amorphous and ill-defined a goal to be seen as a compelling government interest that conceivably could be used to justify "racial preferences" forever. In rejecting such arguments, however, the judge in *Gratz* stated that the university's testimony convinced him that "diversity in higher education, by its nature, is a permanent and ongoing interest."[109]

In February 2001, the *Gratz* court issued a second ruling, this time on the rationale, offered by minority students intervening in the case, that affirmative action is necessary to remedy the effects of past and present racial discrimination.[110] The judge rejected this rationale, stating that though minority students and particularly black students had been mistreated in the past by the university and continued to face racial hostility in the present from the campus community, they had never been explicitly or implicitly discriminated against in the admissions process. Furthermore, even if discrimination were identified, the judge held that remedial action was not shown to be necessary, since it did not serve as the "actual purpose" behind the university's race-conscious admissions policies. Though the university asserted that the "actual purpose" of race-conscious admissions was to increase diversity, student intervenors argued that remedial action may have also motivated the admissions policy. But the district court stated that it is not enough that remedial measures "may have" motivated a race-conscious policy. As part of their burden, student intervenors must have established that remedial measures "actually" motivated the challenged program.[111]

In March 2001, one month after the second *Gratz* ruling, the federal district court in the law school case (*Grutter*) issued its opinion. Holding a starkly different view of the diversity rationale, the *Grutter* judge ruled that diversity was *not* a compelling interest.[112] Echoing the Fifth Circuit, the judge stated that because Justice Powell was not explicitly joined by the other justices in *Bakke*,[113] and because the Supreme Court has since taken a restrictive view of race-conscious decisions,[114] the University of Michigan Law School could not now use the diversity rationale to justify affirmative action.[115] The judge acknowledged the educational and societal benefits derived from a diverse student body, but stated that the consideration of race is nonetheless impermissible. The court added that even if diversity were to constitute a compelling state interest, the law school's admissions program would be found illegal because, among other factors, it employed percentage goals which are, according to the court, "practically indistinguishable from a quota system."[116]

In the same opinion, the court ruled that the necessity to remedy past and present discrimination *also* did not justify affirmative action at the law school. The court noted, "[T]here is no question about the long and tragic history of race discrimination in this country." While public policy has sought to eradicate racial discrimination, the court stated, its lingering effects are apparent in, among other areas, lower education rates and higher poverty rates for some minority groups as compared to whites. Explaining one effect of lingering discrimination—the gap in undergraduate grade point averages (UGPAs) between underrepresented minority and white applicants—the court stated,

[T]he evidence at trial clearly indicates that much of the [U]GPA gap is due to the fact that disproportionate numbers of Native Americans, African Americans, and Hispanics live and go to school in impoverished areas of the country. It should not surprise anyone that students who attend schools where books are lacking, where classrooms are overcrowded, and where Advanced Placement or other higher level courses are not offered are at a competitive disadvantage as compared with students whose schools do not suffer from such shortcomings. An educational deficit in the K-12 years will, for most students, have a negative ripple effect on academic performance in college.[117]

Furthermore, the court acknowledged that the gap in LSAT scores—which the court found harder to explain—was caused in part by subjecting underrepresented minority students, many of whom do not speak English or do not speak standard English as their first language, to tests written in "academic English." The court also found persuasive the explanation that underrepresented minority students are less likely to take an LSAT preparation course because they cannot afford to do so (the cost is roughly $1,000) or are less aware than white students of the benefits that such a course can provide (allegedly increasing LSAT scores by an average of seven points). Citing insufficient evidence, however, the court did not find bias in the content or design of the test itself, or in the conditions in which it is administered, but the court did not rule out that such bias may exist.

The district court concluded that the comparatively lower grades and test scores of underrepresented minorities are attributable, at least in part, to general, societal racial discrimination—a condition which the Supreme Court has said cannot constitutionally be remedied by race-conscious decision making. The intervenors had argued, however, that it is the *overuse* of potentially biased and invalid predictors (and not their mere existence) that has a disparate impact on underrepresented minority students and is attributable not to society in general, but to the law school in particular. The court did not address this point directly but suggested that even if the law school were found to use grades and test scores in a discriminatory manner, affirmative action would not be necessary to remedy such discrimination, since the law school could simply relax, or even eliminate, reliance on these factors.[118]

The *Grutter* court issued an injunction calling for an immediate end to the law school's race-conscious admissions practices. But in April 2001, the law school appealed the decision to the Sixth Circuit Court of Appeals and asked the district court to stay its injunction until the appeal is decided. The district court judge refused.[119] However, a three-judge panel of the Sixth Circuit overruled the district court, allowing the law school to retain its race-conscious admissions policy until the case was resolved. On May 14, 2002, the Sixth Circuit (en banc) decided the case in favor of affirmative action. In a 5-to-4 vote the majority held that the diversity rationale in *Bakke* remains good law and the race-conscious admissions policy employed at the law school is necessary for the law school to maintain enough racial and ethnic diversity in enrollment to offer students an educationally diverse learning environment. In addition, responding to the argument offered by student intervenors that affirmative action is necessary to remedy past and present discrimination, the concurring opinion acknowledged that standardized test scores are not race neutral.[120]

The Sixth Circuit will rule on *Gratz* later, but its decision in *Grutter,* which conflicts with other appeals court decisions, increases the probability that the Michigan cases, separately or together, will reach the Supreme Court. The two other cases—*Hopwood* in Texas and *Johnson* in Georgia—which had been en route to the Supreme Court will now not be heard by the Court. In July 2001, a federal judge closed the nine-year-old *Hopwood* case, after the Supreme Court declined for a second time to hear an appeal by the University of Texas.[121] Several months later, in November 2001, the University of Georgia announced it would not appeal an Eleventh Circuit ruling upholding a lower court decision that struck down the affirmative action program at the university.[122]

As the likely vehicles to decide whether universities across the country can use affirmative action, the Michigan cases are being closely watched. These cases most thoroughly explore the legality of affirmative action under the Constitution and squarely present the contested question of whether diversity is a compelling state interest that justifies the use of race in admissions. Not since 1978, in *Bakke,* has the Supreme Court examined race-conscious admissions in higher education. But with disagreement between the lower courts, the Supreme Court may now revisit the issue. The possibility of a Supreme Court review comes at a time, however, when California—the first state to eliminate race-conscious admissions practices—is rethinking its decision.

While other states are considering whether to eliminate race-conscious policies in their university admissions programs, California—which first did so in 1995, at the University of California, through a vote of the regents—is having second thoughts. Less than six years after the UC regents voted to adopt SP-1, banning the use of race in admissions, the regents have repealed their policy in an attempt to dispel the notion that the University of California does not welcome underrepresented minority students. The repeal is only a symbolic gesture, however, since the use of race is still barred by Proposition 209, which was voted into law in 1996. But as Regent William Bagley—the regent who spearheaded the effort to rescind SP-1—stated, the repeal makes a profound statement: "The message...is that the University of California is no longer a sponsor of anti-affirmative action movements around the nation."[123]

Regent Bagley, a moderate Republican and prominent San Francisco attorney who opposed the elimination of affirmative action at the university, began his campaign to get the regents to reconsider their position in January 2000.[124] Bagley, the 1949 Berkeley valedictorian and a 1952 Boalt alumnus, stated that the ban on race damaged the reputation of his alma mater. He observed, "Our flagship campuses are becoming more and more segregated. That's just a plain fact."[125] By reversing their vote, Bagley asserted that the regents would send a powerful message to students and faculty that minorities were welcome at the university. He worried that underrepresented minorities would never feel truly welcome unless the regents publicly disavowed their decision. "[We] are going to lose a generation of qualified minority applicants without reaching the changing demographics," he stated. "Too many qualified students are unwilling to go to an institution where they perceive that they are not wanted."[126] Regent Ward Connerly disagreed, asserting that "[t]his argument that minority students don't feel welcome is bogus. There is no evidence of it. Why would students spend the hours and hours they do applying to UC if they don't feel welcome?"[127]

Bagley counted on the shifting composition of the board of regents to win approval for his proposal. Seven of the fourteen regents, including former Governor Pete Wilson, who supported the 1995 resolution, were off the board, and Bagley felt that a majority of the regents were now inclined to vote for a repeal. A reversal of the ban on affirmative action would not have any practical effect on admissions while Proposition 209—a constitutional amendment which overrides regential policies—remained in place. But Bagley hoped it would persuade more minority students to apply to the university and attend if they were admitted. A reversal would also be a significant blow to the growing efforts to dismantle affirmative action around the country, and supporters of affirmative action hoped it would provide valuable momentum to launch another initiative campaign to overturn at least the educational portions of Proposition 209 in California. For this reason, Ward Connerly initially opposed any move to reverse the ban, saying that it would only fuel a campaign already under way to overturn Proposition 209. "It would be the dumbest thing we could do. The movement to turn around 209 will come alive...the day after the regents meet."[128]

But the proposal to rescind the 1995 vote had the support of a number of prominent figures, including Lieutenant Governor Cruz Bustamante—the first Latino to be elected to a statewide office in California in 120 years—who also sat on the board of regents. In an opinion piece published in the *Los Angeles Times,* in January 2000, Bustamante wrote,

Five years ago, the University of California declared itself a "colorblind meritocracy" by eliminating all of its affirmative action programs. Educators, political leaders and anyone who cares about the future of California must now ask whether we are better off as a society than we were five years ago. I believe we are not. Indeed, the results of this five-year social experiment suggest serious, long-term repercussions for California's social fabric. Diversity, once a hallmark of the UC, is now an afterthought.[129]

Bustamante called on the regents to take down the "Not Wanted" sign. Stating that "[d]iversity is California's destiny," he suggested that the regents take the necessary steps to ensure that the university "reflects our state's highest aspirations as well as its demographic realities." William Bagley indicated that he would put the proposal on the agenda as soon as he had secured a majority of support for it from the regents, but the delay in doing so frustrated many students, reviving a dormant movement to bring affirmative action back to public education. In March 2001, in the largest protests since the regents voted to end race-conscious admissions, several thousand university and high school students converged on the Berkeley and UCLA campuses to call on the regents to repeal their 1995 ban at their subsequent meeting.[130] In addition, student-of-color organizations at Berkeley—which have traditionally played an important role in recruiting minority students to campus—threatened to withhold their recruiting assistance if the regents did not take action.[131] Under pressure from students as well as state lawmakers—most notably the Latino Caucus—and following intense negotiations among themselves, the regents voted unanimously at their May 2001 meeting to repeal SP-1. In voting for the repeal, Ward Connerly told his fellow regents that he remained convinced that the 1995 resolution was "the right thing to do," and he reminded them that they remain bound by the ban on affirmative action adopted into the state constitution by the voters of California. But Connerly said he was willing to rescind the resolution to help restore peace to the university. "In a civilized democracy, as long as we are true to our convictions, I think it is appropriate to reach out to other people to try to accommodate them," he stated.[132]

In a further effort to mitigate "race-blind" policies that are still in place and to more equitably distribute seats at the University of California, UC President Richard Atkinson has made two proposals which could increase diversity at some (but not all) undergraduate campuses. The first proposal (perhaps inspired by the limited success of the 20 percent plan in Florida)[133] is to convert the 4 percent plan in California to a 12.5 percent conditional plan similar to a plan rejected earlier by the UC regents. Under the proposed plan, the University of California would give conditional admission to the top 12.5 percent of seniors at *every* high school who did not make the first cut under the 4 percent plan, enrolling these students upon completion of two years of community college.[134]

President Atkinson asserts that the proposed plan would help many high-achieving minority students in low-performing high schools reach the university by allowing them to transfer in as upper-division students. Atkinson points out that the plan would also alleviate the pressure of population growth on the university, by relying on the community college system to reduce the load. But a reading of the proposal indicates that the plan would not necessarily increase diversity at the most competitive campuses. Students given conditional admission would still have to compete to gain admission to the campus of their choice, and to the extent that high school grades and standardized tests were used in this process, minority students would still be subject to traditional barriers. In addition, as is true with other percentage plans, the 12.5 percent conditional plan would not apply to graduate school admissions and would do nothing to increase diversity at those schools. Nonetheless, the plan would make the university more accessible to minority students, and Ward Connerly has thus been hesitant to support it. Concerned that the plan is another "preference-based program," Connerly states, "If I get any suspicions at all that this is all orchestrated to increase the pool of underrepresented minorities, then I [will] have to vote against it."[135]

The second and more daring proposal (perhaps motivated by the recent issuance of guidelines by the Office for Civil Rights warning against overreliance on standardized tests)[136] is to drop the general (math and verbal) SAT requirement for incoming freshmen. Atkinson contends that the SAT does not accurately measure students' mastery of high school curriculum, nor does it adequately predict students' ability in college.[137] In a speech before the American Council on Education in February 2001, Atkinson stated that the University of California must be "mindful that it serves the most racially and ethnically diverse college-going population in the nation" and "must be careful to make sure that its standards do not unfairly discriminate against any students."[138]

"The problem," states Atkinson, "is not the use of standardized tests to assess knowledge in well-defined subject areas. The problem is tests that do not have a demonstrable relationship to the student's program of study—a problem that is amplified when tests are assumed to measure innate ability." Instead of the general SAT, Atkinson proposes developing admissions tests that would "create a stronger connection between what students accomplished in high school and their likelihood of being admitted to [the university], and [would] focus student attention on mastery of subject matter rather than test preparation."[139] The university presently requires subject matter tests (known as the SAT II) in writing, mathematics, and a third subject of the student's choice, but these tests are not presently tied to courses required by the university and, though they are an improvement on the general SAT, do not adequately predict student performance.

In addition to substituting the general SAT with a more appropriate standardized test, Atkinson would also like the university to develop guidelines governing the use of tests to make sure that they are not overvalued in the admissions process. He proposes a "holistic" evaluation of applicants, using criteria that recognize a wider range of academic and individual achievement and that assess what students have made of the opportunities available to them. Ward Connerly is wary of this approach. He believes that moving away from standard measures like the SAT will mean colleges lose their fundamental goal of academic excellence. He states disapprovingly, "Looking at a student's potential and the adversity they've overcome—what I call the Academic Misery Index—has the potential of totally reforming college," turning campuses into institutions that value diversity and community service over learning.[140]

But many employers take a different view. In a strongly worded letter sent to college presidents in April 2001, a group of corporate leaders urged academic officials to place less emphasis on the SAT and other standardized tests when evaluating applicants. Executives from companies like Shell Oil and Verizon Communications, joined by members of the National Urban League, said in the letter that entrance exams do not measure the qualities most crucial for success in the business world. The letter did not recommend abandoning the SAT altogether, but urged universities to improve admissions tools that measure applicants' creativity, leadership skills, and commitment to their communities. In defense of the SAT, a spokeswoman for the College Board conceded that standardized tests do not measure leadership skills, but stated that "they aren't intended to." In light of the shortcomings of the SAT and other standardized tests, business leaders called on university officials to invest the necessary energy and resources to forge a "sensible and fair balance in admissions practices."[141]

Atkinson's proposal to drop the SAT may be one step in that direction, as it could increase the prospects of admission for minority students who are disproportionately hindered by the SAT. Because of its possible implications, the proposal has caught national attention, fueling the debate over the relationship between race and standardized tests. Were the regents and faculty to adopt the proposal, the University of California would become the first large public university with competitive admissions to drop the SAT. This has the College Board (which owns the SAT) and the Educational Testing Service (which administers it) very concerned, since more students take the SAT in California than in any other state.[142] A move by the University of California could prompt other large, competitive universities to drop the SAT. Such a move might also influence competitive graduate and professional schools, such as Boalt, to lessen the weight of existing standardized tests and to develop new ones more closely correlated to the field of study for which they select.

The development of new tests, however, is still a long way off. Large, competitive universities have not invested significant energy or resources to find appropriate alternatives to existing standardized tests. Nor have they moved far enough from a test-based admissions policy to a whole person-based admissions policy, which would enable admissions officers to admit students with a wider array of qualifications. New tests and new ways to use tests have the potential to correct for test-based biases and to generate classes of students skilled in a number of ways. But they are only part of what is needed to create a more equitable admissions process. Forms of discrimination appear not only in testing, but in other areas of the admissions process. In some cases, the discrimination is well understood and can be corrected. For example, universities can choose to cap high school GPAs at 4.0 to avoid rewarding students at predominantly white schools who have the opportunity to take Advanced Placement courses graded on a 5.0 scale, and penalizing students at predominantly minority schools who lack that same opportunity. In other cases, the discrimination is less well understood and cannot as easily be corrected. For example, at times, admissions committee members exercise conscious or unconscious prejudices by making value judgments that have a discriminatory effect, such as granting more weight to an applicant who has majored in classics (who is likely to be white) than to an applicant who has majored in ethnic studies (who is likely to be a student of color).

Until the vestiges of past discrimination and the instances of present discrimination are eradicated—which may take some time, since little more than 30 years in the 230-year history of this country have been spent without the yokes of official segregation—racial diversity will not occur naturally in the admissions process. Under these circumstances, universities that hold racial diversity to be a compelling educational interest have no alternative but to select for it. Where racial diversity does not occur naturally—because of past or present discrimination—race must be considered in order to generate a diverse student body. Case studies have shown that neither socioeconomic considerations nor random selection will resolve the problem. Though these solutions and other "race-blind" measures may increase racial diversity at the margins, they will not generate the kind of diversity that can be achieved under affirmative action.

This is the reality that the Supreme Court will have to grapple with should it choose to consider a case challenging affirmative action in higher education. "Race-blind" admissions policies have been disastrous for universities that seek to enroll a diverse student body. At the University of California, for example, in the first year of "race-blind" admissions, the number of underrepresented minorities admitted to Boalt Hall dropped 66 percent and the number admitted to the undergraduate school at Berkeley dropped 57 percent. Now, universities are beginning to graduate post–affirmative action classes and the consequences of "race-blind" policies are compounding. With fewer minorities coming through the universities, employers and graduate and professional schools are having a harder time finding racially diverse candidates. Law schools are a case in point: of the undergraduate schools that have historically produced the highest number of law school applicants nationally—UCLA, UC Berkeley, University of Texas at Austin, University of Michigan at Ann Arbor, and the University of Florida—all are either currently prohibited from taking race into account in admissions or face legal challenges to their affirmative action programs.[143]

If the Supreme Court takes up an affirmative action case, as is likely in the next several years, it will have to decide not only whether race-conscious admissions policies are constitutionally permissible, but also whether they are appropriate (that is to say, effective and necessary) to increase minority representation in higher education. The former question involves an interpretation of the law, while the latter involves an evaluation of history. On this latter question, the story of Boalt Hall sheds much light. The story demonstrates that affirmative action has worked. While it was in place, affirmative action enabled Boalt to create a racially diverse and academically vibrant law school that ranked among the top law schools in the country. Diverse graduates who were trained in a diverse setting went on to become professional, civic, and political leaders. Of these graduates, many minorities broke through the color line, becoming some of the first nonwhite law firm partners, state and federal court judges, congressional representatives, public interest law firm directors, corporate executives, and law professors in the country. Many more served as role models to a new generation of minority students who dreamed of following in their footsteps, and still more challenged stereotypes and broadened perspectives in a multiracial society.

But without affirmative action, Boalt has been unable to maintain the same level of racial diversity that it once did, resulting in substantially fewer minorities graduating from the law school and entering the legal profession. The story of Boalt Hall demonstrates not only that affirmative action works, but also that it is necessary to generating a diverse student body. Following the ban on the consideration of race at the University of California, Boalt lessened the weight of the LSAT (though only slightly) and ended the adjustment of UGPAs (which had been adjusted based on the average LSAT scores from an applicant's undergraduate institution). These and other modest changes increased diversity only marginally. Boalt subsequently experimented with socioeconomic criteria, as did the UCLA Law School (to a far greater extent), but the results of these experiments proved no more successful than the other changes made by Boalt. Despite various efforts to increase diversity, the number of underrepresented minority students at Boalt remains only half of what it was under race-based affirmative action. These efforts and additional research show that there is no substitute for race. Until embedded preferences are removed throughout the admissions process and diversity occurs naturally, the consideration of race appears necessary to admit a diverse student body.

Without affirmative action, Boalt is at a loss. The consequences of eliminating race-conscious policies are disconcerting. The "race-blind" policies implemented at the law school have been anything but race-neutral, and the voices of underrepresented minority students have largely disappeared. A hushed silence—the silence of students, faculty, and administrators unwilling and unable to discuss the difficult issues of race— now hangs over Boalt. For anyone who is willing to listen, the silence is telling. As discussions of race vanish, so do records of racial statistics. In the past several years, records tracking the racial diversity of students over time have disappeared or are no longer accessible through the University of California, Berkeley, or Boalt web sites. Ward Connerly, who was instrumental in ending affirmative action at the university, now seeks to ensure through a ballot initiative that data on race is not even collected. "I find it hard to understand why they need this information," Connerly has stated.[144] But without the ability to keep records on race, it will be difficult to monitor, let alone discuss, race-based inequalities. That may be exactly what Connerly and his supporters want.

The battle of attrition that has taken place at the law school suggests what may lie ahead for other institutions as the debate over affirmative action becomes national in scope. In the next several years, the Supreme Court may settle the legal question of whether affirmative action is permissible and appropriate in higher education. If the Court decides that it is, the states will still have to settle the political question of whether it is desirable. This question has been made moot in California with the prohibition of race-conscious decisions. But to the extent that the regents and voters are willing to reconsider their position, the question remains highly relevant. In other states, not subject to the same laws but undergoing the same analysis, the question of whether affirmative action should be used to keep the doors of higher education open for all is also relevant.

What has happened at Boalt is instructive, and universities, voters, and politicians alike would be wise to take heed. The lessons of this story are many. But perhaps the most important is how far we have yet to go if we are to make our institutions of higher education representative of and relevant to a racially diverse nation.

Notes

Chapter 1: Balancing the Scales

1. Throughout the book, I use the term *minority* to refer to African Americans, Native Americans, Asian Americans, and Latinos. Later in the book, when discussing events from 1975 on, I use the phrase *underrepresented minority* to refer to African Americans, Native Americans, and Latinos only. Asian Americans are not considered underrepresented unless specifically noted (e.g., in discussing Filipinos and other Southeast Asians).

2. Martin Luther King Jr., "I Have a Dream" (1963), in James Melvin Washington, ed., *I Have a Dream: Writings and Speeches That Changed the World* (San Francisco: Harper San Francisco, 1992), p. 101.

3. Though the terms *race* and *ethnicity* are distinguished in the Civil Rights Act, I use the term *race* in this book to refer to both race and ethnicity.

4. Martin Luther King Jr., "The Playboy Interview" (1965), in James Melvin Washington, ed., *A Testament of Hope: The Assembled Writings of Martin Luther King, Jr.* (San Francisco: Harper and Row, 1986), p. 367.

5. Section 14 of Organic Act of 1868, California Stats 1867–68, p. 248.

6. "UC's Unusual Tribute," *San Francisco Chronicle,* April 5, 1968, p. 6.

7. "Heyns Calls on Faculty to Lead Fight against Discrimination Here," *Daily Californian,* April 9, 1968, p. 16.

8. Dean Walkley, dean of admissions, to Dean Edward Halbach, memorandum, "Report on Minority Student Program," May 28, 1969, p.1 (recounting the development of an affirmative action program in 1968).

9. The Boalt Hall School of Law opened for its first classes on January 17, 1911; see Susan Epstein, *Law at Berkeley* (Berkeley: Institute of Governmental Studies Press, 1997), p. 60. The number of students enrolled between 1911 and 1968 is estimated from first-year enrollment figures provided by Epstein (pp. 171–77, 221–22, 250), indicating that in the years 1911–1921, at least 25 students entered each year; in the years 1922–1960, an average of 100 students entered each year; in the years 1961–1964, a minimum of 185 students entered

each year; and in the years 1964–1968, approximately 285 students entered each year.

10. I use the term *Latino* in general to refer to Latinos/Latinas as well as Chicanos/Chicanas, Hispanics, and all subcategorizations, such as Mexicans and Puerto Ricans. When describing a particular person, I use the gendered *Latino* to refer to a male and *Latina* to refer to a female.

11. Herma Hill Kay, interview, September 22, 1999 (African American enrollment); La Raza Law Students Alumni Directory (Latino enrollment); Epstein, *Law at Berkeley,* p. 276 (estimating that at least twelve Asian students had enrolled at Boalt). No figures were available for Native American enrollment.

12. Dennis J. Roberts, "A Southern Journey," *Writ,* October 1963, p. 1; Dick Duane, "Legal Report: Albany, Georgia," *Writ,* December 1964, p. 1. The *Writ* was the Boalt student newspaper at the time.

13. Al Katz, "Civil Rights Reflections," *Writ,* April 1965, p. 4.

14. Robert Cole, interview, May 3, 2000.

15. W. J. Rorabough, *Berkeley at War: The 1960s* (New York: Oxford University Press, 1989), pp. 50, 18.

16. See *Swann v. Burkett,* 209 Cal. App.2d. 685 (1962).

17. The Congress of Racial Equality was a national organization with which Berkeley activists were associated. I use the acronym CORE to refer only to the Berkeley organization.

18. Rorabough, *Berkeley at War,* pp. 18–22, 72, 10.

19. Michael Omi and Howard Winant, *Racial Formation in the United States: From the 1960s to the 1990s* (New York: Routledge, 1994), p. 69.

20. President Lyndon B. Johnson, "To Fulfill These Rights," speech delivered on June 4, 1965, at Howard University; printed in George E. Curry, ed., *The Affirmative Action Debate* (New York: Addison-Wesley, 1997), pp. 17–18.

21. J. Bradley Klemm, "Law Education among Minority Groups Studied by Boalt Group," *Writ,* December 1965, p. 5.

22. Ibid.

23. Edward Halbach, interview, April 18, 2000.

24. Report of the Post-Bakke Committee, appointed by Dean Sanford Kadish on July 31, 1978, pp. II-1p, III-10.

25. Homer Mason, interview, April 17, 2000.

26. Homer Mason, interview, November 9, 1999.

27. Edward Halbach, interview, September 27, 1999.

28. Edward Halbach, interview, April 18, 2000.

29. Albert Moreno, interview, November 9, 1999.

30. Edward Halbach, interview, April 18, 2000.

31. In 1965, the enrollment of women began to increase at Boalt and at law schools around the country. In the decade prior, the enrollment of women at Boalt hovered around 5 percent. In 1965, it was 6 percent and in 1968, women comprised 11 percent of the entering class at Boalt. In subsequent years, enrollment grew to 28 percent in 1980, 46 percent in 1992, and more than 50 percent in 2000; see Epstein, *Law at Berkeley,* p. 320; Boalt Admissions Statistics (2000).

32. Epstein, *Law at Berkeley,* p. 274.

33. Boalt Admissions Committee to Faculty, Students, and Staff, memorandum, "Study of Special Admissions Program," November 6, 1972, p. 1.

34. Edward Halbach, interview, April 18, 2000.

35. Kerner Commission, *Report of the National Advisory Commission on Civil Disorders* (Washington, DC: GPO, 1968, p. 1).

36. Ibid.

37. Ibid., p. 11.

38. "President Acts to Avert a National Catastrophe," *San Francisco Chronicle,* April 6, 1968, p. 1.

39. "King's Widow Pleads for His Dream," *San Francisco Examiner,* April 7, 1968, p. 1.

40. "A Call to Make Good His Dream," *San Francisco Chronicle,* April 6, 1968, p. 5.

41. Barbara Rhine, "An Empty Feeling," *Writ,* May 8, 1968, p. 3.

42. Herma Hill Kay, "Testimony before the University of California Regents," May 18, 1995.

43. In 1968, the law school was fifty-seven years old, and the estimated number of minorities enrolled up to that point was at least 56 (22 African Americans, 20 Latinos, at least 12 Asians, and an unknown number of Native Americans).

44. Herma Hill Kay was hired in 1960 and granted tenure in 1963. She replaced the first woman ever hired to teach at the law school, Barbara Armstrong, who retired in 1957 and let it be known that she expected at least one other woman to be appointed to the law school faculty to replace her. Armstrong had been hired in 1919, and was the first full-time female professor at a major American law school; see Epstein, *Law at Berkeley,* pp. 84, 224, 254, 319.

45. Herma Hill Kay, interview, September 22, 1999.

46. Walkley to Halbach, "Report on Minority Student Program," p. 1. Because of the dearth of written material documenting this time period and the incomplete memories of senior faculty, I rely heavily on this memo for the history of the first year of a formal affirmative action program (1968–69).

47. "Minority Recruitment: New Program at Boalt," *Writ,* October 2, 1968, p. 1.

48. Walkley to Halbach, "Report on Minority Student Program," p.1.

49. See University of California Berkeley, School of Law (Boalt Hall), "Report on Special Admissions at Boalt Hall," 28 *J. Legal Educ.* 363, 365 (1977). The 70–30 weighting of the LSAT was later changed to 50–50.

50. Bruce Blumberg, "Admissions: UGA PGA LSAT," *Writ,* April 22, 1970, p. 10 (discussing the validity of the PGA).

51. See W. B. Schrader, "Summary of Law School Validity Studies, 1948–1975," in *Reports of LSAC-Sponsored Research,* vol. 3 (1975–1977), 519; 530, table 1 (1977), citing validity figures of .33 for 1963–70 and .35 for 1971–74, based on data from seventy-nine schools. In more recent years, the national correlation between the LSAT and first-year grades has approached .40.

52. Susan Sturm and Lani Guinier, "The Future of Affirmative Action: Reclaiming the Innovative Ideal," 84 *Cal. L. Rev.* 953, 970–71 (1996).

53. David Owen, *None of the Above: Behind the Myth of Scholastic Aptitude* (Boston: Houghton-Mifflin, 1985), p. 207.

54. William C. Kidder, "The Rise of the Testocracy: An Essay on the LSAT, Conventional Wisdom, and the Dismantling of Diversity," 9 *Tex. J. Women & L.* 167, 189–97 (2000).

55. Nicholas Lemann, *The Big Test* (New York: Farrar, Straus, and Giroux, 1999), p. 33.

56. Daria Roithmayr, "Deconstructing the Distinction between Bias and Merit," 85 *Cal. L. Rev.* 1450, 1488 (1997).

57. Lemann, *Big Test,* p. 30.

58. Roithmayr, "Bias and Merit," p. 1489 (quoting segregationist Cornelia James Cannon in a 1922 *Atlantic Monthly* article).

59. David M. White, "The Definition of Legal Competence: Will the Circle Be Unbroken?" 18 *Santa Clara L. Rev.* 641, 663 (1978).

60. See Roithmayr, "Bias and Merit," pp. 1483–85, 1491 (discussing among other things, the formation of the American Bar Association as an effort to prevent both immigrants and African Americans from gaining admission to practice law and the implementation of policies at almost half of all accredited law schools to exclude blacks).

61. White, "Definition of Legal Competence," 668.

62. David M. White, "An Investigation into the Validity and Cultural Bias of the Law School Admission Test," in David M. White, ed., *Towards a Diversified Legal Profession,* sponsored by the National Conference of Black Lawyers (San Francisco: Julian Richardson Associates, 1981), pp. 202–3, 207 n. 29.

63. "Huerta 'Raps' about Black and Brown at Boalt," *Writ,* May 22, 1968, p. 3.

64. Ibid.

65. Kathryn Hill, "Admissions Policy Cleared Up," *Writ,* December 17, 1969, p. 2.

66. Walkley to Halbach, "Report on Minority Student Program," p.1 ("Our initial efforts were quite successful. The new students, when added to those already in the second and third-year classes, produced some startlingly promising results. For example, this year we have more black students enrolled than we have graduated in all Boalt history. Although the information is less reliable, we believe that a similar statement could be made for Mexican-American students").

67. Ibid., p. 3.

68. Hill, "Admissions Policy Cleared Up," p. 2.

69. Walkley to Halbach, "Report on Minority Student Program," p. 1.

70. Ibid.

71. Neil Gotanda, interview, May 24, 2001.

72. Epstein, *Law at Berkeley,* p. 277.

73. L. T. Surh, "Make Room for More," *Writ,* May 11, 1972, p. 3.

74. Afro-American Student Union, "Open Letter to the Campus," *Daily Californian,* Berkeley, January 15, 1969, p. 1; "Third World Votes—Strike Wednesday," *Daily Californian,* January 20, 1969, p. 1.

75. Ray Tisdale, "Boalt Minority Students Favor TWLF, Go on Strike to Explain Demands," *Writ,* February 13, 1969, p. 1.

76. Jimmy Dale Lofton III, "College of Ethnic Studies and Right of Self-Determination," *Writ,* February 13, 1969, p. 3.

77. "Huerta 'Raps' About Black and Brown," p. 3.

78. Ibid.

79. Robert Cole, interview, September 22, 1999; Epstein, *Law at Berkeley,* p. 267.

80. Bill Soria, "Chicano Association Organized," *Writ,* October 15, 1969, p. 3; Al Escobedo, "La Clinica de la Raza," *Writ,* April 19, 1971, p. 4.

81. Edward Halbach, interview, April 18, 2000.

82. Robert Cole, interview, September 22, 1999.

83. John Huerta, interview, November 3, 1999.

84. Robert Cole, interview, September 22, 1999.

85. John McNulty, interview, June 25, 2000.

86. John McNulty, interview, September 24, 1999.

87. "All Quiet on the First Year Front," *Writ,* November 9, 1971, p. 4.

88. Richard Delgado, interview, November 2, 1999.

89. Ibid.; and Richard Delgado, interview, April 25, 2000.

90. Jesse Choper, interview, April 25, 2000.

91. "Huerta 'Raps' About Black and Brown," p. 3.

92. Boalt Admissions Committee, "Study of Special Admissions Program," p. 3.

93. Ibid., p. 2.

94. Hazel Harper, "Third World Cutbacks at Boalt Hall Black Law Student Association Protests," *Daily Californian,* April 19, 1972, p. 1.

95. "Faculty Fiddles While Students Burn," *Writ,* May 11, 1972, p. 1.

96. Robert Cole, interview, May 3, 2000.

97. Strike Support Committee, "Response to Faculty Decisions on Special Admissions," *Writ,* May 11, 1972, p. 5.

98. "Faculty Fiddles," p. 1.

99. "Faculty Policy Governing Admission to Boalt Hall" (1973).

100. Ibid.

101. Epstein, *Law at Berkeley,* p. 278. Other Asian subgroups who continued to receive special consideration under affirmative action included Southeast Asians such as Vietnamese, Cambodians, and Filipinos.

102. Ibid., pp. 274–75

103. Boalt Admissions Committee, "Study of Special Admissions Program," pp. 1–2. The rise in Boalt applicant credentials paralleled national trends. In 1961, the median LSAT score of students at 81 percent of the nation's law schools was below 485. In 1975, not one of the 128 law schools approved by the American Bar Association had an entering class with a mean below 510. Seventy percent of them had means between 572 and 693. In comparative terms this means that most American lawyers and judges practicing today would never have been admitted into law school had they had to compete against the standards which have governed admissions since the mid-1970s. See Allan Nairn, "Standardized Selection Criteria and a Diverse Legal Profession," in White, ed., *Towards a Diversified Legal Profession,* p. 375 (quoting statistics from the Educational Testing Service).

104. Report of the Post-Bakke Committee, p. III-7.

105. Omi and Winant, *Racial Formation in the United States*, p. 70.

106. *DeFunis v. Odegaard*, 416 U.S. 312 (1974).

107. Ibid., pp. 320–44 (Douglas, J., dissenting).

108. Ibid., pp. 324–25.

109. Ibid., p. 330 (quoting Rosen, "Equalizing Access to Legal Education: Special Programs for Law Students Who Are Not Admissible by Traditional Criteria," *U. Tol. L. Rev.* 321, 332–33 [1970]).

110. Ibid., pp. 334–35.

111. Ibid., p. 336 (emphasis included).

112. *Regents of the University of California v. Bakke*, 438 U.S. 265 (1978).

113. The brief for the University of California was coauthored by Paul Mishkin and two other attorneys not affiliated with Boalt, the *amicus* brief for the Association of American Law Schools was coauthored by David Feller and five other attorneys not affiliated with Boalt, and the *amicus* brief for the UC law schools was coauthored by David Feller and Jan Vetter.

114. "Brief for Petitioner," *Bakke*, pp. 13–14.

115. Statistics regarding law school enrollment over the years can be found at the National Center for Education Statistics website, http://www.nces.ed.gov.

116. "*Amicus* Brief for the Association of American Law Schools (AALS) in Support of Petitioner," *Bakke*, p. 3.

117. Ibid., p. 4.

118. Ibid., pp. 45–46.

119. Ibid., pp. 49–52.

120. *Bakke*, p. 395 (Marshall, J.).

121. Ibid., p. 396 (Marshall, J.).

122. Ibid., p. 307 (Powell, J.).

123. Ibid., p. 306, n. 43.

124. Derrick A. Bell, "Awakening after *Bakke*," 14 *Harvard Civil Rights-Civil Liberties Law Review* 1–6, 2–3 (1979).

125. David M. White, "Culturally Biased Testing and Predictive Invalidity: Putting Them on the Record," 14 *Harvard Civil Rights-Civil Liberties Law Review* 89–132, 124 (1979), explaining that, for example, the Association of American Medical Colleges supplied the Court with clear evidence of bias on the Medical College Admission Test (MCAT) and studies indicating "differential validity" for black and white students in predicting medical school performance.

126. See White, "Culturally Biased Testing," pp. 124–25; Bell, "Awakening after *Bakke*," p. 3.

127. Bell, "Awakening after *Bakke*," pp. 3–4.

128. Ibid., p. 5.

129. "*Amicus* Brief of the Black Law Students Association (BLSA)at the University of California, Berkeley School of Law," *Bakke*, p. 2.

130. Ibid., pp. 9–13.

131. Ibid., pp. 14–15.

132. See *Griggs v. Duke Power Co.*, 401 U.S. 424, 431 (1971).

133. "Brief of the BLSA," *Bakke*, p. 10.

134. Ibid., pp. 4, 16–18.

135. Ibid., p. 20 ("To ignore the racial bias in the MCAT would itself be racial discrimination. A University can constitutionally avoid that discrimination").

136. Ibid., p. 4; see also *Sweatt v. Painter,* 339 U.S. 629 (1950); *Brown v. Board of Education,* 347 U.S. 483 (1954).

137. "Brief of the BLSA," *Bakke,* p. 4.

138. See White, "Culturally Biased Testing," p. 125 ("That amici raised the issue was insufficient, because the evidence must appear in the record to satisfy some of the Justices").

139. *Bakke,* 438 U.S. at 312.

140. Ibid., p. 314 (Powell, J., citing *Sweatt v. Painter,* 339 U.S. at 634 [1950]).

141. David M. White, interview, October 2, 2000. During the *Bakke* case, White was working as a staff associate at the Childhood and Government Project at Boalt Hall. He subsequently left Boalt and some years later started a nonprofit organization, Testing for the Public, presently located in Berkeley.

142. White, "Culturally Biased Testing," p. 119.

143. White, "An Investigation into the Validity," p. 114.

144. White, "Culturally Biased Testing," p. 120.

145. Ibid., pp. 108–14.

146. Ibid, p. 113.

147. Report of the Post-Bakke Committee, p. III-13.

148. Ibid., appendix 11, "Median LSAT/GPAs by Ethnicity from 1974 to 1978."

149. Ibid., p. III-10.

150. "Faculty Policy Governing Admission to Boalt Hall" (1978).

151. Report of the Post-Bakke Committee, p. III-9.

Chapter 2: Pursuing Excellence

1. Michael Omi and Howard Winant, *Racial Formation in the United States: From the 1960s to the 1990s* (New York: Routledge, 1994), pp. 128–32.

2. Barbara Franklin, "Boalt Hall Hit by Sit-in Strike," *Daily Californian,* March 21, 1978, p. 1.

3. Report of the Post-Bakke Committee, appointed July 31, 1978, appendix 8, "Diversity in First Year Classes, 1970–1978."

4. Franklin, "Boalt Hall Hit," p. 1 (emphasis added).

5. Ibid.

6. In addition to *Regents of the University of California v. Bakke,* 438 U.S. 265 (1978), see *Washington v. Davis,* 426 U.S. 229, 248 (1976).

7. See *Bakke,* p. 387 (Marshall, J., dissenting); *Washington,* p. 256 (Marshall, J., joining in dissent).

8. Omi and Winant, *Racial Formation in the United States,* pp. 133–34.

9. Ibid., pp. 134–35.

10. Ibid., p. 134.

11. Ibid., p. 113.

12. Ibid., p. 131.

13. Ibid., p. 130.

14. Dana Y. Takagi, *The Retreat from Race* (New Brunswick: Rutgers University Press, 1992), p. 46.

15. Nicholas Lemann, *The Big Test* (New York: Farrar, Straus, and Giroux, 1999), pp. 241–42.

16. Takagi, *Retreat from Race*, p. 46.

17. Ibid., p. 34.

18. Ibid., p. 53.

19. However, Asian Americans are caught in a double bind when universities attempt both to preserve high white enrollment and to maintain affirmative action. See Mari Matsuda, "We Will Not Be Used," 1 *Asian Am. & Pac. Islands L. J.* 79, 81 (1993): "When university administrators have secret quotas to keep down Asian admissions, this is because Asians are seen as destroying the predominantly white character of the university. Under this mentality, we can't let in all those Asian over-achievers *and* maintain affirmative action for other minority groups."

20. Sumi Cho, interview, July 10, 2000.

21. Takagi, *Retreat from Race*, p. 93.

22. Ibid., p. 128.

23. See, for example, John H. Bunzel and Jeffrey K. D. Au, "Diversity or Discrimination?—Asian Americans in College," 87 *Public Interest* 49–62 (spring 1987).

24. See James Gibney, "The Berkeley Squeeze: The Future of Affirmative Action Got to the University of California First," *New Republic*, April 11, 1988, pp. 15–17; see also Takagi, *Retreat from Race*, p. 115.

25. Takagi, *Retreat from Race*, p. 110.

26. Ibid., pp. 110–11.

27. An additional 8 percent or so of students admitted were categorized as "Other," "Foreign," or "Decline to state."

28. Takagi, *Retreat from Race*, pp. 154–55.

29. Tomas Rivera, the chancellor at UC Riverside, had been the first person of color to hold such a position.

30. Mike Gonzalez, "Dr. Tien Appointed U.C. Chancellor; Ford, Kadish Lobby for Influence," *Cross Examiner*, March 1990, p. 5. The *Cross Examiner* took the place of the long-defunct student newspaper, the *Writ*.

31. Dinesh D'Souza, "Sins of Admission," in Nicolaus Mills, ed., *Debating Affirmative Action* (New York: Delta, 1994), pp. 230–36.

32. Chancellor Chang-Lin Tien, "Diversity in Higher Education," in Nicolaus Mills, ed., *Debating Affirmative Action* (New York: Delta, 1994) pp. 237–46. Essay is based on keynote address, "The Mutuality of Excellence and Equity Conference," University of Southern California, March 31, 1991.

33. Ibid., pp. 238–39.

34. Ibid., p. 243.

35. Graduation rates refer to students graduating in five years or less.

36. Tien, "Diversity in Higher Education," p. 245.

37. Ibid.

38. See University of California, Berkeley, Institute for Study of Social Change, "The Diversity Project: An Interim Report to the Chancellor" (1990).

39. Takagi, *Retreat from Race,* pp. 145–47 (discussing the findings of the Diversity Project).

40. Troy Duster, "They're Taking Over!—Myths about Multiculturalism," *Mother Jones,* September/October 1991 (discussing some of the findings of the hundreds of student interviews conducted for the Diversity Project).

41. Omi and Winant, *Racial Formation,* pp. 70–71.

42. Dean Choper in "Point Counter Point: Dean Choper and Renee Saucedo," *Cross Examiner,* September 1989, p. 5.

43. Dan Saunders, "Wrestling with Racism," *Cross Examiner,* February 1990, p. 4.

44. Evangeline Nichols, "Academic Support Program Director Responds to Saunders," *Cross Examiner,* March 1990, p. 3.

45. Saunders, "Wrestling with Racism," *Cross Examiner,* February 1990, p. 4.

46. Nichols, "Director Responds," *Cross Examiner,* March 1990, p. 3.

47. Gonzalez, "Dr. Tien Appointed U.C. Chancellor," p. 5.

48. Ibid.

49. Though James Crawford was new to the Boalt faculty, hired laterally as a tenured professor in 1979, he did not increase the number of minorities at the law school, since Henry Ramsey Jr., the one African American, had left in 1980 to accept a seat on the California Superior Court. Ramsey had been hired in 1971, shortly before John Wilkins, the first African American professor at Boalt, passed away. Aside from Wilkins and Ramsey, the only other minority professor to hold a tenured faculty position at Boalt was Sho Sato, a Japanese professor hired in 1951; see Susan Epstein, *Law at Berkeley* (Berkeley: Institute of Governmental Studies Press, 1997), pp. 279–80.

50. Sumi Cho and Robert Westley, "Historicizing Critical Race Theory's Cutting Edge: Key Movements That Performed the Theory," *UC Davis Law Review* (forthcoming), draft, p. 18.

51. Derrick A. Bell Jr., "Application of the 'Tipping Point' Principle to Law Faculty Hiring Policies," 10 *Nova Law Journal* 319–27, 319 (1986), noting that in a 1984 survey of law schools, excluding the historically black schools, there were only 14 schools with more than two minorities—10 schools with three, 3 with four, and 1 with five—and there were at least 28 schools with no minorities.

52. Ibid., pp. 319–20.

53. Ibid., pp. 321, 325. Bell more specifically recommended the application of the "tipping theory" to faculty hiring, wherein the hiring goal would represent a ratio of minorities to whites beyond which whites would leave the school, causing resegregation. The "tipping theory" is drawn from attempts to integrate housing. Bell writes, "[J]ust as policies of controlled racial occupancy enabled a degree of housing integration in areas that otherwise would have remained all-white or become all-black, so adopting similar procedures in legal education could result in a much needed increase in the number of truly integrated law faculties, and a far more productive and humane career for all teachers of color" ("Application of the 'Tipping Point' Principle," p. 326).

54. The CDF was organized in 1986 without previous knowledge of the former student organization by the same name.

55. David Ginsborg, "Boalt Students Call for Boycott of Law Classes," *Daily Californian,* March 22, 1988, p. 1; Marjorie Shultz, interview, April 28, 2000.

56. At the time she was hired, Professor Shultz was one of only two faculty members who had graduated from Boalt. The other was Henry Ramsey Jr., the one African American on the faculty. A large number of the other professors at the time had earned their law degrees from Harvard. See Epstein, *Law at Berkeley*, p. 286. Subsequently, Boalt hired more of its own graduates as well as graduates from other non–Ivy League law schools.

57. Marjorie Shultz, interview, April 28, 2000.

58. The official title of the position was "lecturer with security of employment," which means a permanent lecturer with life tenure.

59. Cho and Westley, "Historicizing Critical Race Theory's Cutting Edge," p. 12. In the few years that Japanese American professor Sho Sato taught at Boalt during this time period, he was an exception to the "one tenured faculty of color" statement. Three African American professors (John Wilkins, Henry Ramsey Jr., and James Crawford), each one apparently hired to replace the former, constituted, in succession, the "one tenured faculty of color."

60. Ginsborg, "Boalt Students Call for Boycott," p. 1.

61. Ibid.

62. David Ginsborg, "Students Arrested at Boalt Hall," *Daily Californian,* March 23, 1988, p. 1.

63. See Eleanor Swift, "Becoming a Plaintiff," 4 *Berkeley Women's L.J.* 245–50 (1988–89).

64. Cho and Westley, "Historicizing Critical Race Theory's Cutting Edge," p. 13.

65. Rene Saucedo, interview, November 2, 1999.

66. Cho and Westley, "Historicizing Critical Race Theory's Cutting Edge," p. 18.

67. Rosy Lee, "Arrests End Boalt Strike," *Daily Californian,* April 7, 1989, p. 1.

68. Robert Westley, "Boalt Hall Students Strike for Diversity," *Daily Californian,* April 6, 1989, p. 4.

69. Rosy Lee, "Boalt Students to Join in Strike," *Daily Californian,* April 5, 1989, p. 1.

70. Lee, "Arrests End Boalt Strike," p. 1.

71. Matt Weil, "Open Letter from Matt Weil," *Cross Examiner,* May 1989, p. 1.

72. "Diversity Protest Continues," *Cross Examiner,* May 1989, p. 1.

73. Doug Warrick, "The New Student-Faculty Diversity Committee," *Cross Examiner,* September 89, p. 1.

74. Robert Berring, interview, June 28, 2000.

75. Warrick, "New Student-Faculty Diversity Committee," p. 1.

76. Jared Slosberg, "The Degeneration of Affirmative Action," *Cross Examiner,* December 1989, p. 3.

77. Jonathon Poisner, "What Is Racism?" *Cross Examiner,* March 1990, p. 2.

78. See Swift, "Becoming a Plaintiff," pp. 245–50.

79. Greg Sterling, "Beyond Memo Wars," *Cross Examiner,* February 1990, p. 1.

80. Ibid.

81. Barry Mitchell and Mathew Weil, "Students, Faculty Debate Hiring," *Cross Examiner,* March 1990, p. 1.

82. Reflecting on the years in which he was dean, Choper stated that he wished he had "handled the issue of diversity differently" and specifically that he had been more receptive to student concerns. Jesse Choper, interview, April 25, 2000.

83. Rey Rodriguez, "A Call for Action," *Cross Examiner,* February 1990, p. 7.

84. Doug Warrick, "Law School: Just for Research?" *Cross Examiner,* March 1990, p. 1.

85. Ibid.

86. Ibid.

87. Jonathon Poisner, "CDF and the Limits of Protest," *Cross Examiner,* November 1990, p. 3.

88. Ibid.

89. Robert Berring to Faculty, memorandum reprinted in "Berring Confronts Faculty on Diversity Inaction," *Cross Examiner,* November 1990, p. 1.

90. "Second Town Meeting on Faculty Diversity Sparks Debate," *Cross Examiner,* December 1990, p. 8.

91. Ibid.

92. Filipino students were a notable exception. Though special consideration given under affirmative action to Filipino undergraduate applicants was reduced in 1990 and then eliminated in 1993, the need for affirmative action seemed to remain. In 1989, under a strong affirmative action program, 227 Filipinos matriculated. In 1990, only 114 matriculated, and in 1993, 54 matriculated. See Jerome Karabel, "No Alternative: The Effects of Color-Blind Admissions in California," in Gary Orfield and Edward Miller, eds., *Chilling Admissions: The Affirmative Action Crisis and the Search for Alternatives* (Cambridge, Mass.: Harvard Civil Rights Project and Harvard Education Publishing Group, 1998), pp. 35–36.

93. Takagi, *Retreat from Race,* pp. 133–34.

94. Herma Hill Kay, interview, April 21, 2000.

95. Epstein, *Law at Berkeley,* p. 330.

96. Ibid., p. 325.

97. See Rachel Moran, chair, "Admissions Policy Statement and Task Force Report," August 31, 1993, p. 24.

98. Ibid., p. 25, citing Admissions Committee to Faculty, Students and Staff, memorandum, "Tentative Report of the Admissions Committee on Special Admissions," January 15, 1973.

99. Ibid., p. 26, citing National Association of Independent Colleges and Universities and National Institute of Independent Colleges and Universities, "Minorities on Campus—Understanding Campus Climate: An Approach to Supporting Student Diversity," 20 (1991).

100. Ibid.

101. Moran, "Task Force Report," pp. 28–30.

102. "Faculty Policy Governing Admission to Boalt Hall" (adopted May 6, 1993); emphasis added.

103. Takagi, *Retreat from Race*, p. 10.

104. Omi and Winant, *Racial Formation in the United States*, p. 50.

105. Ibid., pp. 152, 156.

Chapter 3: Dismantling Diversity

1. Lydia Chavez, *The Color Bind* (Berkeley: University of California Press, 1998), pp. 8–11.

2. Ibid., pp. 13, 14.

3. Peter Schrag, *Paradise Lost* (Berkeley: University of California Press, 1998), p. 11.

4. Chavez, *Color Bind*, pp. 17–22.

5. Ibid., p. 24.

6. See Barry Bearak, "Questions of Race Run Deep for Foe of Preferences," *New York Times*, July 27, 1997, p. 1.

7. Chavez, *Color Bind*, pp. 26–27.

8. Ibid., pp. 28–29.

9. Ibid., pp. 29–30.

10. Ibid., pp. 31–32.

11. John E. Morris, "Boalt Hall's Affirmative Action Dilemma," *American Lawyer*, November 1997, p. 5.

12. Chavez, *Color Bind*, p. 34.

13. Schrag, *Paradise Lost*, pp. 229–31.

14. Ibid., p. 233.

15. Chavez, *Color Bind*, p. 38 (quoting Bill Stall and Cathleen Decker, "Wilson and Prop. 187 Win," *Los Angeles Times*, November 9, 1994, p. 1).

16. Ibid., p. 39.

17. Ibid., pp. 40–41, 44–45, 47.

18. Dexter Wah, "UC Agrees to Review Affirmative Action," *San Francisco Examiner*, January 20, 1995, p. A14.

19. Chavez, *Color Bind*, p. 49.

20. Dirk Tillotson, interview, November 12, 1999.

21. Joe Jaramillo, interview, April 22, 2000.

22. Ibid.

23. Ibid.

24. Chavez, *Color Bind*, p. 50.

25. Nicholas Lemann, *The Big Test* (New York: Farrar, Straus, and Giroux, 1999), p. 290.

26. Chavez, *Color Bind*, pp. 51, 52.

27. Schrag, *Paradise Lost*, p. 235.

28. Ward Connerly, "UC Must End Affirmative Action," *San Francisco Chronicle*, May 3, 1995, p. A19.

29. Larry Hatfield, "Impact of Affirmative Action at UC Detailed," *San Francisco Examiner,* May 16, 1995, p. A1.

30. Jan Vetter, interview in Boalt Transcript, Boalt Hall School of Law, 1995.

31. Jan Vetter, interview, April 21, 2000.

32. Ibid.

33. Joe Jaramillo, interview, April 22, 2000.

34. The term *Chicano* signifies a person of Mexican descent who was born and raised in the United States.

35. Jan Vetter, interview, April 21, 2000.

36. Dean Herma Hill Kay, Testimony before the University of California Board of Regents, May 18, 1995.

37. Though Southeast Asians were considered underrepresented at the law school and given special consideration under affirmative action, Boalt did not and still does not generally provide separate statistics on Southeast Asians and instead incorporates statistics on Southeast Asians into statistics on Asians.

38. Dean Herma Hill Kay, Testimony before the University of California Board of Regents, May 18, 1995.

39. Erin McCormick, "Affirmative Action Rally Disrupts US Regents Panel," *San Francisco Examiner,* May 18, 1995, p. A25.

40. Pamela Burdman, "Regents Plan to Kill UC Race Preferences," *San Francisco Chronicle,* July 6, 1995, p. A1.

41. Dexter Wah, " 'Mistake' to End UC Racial Policy," *San Francisco Examiner,* July 11, 1995, p. A8.

42. "Statement Supporting Affirmative Action by UC President, Chancellors, and Vice Presidents," available online at http://www.inform.umd.edu/EdRes/Topic/Diversity/Response/Action/policy.

43. *Adarand Constructors v. Pena,* 515 U.S. 200 (1995).

44. Lemann, *Big Test,* p. 307.

45. Joe Jaramillo, interview, April 22, 2000.

46. Lance Williams, "UC Affirmative Action Face-off in the City," *San Francisco Examiner,* July 20, 1995, p. A1.

47. Chavez, *Color Bind,* p. 65.

48. Notably, Regent William Bagley, believing the outcome to be a foregone conclusion, abstained from voting on SP-1 so that he could later bring a motion to rescind it. Under the regent bylaws, a regent voting against a successful resolution cannot bring a subsequent resolution to rescind the original resolution.

49. The full text of Resolution SP-1 is available online at the University of California website: http://www.ucop.edu.

50. Lance William, "Over Virulent Protests, Wavering Regents Side with Wilson, End UC Affirmative Action," *San Francisco Examiner,* July 21, 1995, p. A1.

51. Susan Yoachum, "UC Scraps Affirmative Action," *San Francisco Chronicle,* July 21, 1995, p. A1.

52. Robert Cole, interview, September 22, 1999.

53. Yoachum, "UC Scraps Affirmative Action," p. A1.

54. Heather McCabe, "Berkeley Streets Remain Calm after Decision," *Daily Californian,* July 21, 1995, p. 1.

55. Homer Mason, interviews, November 9, 1999, and April 17, 2000.

56. Yoachum, "UC Scraps Affirmative Action," p. A1.

57. Chavez, *Color Bind*, p. 67.

58. Lemann, *Big Test*, p. 307.

59. Chavez, *Color Bind*, pp. 68, 69.

60. Ibid., p. 69.

61. Daniel Tellalian, interview, November 14, 1999; Tellalian, interview, July 10, 2000.

62. Herma Hill Kay, interview, September 22, 1999.

63. Matt Morbello, "One Place to Be," *Cross Examiner*, October 1995.

64. "UC Students Rally for Affirmative Action," *San Francisco Chronicle*, October 13, 1995, p. A1.

65. Ryan Tate, "UC Regents Say Protests Will Not Change Their Minds or Policy," *San Francisco Chronicle*, October 13, 1995, p. A1.

66. Daniel Tellalian, interview, November 14, 1999.

67. Heather McCabe, "5,000 Flock to Sproul Plaza for Affirmative Action," *Daily Californian*, October 13, 1995, p. 1.

68. Edward Epstein, "Faculty Opposes Getting Affirmative Action at UC," *San Francisco Chronicle*, October 21, 1995, p. A13.

69. Chavez, *Color Bind*, p. 73.

70. Ibid., p. 72.

71. Yumi Wilson, "Affirmative Action Fight Seeks Regent," *San Francisco Chronicle*, November 23, 1995, p. A1; and "Regent to Lead," *San Francisco Chronicle*, December 1, 1995.

72. Chavez, *Color Bind*, p. 73.

73. Ibid., pp. 74–75.

74. Regents of the University of California, Meeting of the Committee on Educational Policy, January 18, 1996.

75. Regents of the University of California, Meeting of the Committee on Educational Policy, March 14, 1996.

76. "Horrid Proposal to End UC Minority Outreach," *San Francisco Examiner*, February 17, 1996, p. A18.

77. Ryan Tate, "Report Says Regents Influenced Admissions," *Daily Californian*, March 18, 1996, p. 1.

78. Richard Russell, interview, April 26, 2000.

79. After the newspapers broke the story in March, Ward Connerly proposed to the regents that donor preferences be eliminated. Connerly was trying to expand his anti–affirmative action message to states beyond California and, arguably, the news accounts hurt his credibility. The proposal appeared to be a political move to offset damage to his credibility. The regents voted his proposal down, however, because the chancellors argued that such preferences were an important tool in fund-raising.

80. Andrea Peterson to Members of the Admissions Policy Committee, memorandum, "Projected Minority Enrollment and Breakdown of the Class by Index Score Using Three Different Hypothetical Admissions Policies," attachment 1, April 5, 1996.

81. See "Faculty Admissions Policy" (1996). The director of admissions acts upon a certain number of applications and, at his or her discretion, administratively admits candidates with high PGAs (combined LSATs and UGPAs) and denies candidates with low PGAs. Under the 1996 policy, the faculty voted to send two hundred more of those files which would presumably be acted upon negatively to the Admissions Committee.

82. Marjorie Shultz to Boalt Faculty, "Admissions," memorandum, April 22, 1996, 1–2.

83. Ibid., pp. 2–3.

84. Richard Delgado, commencement speech, May 1996; see also Richard Delgado, "1998 Hugo L. Black Lecture: Ten Arguments against Affirmative Action—How Valid?" 50 *Alabama Law Review* 135–54 (1998).

85. Lemann, *Big Test,* p. 318.

86. Carla Marinucci and Steven A. Capps, "Urges GOP Crusade against Discrimination," *San Francisco Chronicle,* August 13, 1996, p. A1.

87. Chavez, *Color Bind,* p. 153.

88. Ibid., p. 120 (emphasis added).

89. Lemann, *Big Test,* pp. 330, 291–92, 326.

90. Ibid., p. 325.

91. Ibid., pp. 178–83.

92. Annie Nakao, "Furor over Dr. King Ad Ignites 209 Fight," *San Francisco Examiner,* October 24, 1996, p. A1.

93. Lemann, *Big Test,* pp. 328, 329

94. Chavez, *Color Bind,* p. 240.

95. Edward Lempinen, "Measure to Cut Back Affirmative Action Wins," *San Francisco Chronicle,* November 6, 1996, p. A1.

96. Of women voting in the election, 52 percent voted "no."

97. *Coalition for Economic Equity v. Wilson,* 946 F. Supp. 1480, 1495 (N.D. Cal. Dec. 23, 1996).

98. Lempinen, "Measure to Cut Back Affirmative Action Wins," p. A1.

99. Chavez, *Color Bind,* p. 237.

100. *Coalition for Economic Equity v. Wilson,* p. 1490.

101. Edward Lempinen, "Affirmative Action Foe Connerly Goes National," *San Francisco Chronicle,* December 4, 1996, p. A1.

102. Edward Lempinen, "Connerly Widens Anti–Affirmative Action Campaign," *San Francisco Chronicle,* January 16, 1997, p. A17.

103. Pamela Burdman, "Connerly Advocates Name-blind UC Admissions," *San Francisco Chronicle,* March 12, 1997, p. A17.

104. Student affidavit included in Office for Civil Rights Complaint (U.S. Department of Education), filed by the Mexican American Legal Defense and Education Fund (MALDEF), NAACP Legal Defense Fund, California Women's Law Center, and Equal Rights Advocates, March 19, 1997.

105. Marcela von Vacano, interview, November 19, 1999; von Vacano was a student member of the Admissions Committee at the time.

106. Office for Civil Rights Complaint, March 19, 1997.

107. Ibid.

108. Ibid.

109. Ibid. See also grade adjustment guidelines provided to 1996 Boalt Admissions Committee, showing the adjustment (or no adjustment) made to UGPAs for every undergraduate institution.

110. Ibid.

111. Joe Jaramillo, interview, November 15, 1999.

112. Harriet Chiang, "The Man behind Infamous Ruling," *San Francisco Chronicle,* August 28, 1997, p. A1.

113. *Coalition for Economic Equity v. Wilson,* pp. 1431, 1437.

114. Kaaryn Gustafson et al., "New Directions in Diversity," report, May 1997 (n.p.).

115. Letter of support from Congressman Ron Dellums sent to authors of "New Directions in Diversity."

116. No statistics were made available for Southeast Asians, who are also underrepresented at the law school.

117. Boalt Hall Law School, Press Release on Admissions, May 14, 1997.

118. The results of "race-blind" admissions at two of the five medical schools at the University of California—San Diego and Irvine—were also disastrous. UCSD admitted zero African Americans (down from 7 in 1996) and 7 Mexican Americans (down from 26); UCI admitted only 1 African American (down from 4 in 1996) and 7 Mexican Americans (down from 13). Pamela Burdman, "2 UC Medical Incoming Classes Have No Blacks," *San Francisco Chronicle,* August 1, 1997, p. 1.

119. Dana Kiyomura, "Boalt Admits Fewer Blacks, Latinos," *Daily Californian,* May 15, 1997.

120. Quotations from Connerly taken, respectively, from Kenneth R. Weiss, "UC Law Schools' New Rules Cost Minorities Spots," *Los Angeles Times,* May 15, 1997, p. 1; Renee Koury, "UC Admissions for Latinos, Blacks Tumble," *San Jose Mercury News,* May 15, 1997, p. 1A; Weiss, "UC Law Schools' New Rules," p. 1; and Koury, "UC Admissions," p. 1A.

121. Julian Guthrie, "Racial Shift at California Law Schools," *San Francisco Examiner,* May 15, 1997, p. A1. For a refutation of the thesis that blacks have a culture that condemns academic success and that this contributes to lower achievement, see Philip J. Cook and Jens Ludwig, "The Burden of 'Acting White': Do Black Adolescents Disparage Academic Achievement?" in Christopher Jencks and Meredith Phillips, eds., *The Black-White Test Score Gap* (Washington, DC: Brookings Institution Press, 1998), pp. 375–400.

122. Leslie Brown, interview, November 1, 1999.

123. Weiss, "UC Law Schools' New Rules," p. 1.

124. Quotations from Dean Kay and Richard Russell taken from Amy Wallace, "UC Law School Class May Have Only 1 Black," *Los Angeles Times,* June 27, 1997, p. 1.

125. Quotations from Ray Marshall and Krystal Denley taken from Annie Nakao, "Big Minority Dip at Boalt Rattles S.F. Law Firms," *San Francisco Chronicle,* July 6, 1997, p. A1.

126. Robert Selna, "Alone in the Spotlight," *San Jose Mercury News,* West, p. 20.

127. Robert Harris and Dean Kay quoted in Nakao, "Big Minority Dip," p. A1.

128. NPR program, *All Things Considered,* aired July 8, 1997.

129. Henry Ramsey, Jr., "Test Scores Aren't 100% of the Picture," reprinted in *San Jose Mercury News,* August 14, 1997, p. 10B.

130. Louis Freedberg, "UC Regent Says Boalt Hall Dean Snubs Minorities," *San Francisco Chronicle,* July 12, 1997, p. A1.

131. Annie Nakao, "Boalt's Dean Kay Caught in the Middle," *San Francisco Examiner,* July 27, 1997, p. A1.

Chapter 4: Reaching for Answers

1. A total of 15 underrepresented minorities matriculated, but 8 were defers (7 Latinos and 1 African American).

2. Though "race-blind" admissions resulted in no African Americans and only a few Mexican Americans at the medical schools at UC San Diego and UC Irvine, these schools had not previously enrolled the same high number of minority students that Boalt had. In 1996, UCSD enrolled only 3 African Americans and 7 Mexican Americans; UCI enrolled only 2 African Americans and 1 Mexican American. See Pamela Burdman, "Two UC Medical Incoming Classes Have No Blacks," *San Francisco Chronicle,* August 1, 1997, p. 1.

3. Bar Association of San Francisco hiring guidelines were adopted in 1989 by the BASF Board of Directors and subsequently by almost one hundred San Francisco employers. See http://www.sfbar.org/about/diversity.

4. Steve Gonzalez, "Who Gets the Call-Backs?" *Cross Examiner,* November 1989, p. 1, citing "Gender, Ethnicity and Grades: Empirical Evidence of Discrimination in Law-Firm Interviews," *Law and Inequality: A Journal of Theory and Practice* 7, no. 2 (March 1989).

5. Eva Paterson, interview, May 23, 2000.

6. Statement for the ABA National Convention, issued by coalition of law students and lawyers identifying themselves as PRIDE (Protecting and Recognizing the Importance of Diversity in Education), San Francisco, July 1997.

7. Eva Paterson, interview, May 23, 2000.

8. Eric Brooks, interview, April 20, 2000.

9. Eric Brooks, statement to the press, August 18, 1997.

10. Norma Aguilar, interview, September 28, 1997.

11. Norma Aguilar, interview, June 20, 2000.

12. Ibid.

13. Pamela Burdman, "Boalt Hall Alumni Blast UC Policy," *San Francisco Chronicle,* August 19, 1997, p. 13.

14. Amy Wallace, "Lone Black in Boalt Hall Class Urges Change," *Los Angeles Times,* August 19, 1997, p. A3.

15. Ibid.

16. Alumni speak-out press release issued by PRIDE, August 18, 1997.

17. Eric Brooks, interview, September 22, 1999.

18. Manjari Chawla, interview, July 11, 2000. Affirmative action programs are not generally extended to South Asians (Indians) in the United States.

19. Alistair Newbern, interview, April 22, 2000.

20. Mike Murphy, interview, April 24, 2000.

21. Burdman, "Boalt Hall Alumni."

22. Eric Brooks, interview, September 22, 1999.

23. Chancellor Robert Berdahl, Message to the Campus Community, "What's Going On?" August 18, 1997.

24. Amy Wallace, "Lone Black in Boalt Hall Class Urges Change," Los Angeles Times, p. A28.

25. Boalt Hall, "Questions and Answers," information sheet, August 18, 1997.

26. Eric Brooks, interview, September 22, 1999.

27. Norma Aguilar, interview, June 28, 2000.

28. Marjorie Shultz, "Excellence Lost," 13 Berkeley Women's Law Journal 26, 26–27 (1998).

29. Manjari Chawla, interview, September 28, 1999.

30. Terri Yuh-lin Chen, interview, November 15, 1999.

31. Sonya Enchill, interview, November 16, 1999.

32. Andrea Guerrero, "Education for the Twenty-first Century: An Ethos of Diversity," San Francisco Lawyers' Committee News, fall 1997, p. 8.

33. Larry D. Hatfield, "Thousands Rally against 209," San Francisco Examiner, August 28, 1997, p. A1.

34. Eric Brooks, interview, September 22, 1999.

35. The failures to conduct targeted outreach and administer or publish information about minority scholarships were haphazard actions that were not uniformly adopted and, as noted, did not last. They appeared to result from confusion within the administration as to what was permissible at that time.

36. Marcela von Vacano, interview, November 19, 1999.

37. John Yoo, interview, April 27, 2000.

38. As a student, it was difficult to know exactly what was going on with the dean and faculty; from their actions, and at times from their own words, their hesitancy appeared to arise from concern that any action that could be perceived as race-conscious would subject them to repercussions.

39. Daniel Tellalian, interview, November 16, 1999.

40. Eric Brooks, interview, September 22, 1999.

41. Annie Nakao, "Entering Boalt Students Chafe at Homogeneity," San Francisco Chronicle, September 13, 1997, p. A3.

42. CDF/SB to Boalt Hall Faculty, "Student Recommendations for Admissions Policy Reform," letter, September 18, 1997.

43. Venus McGhee, interview, September 10, 2000.

44. Norma Aguilar, interview, September 28, 1999.

45. Before leaving the room, a third-year African American student from Boalt criticized the professor for not calling on minority students who had entered the class. In all fairness, the professor had called on a few, but perhaps the student

felt not enough, of the visiting minority students. This criticism led some student observers in class to rebuke the protesters later as aggressive and hostile. Having been one of the visiting minority students in that class, I feel that the rebuke was excessive. Emotions were high, and the African American student may have over-stated her criticism, but the visiting minority students on the whole conducted themselves in a civil and respectful manner, raising their hands, waiting to be called on, and responding to the subject matter being taught. In the other class in which visiting minority students entered, a minority student made a similar criticism of the professor and was also rebuked. In that instance, the professor had in fact refused to call on visiting minority students, and a minority student only spoke when a white student in the class was called on and gave the floor to the minority student.

46. Protesting students to dean and faculty, "Demand Statement," October 13, 1997.

47. Video footage taken by Hotbed Media, October 13, 1997.

48. Daniel Tellalian, interview, November 16, 1999.

49. "53 Students Arrested," *Cross Examiner*, October 1997.

50. Recounting the arrest procedure, Dean Kay stated, "I consulted with Vice Chancellor Horace Mitchell, who was observing the situation at Boalt, and we de-cided together that since the students had refused to leave the Registrar's Office, the arrests were necessary." Kay e-mail to author, December 20, 1999.

51. Police Captain William S. Cooper, letter to author, March 13, 1998.

52. Norma Aguilar, interview, September 28, 1999.

53. Sonya Enchill, interview, November 16, 1999.

54. Manjari Chawla, interview, September 28, 1999.

55. Glen Turner, open letter to students, October 1997. Turner was a first-year student at Boalt at the time.

56. Terri Yuh-lin Chen, interview, November 15, 1999.

57. Anthony Patel, "The Great Buzzword," in David Wiener and Marc Berley, eds., *The Diversity Hoax* (New York: FAST, 1999), p. 44.

58. Siri Shetty, interview, September 28, 1999.

59. Norma Aguilar, interview, September 28, 1999.

60. Dean Herma Hill Kay, "Town Hall Meeting on Admissions," *Boalt Bul-letin Board,* October 27, 1997.

61. Lloyd Farnham and Todd Jackson, Editorial, *Cross Examiner*, October 1997.

62. Garner Weng, "How Stella Got Her Character," 13 *Berkeley Women's Law Journal* 19, 24–25 (1998).

63. Associate Dean Robert Cole, Chair, "Report of an Ad Hoc Task Force on Diversity in Admissions," Boalt Hall, October 14, 1997.

64. Daniel Tellalian, interview, November 16, 1999.

65. Robert Selna, "Alone in the Spotlight," *San Jose Mercury News,* p. 8.

66. Ibid., p. 12.

67. Aman Thind, interview, November 11, 1999.

68. Dawn Mann Valentine, interview, November 10, 1999.

69. The requirements for an initiative campaign in California can be found at the secretary of state's website, http://www.ss.ca.gov. For further insight into running an initiative campaign, see Jim Shultz, *The Initiative Cookbook,* available online, http://www.democracyctr.org/cookbook.html.

70. Aman Thind, interview, November 11, 1999.

71. Dawn Mann Valentine, interview, November 10, 1999.

72. Eva Paterson, interview, May 23, 2000.

73. Adam Murray, interview, November 14, 1999.

74. For a description of the programs targeted by Wilson, see American Civil Liberties Union, *Reaching for the Dream: Profiles in Affirmative Action* (San Francisco: ACLU, 1998).

75. Aman Thind, interview, November 11, 1999.

76. SEO press release, "Thousands of Students across California Mobilize to Place the Equal Educational Opportunity Initiative on the Ballot," February 9, 1998.

77. Editorial, "Promoting Educational Opportunities," *Stanford Daily,* January 20, 1998.

78. Renee Koury, "Jesse Jackson Joins Students' Initiative Drive," *San Jose Mercury News,* February 19, 1998, p. 1B.

79. Barbara Lee was elected into office in a midterm election on April 7, 1998, to replace retiring Congressman Ron Dellums. Lee supported the EEOI as a U.S. congresswoman and, prior to that, as a California state senator.

80. Randy Parraz, "Letter from the Editor," *Hispanic National Bar Noticias* (winter 1998): 2.

81. Adam Murray, interview, November 14, 1999.

82. Aman Thind, interview, November 11, 1999.

83. Adam Murray, interview, November 14, 1999.

84. Dawn Mann Valentine, interview, November 10, 1999.

85. Sandra Alvarez, interview, November 9, 1999.

86. Laura Schiebelhut, "Dramatic Drop in Minority Admits," *Daily Californian,* April 1, 1998, p. 3.

87. Advanced Placement courses in California are graded on a 5.0 scale, making it possible for students who take such courses to have a grade point average above 4.0.

88. Schiebelhut, "Dramatic Drop," *Daily Californian,* April 1, 1998, p. 3.

89. Laura Schiebelhut, "Campus Reacts to Admissions," *Daily Californian,* April 1, 1998, p. 3.

90. Henry K. Lee, "Oakland Teachers Decry UC Rebuff of Top Students," *San Francisco Chronicle,* April 17, 1998.

91. Kevin Leung, "Students Express Support for Lawsuit," *Daily Californian,* February 3, 1999, p. 5.

92. Schiebelhut, "Campus Reacts," *Daily Californian,* April 1, 1998, p. 3.

93. SEO press release, "Students Gain Support for Drive to Qualify Affirmative Action Initiative," April 12, 1998.

94. Andrea Guerrero, "The Equal Opportunity Initiative," in San Francisco La Raza Lawyers' Association, *La Voz* (spring/summer 1998): 9.

95. David S. Broder, *Democracy Derailed: Initiative Campaigns and the Power of Money* (New York: Harcourt, 2000), pp. 91–92.

96. See Kenneth Howe, "Big Money Swamps the Ballot Initiative" and "Well-Paid Armies Wielding Clipboards," *San Francisco Chronicle,* May 19, 1998, p. 1 (parts of a series on the California initiative process).

97. Khari Tillery, interview, November 13, 1999.

98. Sonya Enchill, interview, November 16, 1999.

99. Khari Tillery, interview, November 13, 1999.

100. Dawn Mann Valentine, interview, November 10, 1999.

101. Testing for the Public, press release and study conclusions, September 29, 1998.

102. William Kidder, interview, April 27, 2000.

103. Note that the scale on which the LSAT is scored changed from a highest possible scaled score of 800 to a highest possible scaled score of 180.

104. Brady R. Dewar and Vasant M. Kamath, "Report Shows LSAT Score Gap," *Harvard Crimson,* October 2, 1998.

105. Claude M. Steele, "Thin Ice: 'Stereotype Threat' and Black College Students," *Atlantic Monthly,* August 1999, p. 50.

106. Chris Jenkins, "Study Highlights Disparities in LSAT Scores," *Daily Californian,* October 29, 1998, page 1.

107. Ibid.

108. "New Definitions of Merit" Committee progress report, Boalt Hall, November 1998.

109. Decreased minority enrollment at Berkeley and UCLA might also diminish the minority applicant pool to law schools nationally, since in the 1997–98 application cycle, UCLA and Berkeley, respectively were the top two producers of law school applicants in the country.

110. The case was originally filed as *Rios v. Regents of the University of California* and is now called *Castaneda v. Regents of the University of California.*

111. Seth Rosenfeld, "Rights Groups Launch Legal Bid on Behalf of Honor Students Denied Admission," *San Francisco Chronicle,* February 2, 1999.

112. *Rios* (now *Castaneda*) *v. Regents,* Complaint, February 1999.

113. Z. Byron Wolf, "Task Force Urges Regents to Drop SAT Requirement," *Daily Californian,* September 19, 1997; Pamela Burdman, "UC Regents May Drop SAT Requirement," *San Francisco Chronicle,* September 19, 1997, p. A6.

114. Kevin Leung, "Crowd Rallies to Support Suit," *Daily Californian,* February 3, 1998, p. 1.

115. Seth Rosenfeld, "UC Berkeley Sued over Minority Admissions," *San Francisco Chronicle,* February 3, 1999.

116. Pamela Burdman, "Two Challenges Set for UC's Race-Blind Admissions," *San Francisco Chronicle,* February 8, 1999.

117. Robert B. Gunnison, "Bill Backing Outreach for Women, Minorities Vetoed," *San Francisco Chronicle,* July 29, 1999.

118. The ACLU asserts that Governor Davis, since taking office, has refused to do anything meaningful to address the problem of racial profiling (the police practice of disproportionately stopping and searching minority motorists); he

has betrayed his promise to support affirmative action; he has blocked the enforcement of antidiscrimination laws; he has appealed a federal court decision striking down Proposition 187; he has turned a blind eye to gross educational inequality; and he has supported a ballot measure (Proposition 21) to prosecute children as young as fourteen as adults and has eliminated juvenile crime prevention programs. See Michelle Alexander, "A Racial Justice Report Card for Governor Gray Davis—Midterm Grade: F," ACLU of Northern California website, http://www.aclunc.org, August 10, 2000.

119. William G. Bowen and Derek Bok, *The Shape of the River: Long Term Consequences of Considering Race in College and University Admissions* (Princeton, NJ: Princeton University Press, 1998), p. 47, citing Thomas J. Kane, "Racial and Ethnic Preferences in College Admissions," in Christopher Jencks and Meredith Phillips, eds., *The Black-White Test Score Gap* (Washington, DC: Brookings Institution, forthcoming). See also Linda Wightman, "The Threat to Diversity in Legal Education: An Empirical Analysis of the Consequences of Abandoning Race as a Factor in Law School Admissions Decisions," 72 *New York Univ. Law Rev.* 1, 39–45 (1997), demonstrating that socioeconomic factors are no substitute for race in the admission of a diverse student body.

120. For an analysis of UCLA's socioeconomic admissions experiment, see Deborah C. Malamud, "Assessing Class-Based Affirmative Action," 47 *J. Legal Educ.* 452 (1997); Richard H. Sander, "Experimenting with Class-Based Affirmative Action," 47 *J. Legal Educ.* 472 (1997); Deborah C. Malamud, "A Response to Professor Sander," 47 *J. Legal Educ.* 504 (1997); Richard H. Sander, "Comment in Reply," 47 *J. Legal Educ.* 512 (1997); Richard D. Kahlenberg, "In Search of Fairness: A Better Way," *Washington Monthly* 26 (June 1998).

121. Dean Herma Hill Kay, commencement remarks, May 1999.

122. The estimate of two thousand is based on the minimum percentage (approximately 25 percent) of minority students entering Boalt from the years 1970 to 1998; the figure assumes a total class size of 270 students.

123. The statement was written principally by third-year student Priya Sridharan and reviewed by about fifty other third-year students.

Chapter 5: Listening to the Silence

1. Rafael Mandelman, interview, September 22, 1999.
2. Rafael Mandelman, interview, July 6, 2000.
3. Rafael Mandelman, interview, September 22, 1999.
4. Oscar Cisneros, interview, April 18, 2000.
5. The *La Raza Law Journal* at Boalt (one of only a few such journals in the country) is also having severe staffing problems that have already led to publication delays. Similarly, the *National Black Law Journal* has been forced to move from the UCLA law school because of staffing problems.
6. Eric Brooks, interview, September 22, 1999.
7. Rafael Mandelman, interview, September 22, 1999.
8. Khari Tillery, interview, November 13, 1999.

9. Rafael Mandelman, interview, September 22, 1999.

10. In 1999, Boalt student David Weiner (class of 2000) and Marc Berley, the executive director of the Foundation for Academic Standards and Traditions (FAST), published a collection of essays attacking the "diversity movement" at Boalt, in a book entitled *The Diversity Hoax: Law Students Report from Berkeley* (New York: FAST, 1999); the essays come predominantly from members of the class of 2000.

11. Rafael Mandelman, interview, September 22, 1999 (recounting a conversation with another student in class).

12. Khari Tillery, interview, November 13, 1999.

13. Eric Brooks, interview, April 14, 2000. The East Bay Community Law Clinic was formerly known as the Berkeley Community Law Center (BCLC).

14. Eric Brooks, "Questions of Difference," reflection piece written for EBCLC class, March 8, 1999.

15. Bernida Reagan, interview, September 24, 1999.

16. Bernida Reagan, "The Impact of Cutbacks in Affirmative Action on Community Lawyering," 14 *Berkeley Women's Law Journal* 6 (1999).

17. Ibid.

18. Ibid.

19. Daniel Tellalian, interview, November 17, 1999.

20. Pedro Noguera, Opinion, "Diversity Forever Changed," *Daily Californian,* November 2, 1999. Noguera subsequently left the University of California.

21. Sunil Gupta, interview, September 22, 1999; Gupta, interview, April 28, 2000.

22. Lujuana Treadwell, interview, September 28, 1999. Treadwell subsequently left Boalt.

23. Sunil Gupta, interview, September 22, 1999.

24. Khari Tillery, interview, November 13, 1999.

25. Norma Aguilar, interview, September 28, 1999.

26. Ibid.

27. Khari Tillery, interview, November 1999.

28. Ibid.

29. Herma Hill Kay, interview, September 22, 1999.

30. Robert Berring, interview, June 28, 2000.

31. Robert Cole, interview, May 3, 2000.

32. Linda Wightman, "The Threat to Diversity in Legal Education," 72 *New York University Law Review* 1–52, 50 (1997).

33. Wightman, "Threat to Diversity," pp. 36–38 (of the students who would have been rejected based on numerical indicators, Wightman found in her study that 79 percent of Native Americans graduated and 76 percent passed the bar; 88 percent of Asians graduated and 88 percent passed the bar; 78 percent of African Americans graduated and 73 percent passed the bar; and 84 percent of Latinos graduated and 83 percent passed the bar).

34. Stephan Thernstrom, "Farewell to Preferences?" 130 *Pub. Interest* 34, 41 (1998).

35. See Nanette Asimov, "Asian American Students Trickle In to Law Schools," *San Francisco Chronicle,* February 23, 2001 (reporting on findings by William Kidder indicating that Asians are *not,* as Stephan Thernstrom suggests, "distinctly better off" in a race-blind admissions process; Kidder accuses Thernstrom of manipulating data to reach his conclusion, and Thernstrom responds, "I don't do that," but admits that he might not have painted the whole picture, stating, "I may have assumed there were no changes in enrollment. I didn't know").

36. William C. Kidder, "Situating Asian Pacific Americans in the Law School Affirmative Action Debate: Empirical Facts about Thernstrom's Rhetorical Acts," 7 *Asian Law Journal* 29, 42–43 (2000).

37. William C. Kidder, "Portia Denied: Unmasking Gender Bias on the LSAT and Its Relationship to Racial Diversity in Legal Education," 12 *Yale J.L. & Feminism* 1, 24 (2000).

38. Ibid., p. 33.

39. Ibid., pp. 33–34.

40. Ibid., pp. 32–34.

41. Ibid., pp. 34–35.

42. Wightman, "Threat to Diversity," pp. 29–31.

43. See Richard O. Lempert, David L. Chambers, and Terry K. Adams, "Michigan's Minority Graduates in Practice: The River Runs through Law School," 25 *Law & Social Inquiry* 395–505 (2000). See also William C. Kidder, "The Rise of the Testocracy," 9 *Tex. J. Women & L.* 198 (2000; discussing Michigan study); Lani Guinier, "Law School Affirmative Action: An Empirical Study of Confirmative Action," 25 *Law & Social Inquiry* 565–83 (2000) (also discussing Michigan study).

44. Kidder, "Rise of the Testocracy," pp. 197–98.

45. *United States v. Fordice,* 505 U.S. 717, 736–37 (1992) (rejecting Mississippi's exclusive reliance on the ACT for college admission purposes where the *ACT Manual* recommended that the test should not be the sole factor in admissions decisions).

46. LSAC, *The Law School Admission Test: Sources, Contents, Uses* (1991), pamphlet.

47. Kidder, "Portia Denied," p. 20.

48. Marjorie Shultz, interview, April 28, 2000.

49. Marjorie Shultz, grant proposal submitted to Law School Admission Council, January 31, 2000.

50. Guinier, "Confirmative Action," pp. 566, 572.

51. Letter to Chancellor Berdahl from eleven student organizations at Boalt opposing the selection of Professor John Dwyer as dean, February 11, 2000.

52. Ibid.

53. Tanya Schevitz, "New Dean Chosen for Boalt: Environmental Law Professor Gets Nod," *San Francisco Chronicle,* February 15, 2000, p. A17.

54. Open forum with Professor John Dwyer, Boalt Hall, hosted by Boalt Hall Students Association, April 13, 2000.

55. Angela Harris, interview, April 27, 2000. James Crawford, the one tenured African American professor at Boalt when Harris was hired, retired in 1997. Bryan Ford, another African American who was hired with Harris, left Boalt several years earlier to take a tenure-track position at another law school.

56. Ave Mince-Didier, interview, April 20, 2000.

57. John Tanghe, interview, April 20, 2000.

58. Angela Harris, interview, April 27, 2000.

59. Robert Berring, interview, June 28, 2000.

60. Dirk Tillotson, "School Colors: The Whitewashing of Boalt Hall Harms Its Students and the Profession," *San Francisco Daily Journal,* October 22, 1999, p. 4.

61. William G. Bowen and Derek Bok, *The Shape of the River* (Princeton, NJ: Princeton University Press, 1998), pp. 285, 281, 168–69.

62. Guinier, "Confirmative Action," pp. 568–69 (discussing Lempert, Chambers, and Adams, "Michigan's Minority Graduates in Practice," p. 395).

63. Bowen and Bok, *Shape of the River,* p. 10.

64. Ibid., p. 11.

65. United States Census Bureau, *Statistical Abstract of the United States,* table 672 (1998).

66. Affirmative Action Committee of the San Francisco Bay Area Chapter of the National Lawyers' Guild, "Affirmative Action" (brochure), July 1997.

67. Bowen and Bok, *Shape of the River,* pp. 267–68.

68. See Thomas J. Sugrue, "Expert Report of Thomas J. Sugrue," 5 *Mich J. Race & L.* 261 (1999). This is one of several expert reports prepared for the University of Michigan in its defense in court of its affirmative action program.

69. University of Michigan, "Expert Report: The Compelling Need for Diversity in Higher Education," 5 *Mich. J. Race & L.* 241, 249 (1999), summarizing "Expert Report of Patricia Gurin," 5 *Mich. J. Race & L.* 363–426 (1999).

70. Patricia Gurin, "Expert Report of Patricia Gurin," 5 *Mich. J. Race & L.* 365–66 (1999).

71. Gary Orfield and John Yun, *Resegregation in American Schools* (Cambridge, MA: Harvard University, Civil Rights Project, June 1999), table 11, p. 15.

72. John Matlock, "Student Expectations and Experiences: The Michigan Study," *Diversity Digest* (summer 1997), p. 11.

73. Gary Orfield and Dean Whitla, *Diversity in Legal Education: Student Experiences in Leading Law Schools,* a report of the Civil Rights Project, Harvard University, August 1999, p. 11 and table 12, p. 17. This study was conducted through a Gallup Poll that surveyed 81 percent of the student bodies at Harvard and Michigan—two of the most competitive law schools in the country, ranking number one and eight, respectively, in the *U.S. News and World Report* rankings. The racial and ethnic composition of the survey population was 6.7 percent African American, 10.3 percent Asian, 4.3 percent Latino, 0.6 percent Native American, 66.9 percent White, 2.8 percent Mixed, 7.6 percent Foreign, 0.9 percent Refused Question/Unknown.

74. Ibid., table 9, p. 15.

75. Ibid., table 16, p. 19; table 18, p. 21; table 20, p. 22; table 19, p. 21.

76. Gurin, "Expert Report," p. 367.

77. State of California, Department of Finance, "County Population Projections with Race/Ethnic Detail" (Sacramento, CA, December 1998).

78. State Bar of California, "Survey Finds Bar Makeup Is Shifting, but Slowly," *California Bar Journal* (November 2001): 1, 11.

79. Tillotson, "School Colors," *San Francisco Daily Journal,* October 22, 1999, p. 4.

80. *Hopwood v. Texas,* 78 F.3d 932 (Fifth Cir. 1996).

81. It is believed, however, that before Louisiana and Mississippi can end affirmative action at their public universities, they must first comply with previous desegregation orders.

82. Order Denying Writ of Certiorari, 518 U.S. 1033 (1996).

83. Christy Hoppe, "Judges Asked to Revisit Affirmative Action Suit," *Dallas Morning News,* June 8, 2000, p. 27A.

84. *Sweatt v. Painter* was the case relied upon by Justice Douglas in *Bakke* to conclude that legal education was an example of the type of program that would benefit from a diverse student body. See Thomas D. Russell, "The Shape of the Michigan River as Viewed from the Land of *Sweatt v. Painter* and *Hopwood,*" 25 *Law & Soc. Inquiry* 507, 507–8 (2000).

85. David S. Broder, *Democracy Derailed* (New York: Harcourt, 2000), p. 173.

86. Broder, *Democracy Derailed,* pp. 177–80.

87. Louis Freedberg, "Connerly Exults at New Affirmative Action Ban: Initiative Wins in Washington State," *San Francisco Chronicle,* November 5, 1998, p. A3.

88. Editorial, "Spare Florida a Prop. 209 Stink," *San Francisco Examiner,* June 8, 1999, p. A18.

89. See Jeffrey Selingo, "What States Aren't Saying about the 'X-Percent Solution,'" *Chronicle of Higher Education,* June 2, 2000, p. A31.

90. Jeffrey Selingo, "U. of Texas at Austin Still Draws Half of Its Students from a Handful of High Schools, Study Finds," *Chronicle of Higher Education,* Monday, April 2, 2001, www.chronicle.merit.edu.

91. Selection criteria adopted by the University of California for its undergraduate admissions in 1988, prior to the repeal of affirmative action.

92. Grace Frank, "University Preferences End," *Tampa Tribune,* February 18, 2000, p. 1.

93. Bill Cotterell, "Connerly: Drive's Off, for Now," *Tallahassee Democrat,* May 8, 2000, p. 1.

94. *Johnson v. Bd. of Regents,* 106 F. Supp. 2d 1362 (S.D. Ga., 2000); see, respectively, pp. 1369–71, 1373, 1371–72.

95. Sara Hebel, "Courting a Place in Legal History," *Chronicle of Higher Education,* November 24, 2000, www.chronicle.merit.edu.

96. See *Adarand Constructors v. Pena,* 515 U.S. 200 (1995) (plurality opinion); *Wygant v. Jackson Bd. of Education,* 476 U.S. 267 (1986).

97. See Sara Hebel, "U.S. Appeals Court Upholds Use of Affirmative Action in Admissions," *Chronicle of Higher Education,* December 15, 2000, www.chronicle.merit.edu.

98. *Smith v. University of Washington Law School,* 194 F.3d 1045 (9th Cir. 1999).

99. *Smith v. University of Washington Law School,* 233 F.3d 1188 (9th Cir. 2000).

100. Ben Gose, "Supreme Court Declines to Review Affirmative Action in Higher Education," *Chronicle of Higher Education,* May 29, 2001, www.chronicle.merit.edu.

101. Hoppe, "Judges Asked to Revisit Affirmative Action Suit."

102. Ibid.

103. *Hopwood v. Texas,* 236 F.3d 256 (Fifth Cir. 2000); see also Mary Ann Roser and Sharon Jayson, "UT Wins Round in Ballet over Affirmative Action," *Austin American Statesman,* December 22, 2000, p. A1; "Full Court Asked to Hear Hopwood Case," *Dallas Morning News,* January 6, 2001, p. 29A.

104. Lee Bollinger and Nancy Cantor, "The Educational Importance of Race," *Washington Post,* April 28, 1998, p. A17.

105. Minority students are represented by the private law firm of Scheff & Washington and civil rights organizations including the NAACP Legal Defense Fund, MALDEF, and the ACLU.

106. See *Grutter v. Bollinger* and *Gratz v. Bollinger,* 188 F.3d 394, 401 (Sixth Cir. 1999) at 6 (ruling on consolidated appeal for intervention of current and potential minority students of the University of Michigan). See also Peter Schmidt, "Court Opens Way for Minority Students to Intervene in Mich. Affirmative-Action Case," *Chronicle of Higher Education,* August 11, 1999, www.chronicle.merit.edu.

107. See Peter Schmidt, "Federal Judge Approves U. of Michigan's Use of Race in Admissions Decisions," *Chronicle of Higher Education,* December 14, 2000, www.chronicle.merit.edu.

108. *Gratz v. Bollinger,* 122 F. Supp. 2d 811, pp. 820, 822 (E.D. Mich., 2000).

109. Peter Schmidt, "Federal Judge Upholds Use of Race in Admissions," *Chronicle of Higher Education,* January 5, 2001, www.chronicle.merit.edu.

110. See Ben Gose, "Minority Students at U. of Michigan Lose Affirmative-Action Case," *Chronicle of Higher Education,* March 2, 2001, www.chronicle.merit.edu.

111. *Gratz v. Bollinger,* 135 F. Supp. 2d 790 (E.D. Mich., 2001).

112. See Jeffrey Selingo, "Federal Judge Finds That U. of Michigan Law School Uses Affirmative Action Unconstitutionally," *Chronicle of Higher Education,* March 28, 2001, www.chronicle.merit.edu.

113. Of the six separate opinions issued by the Supreme Court in *Bakke,* only the one written by Justice Powell discussed the diversity rationale.

114. Though the Supreme Court has not considered whether diversity is a compelling interest.

115. *Grutter v. Bollinger,* 137 F. Supp. 2d 821, 849 (E.D. Mich., 2001).

116. Ibid., pp. 850, 851.

117. Ibid., pp. 863, 863–64, 864.

118. Ibid., pp. 870–71. With respect to the LSAT, the court stated, "The evidence presented at trial indicated that the LSAT predicts law school grades rather poorly (with a correlation of only 10–20 percent) and that it does not predict success in the legal profession at all. If, as its admissions policy states, the law school seeks students who 'have substantial promise for success in law school' and 'a strong likelihood of succeeding in the practice of law,' one must wonder why the

law school concerns itself at all with an applicant's LSAT scores." With respect to undergraduate grades, the court stated, "The law school's admissions policy acknowledges that, even in combination, the LSAT score and undergraduate GPA are 'far from perfect' predictors of success in law school. In fact, the policy asserts that the correlation between the index score and first-year law school grades may overstate an applicant's academic achievements or promise, and that low grades may understate them."

119. Peter Schmidt, "U. of Michigan Law School Is Allowed to Continue Using Affirmative Action Pending Appeal," *Chronicle of Higher Education,* April 6, 2001, www.chronicle.merit.edu.

120. See *Grutter v. Bollinger,* 2002 FED App. 0170P (6th Cir.).

121. Sara Hebel, "U. of Georgia Won't Ask Supreme Court to Reverse Decision Striking Down Use of Race in Admission," *Chronicle of Higher Education,* November 12, 2001. The Eleventh Circuit Opinion is found at *Johnson v. Bd. of Regents,* 263 F.3d 1234 (11th Cir. 2001).

122. *Grutter v. Bollinger,* 247 F.3d 631 (Sixth Cir. 2001).

123. Peter Schmidt, "In a Largely Symbolic Act, U. of California Regents Rescind Their Ban on Affirmative Action," *Chronicle of Higher Education,* May 17, 2001, www.chronicle.merit.edu.

124. Tanya Schevitz, "Preferences Ban Faces Battle from UC Regent," *San Francisco Chronicle,* January 29, 2000, p. A3.

125. Dana Hull, "Debate over Race Policies Continues: Supporters Urging UC to Bring Back Affirmative Action," *San Jose Mercury News,* May 1, 2000, p. A1.

126. Schevitz, "Preferences Ban Faces Battle," p. A3.

127. Tanya Schevitz, "Protesters Slam UC Admissions Policy," *San Francisco Chronicle,* March 15, 2001, p. A3.

128. Jeffrey Selingo, "University of California Regents May Revisit Ban on Affirmative Action in Admissions," *Chronicle of Higher Education,* January 9, 2001, www.chronicle.merit.edu.

129. Cruz M. Bustamante, "UC, Take Down the 'Not Wanted' Sign," *Los Angeles Times,* January 31, 2000, p. B5.

130. See Schevitz, "Protesters Slam UC Admissions Policy," p. A3; Justino Aguilar, Henry K. Lee, and Tanya Schevitz, "UC Protest Rips Policy on Minorities," *San Francisco Chronicle,* March 9, 2001, p. A19. See also Megan Cohen, "Throngs Show Support for Affirmative Action," *Daily Californian,* March 21, 2001, p. 1; Robert Salonga, "Activists Demand Repeal in Day of Protest," *Daily Bruin,* March 15, 2001, p. 1.

131. Aguilar, Lee, Schevitz, "UC Protest Rips Policy on Minorities," p. A19.

132. Schmidt, "U. of California Regents Rescind Their Ban on Affirmative Action."

133. In late August 2000, Governor Jeb Bush announced that his new admissions policy had yielded a 12 percent increase in the number of minority freshmen enrolling at the ten public universities in Florida. But the surge in enrollment was less likely the result of the "20 percent plan" than the result of increased funding from the state legislature that allowed for an 11 percent overall increase

in freshman enrollment and for greater student recruitment and race-targeted scholarships. Thus, though the numbers of African Americans and Latinos enrolling in the public universities went up, the percentage of African Americans in the entering class stayed constant at 17.6 percent and the percentage of Latinos decreased slightly from 14.0 percent to 13.6 percent. Jeffrey Selingo, "Florida's Universities See Rise in Minority Enrollment after End of Racial Preferences," *Chronicle of Higher Education,* September 8, 2000, www.chronicle.merit.edu; David Wason, "Bush, Democrats Differ on One Florida Results," *Tampa Tribune,* August 30, 2000, p. 1; Scott Powers and Linda Kleindienst, "Bush Declares Victory for One Florida Plan," *Orlando Sentinel,* August 29, 2000, p. 1.

134. Tanya Schevitz, "New UC Plan to Raise Minority Enrollment, Conditional Admission to Be Offered," *San Francisco Chronicle,* September 22, 2000, p. A1.

135. Ibid.

136. In guidelines issued December 2000, the OCR warns universities that overreliance on standardized tests may constitute a violation of federal nondiscrimination regulations which could jeopardize a university's federal funding. See U.S. Department of Education Office for Civil Rights, "The Use of Tests as Part of High-Stakes Decision-Making for Students" (December 2000). The heavy reliance on standardized tests and the disparate impact of that reliance on students applying to law school and other graduate programs at the University of California form the basis of the complaint that was filed by MALDEF and other civil rights organizations with OCR in March 1997. The complaint is still pending and, given the political will that would be necessary to withhold the $1 billion in federal funds that the UC now receives, is unlikely to be resolved soon. Nevertheless, the new OCR guidelines, which reiterate existing federal regulations, may provide added pressure to compel UC and other highly selective universities to voluntarily change the way they use standardized tests.

137. See Jeffrey Brainard, "University of California's President Proposes Dropping the SAT Requirement," *Chronicle of Higher Education,* February 19, 2001, www.chronicle.merit.edu. The SAT is divided into two kinds of tests: the general math and verbal test which is referred to as the SAT or SAT I test, and subject matter tests which are referred to as the SAT II tests. UC President Atkinson proposes dropping the SAT I and retaining the SAT II.

138. Richard C. Atkinson, University of California President, "Standardized Tests and Access to American Universities," speech delivered to the American Council on Education, Washington, DC, February 18, 2001.

139. Brainard, "UC President Proposes Dropping SAT."

140. John Cloud, "Should SATs Matter?" *Time* (special report), March 12, 2001, p. 62.

141. Eric Hoover, "Business Leaders Urge Colleges to Give Less Weight to Standardized Tests in Admissions," *Chronicle of Higher Education,* April 12, 2001, www.chronicle.merit.edu.

142. Jeffrey Selingo, "Call to Eliminate SAT Requirement May Reshape Debate on Affirmative Action," *Chronicle of Higher Education,* March 2, 2001, www.chronicle.merit.edu.

143. "The Leading Undergraduate 'Feeder Schools' for Black and White Law School Applicants," *J. Blacks Higher Education* 85 (winter 1999/2000). See William C. Kidder, "Affirmative Action in Higher Education: Recent Developments in Litigation, Admissions and Diversity Research," a report for the Society of American Law Teachers (SALT) Conference, San Francisco, California (January 4, 2001), pp. 16–18.

144. Jeffrey Selingo, "Foe of Affirmative Action Seeks to Bar Colleges in California from Collecting Data on Race," *Chronicle of Higher Education,* February 14, 2001, www.chronicle.merit.edu.

Index

Note: Italicized page numbers indicate tables.

Text:	10/13 Galliard
Display:	Galliard
Compositor:	Impressions Book and Journal Services, Inc.
Printer and binder:	Maple-Vail Book Manufacturing Group
Indexer:	Margie Towery